OHIO STATE UNIVERSITY
LIMA CAMPUS LIBRARY

A Book of Readings
FOR MEN AGAINST SEXISM

Jon Snodgrass, editor

TIMES CHANGE PRESS
Albion, CA 95410

D0162312

Copyright ©1977 by Jon Snodgrass

Printed in the U.S.A.
Fourth Printing

Times Change Press
Albion, CA 95410

Library of Congress Cataloging in Publication Data

   Main entry under title:
For men against sexism: a book of readings.

   Includes bibliographies.
1. Sexism—Addresses, essays, lectures.
2. Masculinity—Addresses, essays, lectures.
3. Feminism—United States—Addresses, essays, lectures.
4. Sex roles—Addresses, essays, lectures.
   I. Snodgrass, Jon.
HQ1067.F65   301.41   77-77388
ISBN 0-87810-531-X hardbound
ISBN 0-87810-031-8 paperback

Times Change Press material is copyrighted to prevent reprinting by
profit-making publishers. When possible, we readily give permission
for its use by people whose purpose is, like ours, to help further personal growth and radical social change.

to
Dawn

Contents

Introduction:
Men and the Feminist Movement

Jon Snodgrass

Who I Am . . .

I am a white working class male who was admitted to college during the boom period of the 1960's. With the aid of the G.I. Bill and a Ford Foundation Fellowship, I attended the University of Pennsylvania where I obtained a Ph.D. in June, 1972. I moved to Los Angeles shortly thereafter to teach sociology in the California State University system.

During the 1960's I was drawn to the New Left and participated in the anti-war movement. I was politicized each year and with every escalation of the war. At times I attempted to affiliate with left organizations, but usually found myself alienated from political groups and intimidated by radical individuals. I often questioned my commitment to social change and concentrated on my graduate career and personal needs.

With the advent of the women's liberation movement, many of my reservations and criticisms of the New Left were demystified and articulated. I identify with Eli Zaretsky when he writes:

> Firestone's book, *The Dialectic of Sex,* along with other products of the women's movement, crystallized many people's dissatisfaction with the traditional politics of the left. Socialism, staking all on a reorganization of the economy, appeared inadequate to the needs of modern men and women. Socialism promised to revolutionize society on the basis of narrow programs that did not touch the inner life of people. Firestone's book spoke to the deep distrust of both bourgeois and radical politics that prevails in our society. Politics promises to affect us in what we share with large numbers of people, but in much of our lives we feel unique or alone. Firestone's stress on the importance of the family evoked a new conception of a political movement: one that would make the inner emotion-

6

al life of its participants part of its practice.[1]

While there were aspects of women's liberation which appealed to me, on the whole my reaction was typical of men. I was threatened by the movement and responded with anger and ridicule. I believed that men and women were oppressed by capitalism, but not that women were oppressed by men. I argued that "men are oppressed too" and that "it's workers who need liberation!" I was unable to recognize a hierarchy of inequality between men and women (in the working class) nor to attribute it to male domination. My blindness to patriarchy, I now think, was a function of my male privilege. As a member of the male gender caste, I either ignored or suppressed women's liberation.

My full introduction to the women's movement came through a personal relationship. While I had read a few feminist books and discussed feminism with a few women in Pennsylvania, it was not until I moved to California that I began to change. Here I met and fell in love with a woman who was being politicized by women's liberation. As our relationship developed, I began to receive repeated criticism for being sexist. At first I responded, as part of the male backlash, with anger and denial. In time, however, I began to recognize the validity of the accusation, and eventually even to acknowledge the sexism in my denial of the accusation.

I do not understand the entire process by which I experienced a change in consciousness from opposition to support of the women's movement, but I do remember one of the incidents that led me to realize that the major component of my identity was associated with my gender. One evening, my lover challenged the male supremacist remarks of a television commentator. I defended the commentator and we argued. I denied that I was being sexist and I denied that my refusal to admit being wrong in an intellectual argument with a woman was also associated with my masculinity. Subsequently, I realized that I had supported the commentator simply because he was a man and *not* because I believed he was correct. Threatened by the challenge to my male dominance, I had identified with him against the person I loved because he and I were genitally males. Thus I dimly recognized patriarchal bonding and faintly perceived my own misogyny. I began to sense the irrationality of sexism, and in my writing I referred to this experience as a "breakthrough in consciousness."

Thus, gradually, I began to accept the accuracy of the accusation that I was a male supremacist, but felt helpless to do anything about it. I devalued myself and felt incapable of change. I wondered how other

7

men were experiencing the women's movement. Only later was I to understand that men of every class, race, sexual preference and political orientation responded to the women's movement in a reactionary way. I sought out and joined men's consciousness-raising groups, but they were not very meaningful and did not last for very long. I rarely found men like myself who were attempting to relate to feminists and yet were reacting to feminism in hostile, frightened and depressed ways. My aloneness was itself a key experience for me at the time.

. . . and Where I am Coming From

To understand my own reaction to the women's movement I read feminist literature and searched for materials written by men. At the same time, in the university, I came under pressures to "publish or perish," and I began to think seriously about preparing an anthology concerning men and the feminist movement.

I continued my search for a meaningful men's group and helped form the Los Angeles Men's Collective in October 1974.[2] In my practice I heard the men's movement criticized for being "subjectivist," "individualistic," and "bourgeois." I also heard radical males criticized for being "masculine-identified" and "dogmatic." Both criticisms seemed correct to me. Bob Lamm captured my position and outlook when he wrote in an April 1974 *Win* "Special Issue on Men,"

I feel very torn. I identify with the men's movement and feel a strong tie to its work and growth. But my friends who work in left politics criticize the men's movement for being lily-white, bourgeois and elitist—and it is—and the criticism hurts me. At the same time, I identify with the left and feel a strong tie to its work and growth. But my friends from the feminist, gay liberation, and men's movement criticize the left for being sexist—and it is—and that criticism also hurts me.[3]

Concerned about the split between the anti-sexist men's and the working class movements, I wrote an article, "The Women's Liberation Movement and the Men," in the fall of 1974. It was an overview and criticism of men's liberation from a Marxist perspective, an attempt to raise class consciousness in the men's movement. In spite of serious reservations about its classist, sexist, and racist composition and biases, which I spelled out and condemned, I basically supported the men's movement. It seemed to hold potential for ultimately contributing to a socialist transformation of society by building unity between the male-dominated left and the autonomous women's movement. My primary loyalty remained with the left and with men. Since that time, however I have become much more critical of *both* the male left and men's liberation.

In the fall of 1975, I wrote "Four Replies to Radical Feminism: Marxism, Revolutionary Effeminism, Gay Marxism and Men's Liberation," an overview and criticism of men's reactions (particularly socialist men's) to the women's movement from a radical feminist perspective. This statement was the obverse of the previous essay. I attempted to demonstrate that persistent sexism in the various male responses had validated radical feminist theory, which holds patriarchy to be the *root* cause of women's oppression. And, I thought, the men's reactions also confirmed the first premise of revolutionary effeminism, that all men are sexist. I addressed the article primarily to the left and showed the need for a male role struggle against male supremacist consciousness among socialist men.

Socialism and Feminism

In both my articles I was attempting to build unity by integrating socialism and feminism, the two movements with which I most closely identify. However, because I believe that men cannot be feminists, I do not call myself a socialist-feminist. Instead, I refer to myself as an antisexist socialist, admittedly an awkward term. I feel that for men to refer to themselves as feminists is equivalent to whites calling themselves black militants; I attempt to respect autonomy by thinking of feminism as a women's movement.

In producing this anthology I continue my concern for the split between the socialist and feminist causes. The basis for the split is the Marxist position on the relationship between sexism and capitalism, especially the explanation for women's oppression. Fundamentally, Marxists adopt the position that women's oppression is a product of the capitalist mode of production and that it originated historically with the development of classes. This perspective relies on Frederick Engel's influential book, *The Origin of the Family, Private Property and the State.*[4] Feminists, however, have analyzed women's oppression as originating in a male supremacist system, as well as in capitalism. Whereas power is centralized in a ruling class according to Marxism, it is concentrated among men according to feminism. Both theories, I think, are basically correct, incomplete and contradictory. Generally, I agree with the conclusion to Juliet Mitchell's *Psychoanalysis and Feminism,* that we are dealing with two distinct but related systems of power: "the economic mode of capitalism" and the "ideological mode of patriarchy," and that we require a "specific struggle against patriarchy" (as well as a struggle against capitalism).[5]

I believe that women were oppressed in pre-class society on the basis of their biological reproductive roles, and—while under capitalism women are oppressed as workers—they are still oppressed, by men, as women. This means that much of women's oppression extends beyond the class system and has its foundation in patriarchal power. Consequently, I support the development of a socialist-feminist movement which synthesizes a Marxist analysis of political economy with a feminist analysis of patriarchy.

Unfortunately, few of the articles in this anthology integrate the struggle against patriarchy with the struggle against capitalism. Most of the materials concentrate exclusively on one struggle or the other, a characteristic itself which reflects the split between socialist and feminist thought. On the whole, there are more articles on the struggle against male supremacy than against capitalism because this is a collection of readings *for men against sexism.* The emphasis on sexism is not meant to imply that capitalism is a secondary contradiction, as radical feminists might argue. Socialists have traditionally ignored women's (and gays') oppression, and in stressing male domination I am attempting to redress the historic subordination of women's oppression to the class struggle.

The collection of readings is divided into two parts. In the first, *Women's Oppression,* are articles about the role of men in the oppression of women. The articles by men were written as a direct result of the influence of the women's movement. The three articles by women are analyses of men's reactions to feminism. The material is organized topically into sections.

The second part of the anthology, *Gay, Class, and Racial Oppression,* is devoted to three forms of oppression that are related to the oppression of women. Unfortunately, theory concerning the relationship between women's oppression and gay, class, and racial oppression is scarcely developed. Consequently, most of the articles describe men's experience of the oppression without much attention to the theoretical inter-connections.

In bringing together this book of readings for men against sexism, I do not intend to replace works by feminists. I have provided an appendix of important feminist publications and several authors of articles have also prepared recommended reading lists. I would like to stress that my knowledge about sexism as a man is deeply endebted to women, personally as well as writers and activists. I would also like to thank Mike Bradley for his editorial work in the preparation of this anthology, and all the authors for donating their work. I hope this collection of readings encourages the growth of men in support of feminism.

Los Angeles—July, 1976

[1] Eli Zaretsky, "Capitalism, the Family and Personal Life," *Socialist Revolution,* Part I, 13 (Jan—Apr 1973), 72-73.

[2] "Statement of the Los Angeles Men's Collective," *Changing Men,* (March 1976), 27-30.

[3] Bob Lamm, "And a Cautionary Note," *Win,* 10 (April 11, 1973), 26.

[4] Frederick Engels, *The Origin of the Family, Private Property, and the State* (New York: International Publishers, 1942).

[5] Juliet Mitchell, "The Cultural Revolution," *Psychoanalysis and Feminism,* (New York: Random House, 1974), 407-416.

Part One:
Women's Oppression

MALE SEXUALITY

Section Introduction

Patriarchy divides males and females into dominant and subordinate castes on the basis of gender and polarizes human sexuality and personality into masculine and feminine dimensions. This division eroticizes power and aggression in men. As a result, male sexual functioning operates as the *instrument* of women's oppression and enforces male rule. The anthology begins with studies of men's sexuality because of its importance to women's oppression.

In the first article, Jack Litewka focuses on the socialization process which conditions male sexuality. The concentration of men's sexual feelings in their genitals and the separation of men's sexuality from emotionality, expressed in the title, "The Socialized Penis," are essential aspects of masculinity. Litewka's article was one of the first and most sensitive responses by a man to the women's liberation movement. In contrast with the vast majority of male reactions, Litewka's essay is more advanced and more rare, because it acknowledges that men are the oppressors of women. Most male reactions have linked male socialization with "male oppression." Litewka, however, connects male socialization with male *supremacy,* and recognizes that men and women are not equally affected by sex role assignments and stereotypes. He sees masculine socialization as the preparation of the male for dominance. Atypically then, his analysis tends to support the women's movement by appreciating the prime source of women's subordination.

Originally writing in 1971, Litewka attempted to communicate some theoretical ideas concerning the origin of male supremacy by concentrating on his own psycho-sexual history. This self-examination was a direct result of encounters with women and the women's movement. Litewka reveals that on three separate occasions over a period of a year and a half, he was unable to obtain an erection during intercourse. Searching for an explanation, he recollects his adolescent initiation into sex by describing the male role in "making out." From the description he infers a principle about the pattern of male socialization: "three elements reappear constantly in every step of the development of male sexual stimulus and response: objectification, fixation, and conquest." The focus on the psychological content of politicized male sexuality and its connection to male supremacy is perhaps the strongest aspect of his article. Litewka reasoned further than he was unable to obtain an erection because he was unable to objectify, fixate, and conquer the women in question. He had caring feelings for all three women. This explanation, which depicts his impotence as a function of his liberation, is one in which he recognizes that "I come off looking pretty good. Looking pretty damn egalitarian."

A woman friend challenged this interpretation, however, and claimed that his lack of an erection meant he could not accept the women as sexual equals. In this view, his impotence was a form of punishment to the women for their sexual assertiveness. Criticized for being sexist, and sensing the validity of the accusation, he raises a series of excellent questions about men and women, which because of the early date of publication and his complete isolation from changing men, he is unable to adequately answer. Litewka's experience reveals the continued re-emergence of misogyny which accompanies men's development of higher levels of consciousness. This persistence initially contributes to pessimism about the ability to change. Litewka suggests that men may change by undergoing "re-socialization," but he does not actually envisage this process. He concludes with a criticism and clarification of his essay:

> Litewka has asked that readers of his essay be aware that, "I am sensitive about what I had to say six years ago being frozen into print today as if it represented my present process, feelings and thoughts. When I wrote my essay, not much had been written by men about their own experiences. Consequently, oversights or omissions or superficialities which seem unforgiveable today did not seem that way to me then. I was, and still am, concerned that my essay did not deal with homosexuality in a substantive way. This was partly deliberate, partly out of ignorance, and mostly because it was not within my realm of experience. I was aware that my brief allusion to homosexuality was written without the benefit of many other people's sensitive explorations into homosexuality, bisexuality and androgyny that have surfaced in the past five years . . . especially the contributions of gays and feminists."

In "Refusing To Be a Man," the next article in this section, John Stoltenberg does not mention the process by which he began to question and then reject his masculinity. Although he is critical of the classification of human sexuality into heterosexual, homosexual or bisexual modes, because these terms objectify sexuality and are themselves the linguistic product of a male-dominated culture, he discloses that he has lived both as a "married man" and as a "gay man." Thus, unlike Litewka, who concentrates almost exclusively on the sexuality of heterosexual males, Stoltenberg has the advantage of his own experience in discussing homosexuality and heterosexuality. He stresses that male sexuality is essentially identical, dependent upon objectification and domination, regardless of sexual preference. Both homosexual and heterosexual males have been treated as males in a male supremacist society and have received a masculine sexual training. Therefore, gay men do not escape the impact of patriarchy in the formation of their sexuality and identity.

Stoltenberg continues by describing two aspects of his own sexuality, the capacity to enjoy multiple orgasms and the ability to appreciate sexual arousal without erection. Both of these capabilities emerged as he began to question what he believes are patriarchal lies about the nature of male orgasms and erections. In effect, these myths function in the interest of male rule. Appreciating the connection between the distortion of his sexuality and the oppression of women by patriarchy, Stoltenberg concludes by renouncing manhood. In repudiating masculinity, he dedicates himself to the overthrow of male supremacy.

"Making Love with Myself," the third article, is written by Jamie Bevson, an activist in the Portland Men's Resource Center. He describes how learning to appreciate masturbation provided him with a way to struggle against his oppressive rape fantasies, a perversion that he believes was acquired through patriarchal socialization. Subjecting himself to the pleasure of his own body released him from the psychological need to objectify and dominate the bodies of others—in his imagination—as a means of erotic stimulation.

In "How Pornography Shackles Men and Oppresses Women," Michael Betzold hypothesizes that the pornography boom is a backlash to the women's liberation movement. He wonders why anti-sexist men have not been more aware of, and active against, this form of misogyny. He explains that pornography reinforces male supremacy by portraying the objectification and domination of women by men. He also discusses the negative effects of pornography on men's emotionality and sexuality and describes areas of cities set aside for the display, torture, and sale of women. The goal of anti-sexist men, he concludes, should be to abolish these areas and practices.

In the final article, "Learning From Women," Bob Lamm describes the lessons he learned from women who took his college classes on men and masculinity. In terms of male sexuality, the most important lesson concerned rape. Rape reveals in miniature, he asserts, the basic relationship of men to women in a male supremacist system. Male sexuality, eroticized by dominance, is epitomized in the act of violent sexual subservience. " . . . Rape is one of the most savage," he writes, "and yet most accurate metaphors for how men relate to women . . ." Thus, rape *is* the behavioral expression of male sexuality under patriarchy. Lamm was also educated in his classes about his own resistance to feminist theory and to women's autonomous organization. He concludes by emphasizing the importance of men learning from women in order to change themselves and develop the struggle against sexism.

The Socialized Penis

Jack Litewka

This is, to a certain degree, a personal story. I felt the need to make it public because I have sensed for a long time, and now see more clearly every day, the disaster of sexuality in its present forms. Some women have been struggling with this reality. They have attempted to expose the male/female myth in the hope of creating a healthier reality. But most men have been (at best) silent or (at worst) dishonest—and often ignorant and defensive. This essay is an attempt to help men begin talking among themselves and hopefully with women.

The people who should have initiated the dialogue are psycho-analysts and psychiatrists: the psycho-healers. But they have failed us. And themselves. By and large, they have concentrated their energies on helping people adapt to the realities of the existing social system rather than examining the foundations of that system. But, like the rest of us, these people are damaged. And being damaged, they are incapable of dealing with their own experience. Have you seen much written or spoken about masturbation? I haven't. The psycho-healers, most of whom are men, always talk about the phenomenon of masturbation as if it was "other," "out there." Have you ever heard a psycho-healer say, "When I masturbate(d) . . ."? Of course not. They are incapable or terrified of dealing with their own experience. So I am attempting to deal with mine, with those of men I know, in an effort to help us begin to deal more honestly with one aspect of male socialization.

Like the psycho-healers, like everyone, I am also damaged. I may be incapable of asking the right questions. I know I'm not able now to supply the "answers" that are needed. Desperately needed. But I'm going to try, and I hope that other men will also begin trying. Through persistence and honesty and perhaps by accident, we'll end up asking the right questions and be better able to answer them.

I'm very grateful to a few close friends, male and female, who are involved in this struggle and who have given me support and encouragement and criticism and chunks of their own lives in the writing of this essay. I'm also very happy that the Women's Movement exists and that many women are committed to undoing the damage done to all of us. I am not going to re-discuss what women writers have already explored. The sexual socialization of men in this century is what I want to deal with. More specifically, socialized sexual response. Still more specifically, the socialized penis. My penis, not just those of other men out there.

***

I was raised in America and learned—as did many other boys in my childhood and men I know now—to perform sexually on desire or request. This performance I think can be considered the norm, an ability that most males wanted to develop or maintain. The males who didn't conform to this norm usually felt incomplete, unskilled, or unmanly. And this insufficiency often resulted in self-damning fear and anxiety, while other "healthy" males who automatically or easily conformed to the norm just cruised along, dropping anchor in this or that port when entertainment's hunger urged.

I think I am typical of most American males when I say that getting aroused, getting an erection, was not a major problem in adolescence. If there was a major problem, it was in not knowing what to do, or not being allowed to do anything, with an erection. So you had to learn how to hide it or deal with the embarrassment of its discovery.

I don't know when I began to be annoyed with the way women and men relate. Like most men, I think, I only dealt with a relationship when I had experienced enough and was troubled enough to look back at a previous relationship. But by the time one seriously begins to examine male/female relationships, it is usually too late. Because one has already been thoroughly socialized. So instead of dealing with male/female relationships, one is incapable of examining them, or refuses to examine them, or represses what one knows, or stands under it intellectually and laughs at the absurdity. Or tragedy.

In the last year and a half, something happened to me on three separate occasions that made me decide to seriously analyze the way I had been sexually socialized. I now understand that the incidents occurred because I was already grappling with the origins of my sexuality.

Incident 1. A woman I liked (and who liked me—"love" may be

a mythic word so it is not being used, especially since it has nothing to do with erection) and I were in bed together for the first time. We talked and hugged and played. To my surprise and dismay, I didn't get an erection. At least not at the propitious moment (I did have erections now and then throughout the night). And I didn't know why. Maybe I was just too tired or had been fucking and masturbating too much (though that had never been a problem before). But it didn't disturb me too much because the woman was supportive and we both knew there would be other nights. So we rolled together, smelled each other, and had a lovely night despite absence of coitus.

In the following year, I had a few relationships and my penis was its old arrogant self, so that one night seemed an unexplained oddity and was pretty much forgotten. My sexual life had the same sexual dynamics as my previous sexual history, so things were back to normal. But then came round two.

Incident 2. Similar in all respects to Incident 1. No erection at the right time. Again, I did have erections now and then throughout the night. Again, I didn't know why. But I knew it wasn't from being too tired or fucking or masturbating too much, since I hadn't slept with a woman in about a month and since I had spent the past week on vacation just reading, resting, doing odd jobs—not masturbating—and enjoying the absence of tension. Again, it wasn't a hassle because the woman knew me and I knew her and we both knew people the other had slept with, so it was chalked off as a freak with neither of us to blame. We touched along the whole length of our bodies and discussed basketball, politics, and our social/sexual histories. She fell asleep. I couldn't, my brain gnawing at me, having scary thoughts about a present (temporary) or impending impotency, and resolving to do something—but not knowing what.

Simplistically, I made an assumption: it had to be me or the woman I was with. But since it had happened with two different women, I figured it was me (though there might have been similarities between the women and the situations). But since I had performed sexually in a normal way many times in the year between these incidents, I assumed that it had to be something about these particular women in combination with me.

My immediate concern was my own fright. The "no erection at the right time" syndrome had happened to me twice. I was scared, very scared. Images of impotence hung in the air and wouldn't disappear. So I got in touch with an old love whom I still spend a loving night or two with every five or six months and with whom I had always had good sexual chemistry. We got together two nights later and history prevailed: my penis had its timing back and I performed like the stud I was always meant to be. Which was a tremendous relief.

But I still had no answer to my question: why didn't I get an erection at the right time on two different occasions when I was with women I wanted to be with and who wanted to be with me, when there was mutual attraction and social/political/intellectual compatibility? I had a few clues, a few hunches, a few theories. But at best they were very partial answers. So I started to do a lot of thinking and isolated myself from old loves and potential new ones. I decided to read a lot of 19th-century porno literature, hoping that there might be repeated patterns (and there were) of male/female sexual activities that I could learn something from. (I realize now that this was a cop-out, a refusal or inability to look at myself, my own sexual experience; and that to look at "other" sexuality, to learn from second-hand experience, was a safer path and one of less resistance. And for that reason, too, it may actually have been the only way I could start the examination.) I also read a lot of feminist writings, and continued to have many and long talks with a few close friends, all of whom are intensely involved with the liberation of people. I learned much during this time (a lot of which I already knew but couldn't make cohere), not all of which lends itself to this essay. But it all fed into an increasingly less diffuse puzzle.

Incident 3. This occasion was similar in almost all respects to Incidents 1 and 2, occurring about 18 months after the first incident and six months after the second. Between the second and third incidents, my sexual life had again been normal (for me).

This time I wasn't as frightened because I had already begun to figure out what the fuck was going on and had the reassurance that I was determined enough to maybe, maybe just, see it through to solution. Again, the woman was supportive and someone whom I had gone through many things with over the years: this was just going to be another thing that we would have to deal with. Also, there was some hope because perceptions were beginning to clump together.

It became increasingly clear to me that in order to find answers to my emerging questions, I would have to go back and retrace the steps that were parts of my sexual history. Simultaneously, I was thinking that if my socialized sexuality was in any way similar to that of other men, then my formulations wouldn't be idiosyncratic to my experience. And as clues found me, I remembered old talks with young male friends and checked them against recent talks with adult male friends. It seemed that we had all gone through a basically similar process (with countless variations). Even those males who had not conformed to the norm, who didn't perform sexually according to the book, were affected by the norm process (sometimes resulting in a devastating social and sexual isolation). So I thought it would be worth the effort to construct a norm, however flawed, to determine what shape that image took. And to see if that image could teach.

***

The Initiation of a Young Male: In looking back on my sexual experiences and those of male friends, a very definite and sequential pattern was evident. I'm talking about actual (overt) sexual events, not subliminal or imagined or representational sexual experiences. I'm thinking of adolescent times in adolescent terms when males begin to experiment and develop their knowledge and expertise. I'm thinking about things you did sequentially as you got older. With a few total exceptions and an odd irregularity or two (like fucking a "whore" before you'd kissed a "girl") among the many men I have known and talked with, the sequence runs roughly as follows.

You kiss a girl. You kiss a girl a number of times. You kiss a girl continuously (make-out). You kiss a girl continuously and get your tongue into the act. All through this process you learn to use your hands to round out the orchestration, at first with simple clumsy chords and later with complex harmonies (with the woman, of course, being the instrument made to respond to the musician). You, as a young male, are told (or figure out) what sensitive spots you should seek, and learn more as the young female (hopefully) responds to your hands. First you just hug and grasp. Then you make little circles on her shoulders with your fingers. Then you go for the back of the neck, and run your fingers through her hair (music, please), and then over her face and throat. Then the outer ear (lobes especially). And middle ear. Then lower back (at which point your tongue might cover the ear as a stand-in for the absent hand). Then the tender sides of the waist above the (maybe-not-yet) hip bones. Then the belly. And after, the upper belly and the rib cage. Here let us take a deep breath before the great leap upward to the breast, which is a bold act broken into a number of ritualistic steps. First the hand over one breast, with blouse and bra between your hand and the female's flesh. This is a move that took special courage (balls?) and was very exciting for it seemed a new level of sensuality (which it was for the female, but for the male? no, only a new level of expectation). Then came a kind of figure-eight roving over the chest from one breast to the other (if your position allowed—how many right-handed lovers out there?). Then a sneaking between buttons (later unbuttoned) so your hand is on the breast with only the bra separating you from flesh. (Or if this procedure was too uncouth or too visible to others in the dusky room or impossible because of a no-button sweater, you worked underneath the garment from a fleshy belly right up to the bra). Then, by means of gradually developed finger dexterity, you begin to attack the flesh of the breast itself, work-ing down from the top of the bra into the cup. And if you hadn't yet picked up any signs of female complicity in your previous experience, it was often clear here. If she sat and breathed normally, your fingers didn't stand a chance (bras were worn very tightly in my junior high school so that nipples were always pointing up at your eyes). If she wanted to be helpful, she would deeply exhale and move her shoulder forward so there was space between the bra and the breast. (Women's cooperation during all these events is an interesting topic and really should be written about by a woman.) And here came the rainbow's gold—the assault on the nipple. While a kiss was exciting, and cupping a breast breath-taking, the conquest of the nipple was transcendent. Partly because it was the only part of a female's anatomy that we have dealt with so far that isn't normally seen or even partly exposed. Also because you knew that when this was achieved, the girl really liked you, and that getting the bra unhooked and off would not be far away. Maybe as soon as next week. When older, the same night. And you also sensed that you were getting closer to the core of sexuality (excuse the geographically mixed metaphor). Then began the assault on the crotch, in steps similar to those of the battle of the breast. You caressed her hip, worked around to her ass, pulled her close to announce (if it hadn't already been discovered) the existence of your penis and give it some pleasurable friction (and provide the girls with a topic of gossip later? if you were erect). Then you worked down to the side of her leg. Then the front of her thigh. Then with a deep breath, and microscopic steps, you slowly progressed toward the vaginal entrance (how many of you had imagined the entrance four inches higher than you found it to be?). Now here there are many variables: was it a swim party when she had on the bottom part of a two-piece suit, or was she wearing jeans, or did she have a skirt on? Whatever the case, you usually ended up rub-bing her crotch through cloth and then worked down from her belly toward her crotch, getting your hand (as one variation of the phrase goes) into her pants. Then you sort of played around above or on top of her slit and eventually got a finger in it, and by accident or design (depending on your previous intelligence briefings) found the "magic button." And soon (usually), all hell broke loose, and more than ever before, you didn't quite know what to do with yourself if fucking wasn't yet in the script.

And that pretty much covers the pre-coital scenario. Except it was described in a semi-humorous manner and, as a male, many of these events were terrifying. You, most often, had to take the first step. And you could be rejected. Refused. Denied. Cold and flat. And that could hurt. Hurt bad. In your eyes and in your male friends' eyes. Being scared to try and therefore not trying could just as easily become the subject of psychological self-punishment and social ostracism. So there was always this elementary duality: while apparently the aggressor and conqueror, you were captive to a judgment by the female who would accept or reject you.

Also important to remember is how these events were reported to/discussed with male friends after the party or date. Or gone over in your own mind, again and again, detail by detail. How every step along the initiation route was stimulating and could/did cause an erection (remember the four-hour erections and blue balls?). How we compared notes, made tactical suggestions, commented on important signs— heavier breathing, torso-writhing, aggressive hands, a more daring tongue, involvement of teeth, goose bumps, erected nipples, and when menstruation occurred or was expected to occur. Which girls liked what, since in those days "relationships" were short-lived and you never knew which female you might be with another time. And if you were ever in doubt as to what came next in the scenario, your friends informed you of the specifics of the next escalation. And sometimes, if that wasn't possible, the female you were with (embarrassingly enough) let you know in any one of a number of subtle (or not-so-subtle) ways what was next on the agenda.

There were, in retrospect, many funny occasions that cropped up in this initiation process. I don't really need to talk about them because you probably have your own to tell. What stuns me now is that origins of the tragedy of sex emerge clearly from that process of socialized sexuality.

Three elements seem to reappear constantly in every step of the development of male sexual stimulus and response: Objectification, Fixation, and Conquest. (Idealization is a romantic concept that is both bible and aspirin for the three basic elements and tends to obfuscate them.) In any given situation, the order of occurrence and importance of these elements varies, but I believe the order given corresponds to the chronological reality (most of the time) and is more easily discussed.

Objectification: From a very young age, males are taught by everyone to objectify females (except Mom?). They generalize the female, in an almost platonic sense. This generalized woman is a concept, a lump sum, a thing, an object, a non-individualized category. The female is always "other." Against this backdrop males begin, when society allows, overtly to exercise bits of their sexuality.

Males learn to objectify through a process of "definition." We identify, and have identified for us, many female attributes. It starts simply: girls have long hair, wear ribbons on it, have on dresses, and like pink and yellow things. And, of course, they play with dolls. Then comes a sexual understanding: females have no penis, bear children, have breasts, thinner waists, and hips that swell. Until we realize the vagina's existence, we think females are missing their penis and in its absence is a void (are they incomplete?). As we accrue this knowledge, the female social role has already been defined everywhere for us. If we play hospital, the little girls are, of course, the nurses and we, of course, the doctors. If it's time for exercise at school, they play hopscotch while we play football. When it's time to learn practical living skills, they sew and bake while we use tools and build. They are easily recognized as different. There's them and there's us. And who'd want to do a silly girl's thing anyhow?

Fixation: Part of male sexual initiation is learning to fixate on portions of the female's anatomy: at first, breasts, and later, that hidden unknown quantity, the vagina. Somewhere, in some deep cavern in our brain, before we consciously know about sexuality, it must register on us that we never see males touching the female chest or lower belly. And in movies, on TV, in advertisements, where else can we look when the camera's eye focuses on breasts? So our eye is trained and we fixate. Emotionally, too. We learn that if we do that, we will eventually get pleasure and have fun. And be men. Be seen as male. Be reacted to as male.

Because of the way we are socialized, erection follows fixation or occurs in a situation in which fixation plays a role. We observe this coincidence. We learn we can *will* an erection without a woman being near us. And since it is pleasurable (and, at first, astounding), since it gives us assurance that we are male, we create erections out of our imagination, by merely objectifying a female of our choice, fixating on the parts of her body that excite, and usually manipulating that body (see Conquest, below). By denying this process, by repressing our desire and fantasy, we avoid embarrassing erections in public, which is vital since we are always "seeing" breasts and vaginas, hundreds of them, which have the potential of putting us into gear. So we exercise control over our penis while often saying that our penis has a mind of its own—all of which is true.

Conquest: To conquer is a highly valued skill in our society. We are taught to alter the enemy into nothingness, to convert the bear into a stuffed head and rug, to gain power and rule. It's very much either/or: you're a winner or a loser, a good guy or a bad guy, someone who has made it or hasn't. Male initiation rites and activities always require trophies (e.g., sports) and the more numerous and advanced your "awards," the more of a man you are. In sexual matters, the male conquers when he succeeds in reducing the female from a being into a thing and achieves some level or form of sexual gratification—a kiss, or your hand on her breast, or intercourse, depending on your age, sexual advancement, and surrounding social norms. Conquest logically (ahem) follows Objectification and Fixation. I mean, after all, what the hell's the sense of objectifying and fixating if you're not going to get off your ass and do a little conquering? And when we do conquer, what is the trophy? In the old days it might have been a lock of hair or a garter strap. A ring can also announce your achievement. But always, your own knowledge of what transpired is your reward—being pleased with yourself and being able to say to yourself, "I am a man." And if others have knowledge of your conquest, your knowing that they know is as great an award as any.

That, in brief, is the Objectification/Fixation/Conquest dynamics. The implications and ramifications of these elements of socialized sexual responses are staggering and too numerous to attempt to list and discuss here. But let me offer one implication (as an example) that seems realistic to me: that male sexual responses have little (or nothing) to do with the specific female we are with at any given moment. Any number of lips or breasts or vaginas would do—as long as we can objectify, fixate, and conquer, an erection and (provided there is some form of penile friction) ejaculation will occur.

If this example rubs you the wrong way, think about the existence and effectiveness of pornography, both verbal and photographic. What pornography does is create a fertile environment that makes it "natural" for the imagination to objectify, fixate on, and conquer a verbally or photographically depicted female. So even without a female being present in the flesh, the penis grows. Now you may say

24

that the female *is* present, that is, in the male mind. And I'd agree, but the female is not physically there. So in a certain sense, most males become a self-contained sexual system—not homo- or heterosexual, but self-sexual.

This shouldn't surprise anyone: it's based in our physiology and it's based in society's denial of sexual gratification. But, on conscious and unconscious levels, this is threateningly close to homosexuality. Because having a penis and getting erections is equivalent to maleness and ego, it seems that what's important to us as males is the male genitalia, and that might appear suspect to the puritan heterosexual mind-set.

How then do we draw the line between our own penis and all those other penises which are virtually identical to our own? The answer: we do to our penis what we do to females. We objectify it, fixate on it, and conquer it. In that way we "thingify" our penis, make it "other," so that we can talk about "it" and apologize for "its" behavior and laugh at "it" as if it were a child on the rambunctious side whom we can't control. So we have confirmed "its" separateness from us. We can even give our penis a name, like John Thomas or Peter, which states positively to the world that our penis is its own man. (And therefore we are not responsible for its actions?)

Because our penis is central to our own sense of ego and manhood, it is natural that anything that causes erections (with the resulting pleasure and power and self-identification) is to be used. Objectification/Fixation/Conquest of females allows us to function this way. Because we have been socialized to respond that way. So we *do* function that way (nothing succeeds like success, etc.).

Now there is a new female before us. Without really knowing her, without really knowing (or caring?) what she thinks or feels, we "like" her. Because she is female. Because she is "other" and with her you will be yourself—a male in a potential relationship that re-establishes, affirms, proves your manhood. Which means that at the moment of meeting, we have already objectified the female. And for our maleness, this is a necessary first step which permits us to fixate and hopefully go on to conquer so that our climax can strengthen our ego and sense of maleness. When you hear a man "complain" that he's slept with his wife "hundreds of times, and each time I have to seduce her as if she were a virgin," you observe a woman who has learned her lessons too well and a man who loves responding to them (though I don't mean this to be an example of a typical relationship). Seduction, in its crudest sense and crassest form, is nothing more than Fixation and

Conquest made possible because the male has already made a generaliz-ed object out of a specific female. (Listen to the language: cunt, tits, pussy, boobs, snatch, jugs . . .) This is the procedure males follow to get their sexual machinery into gear (with many personal idiosyncrasies, which is why prostitutes keep careful notes on the likes and dislikes of their clientele). Again, pornography and its effectiveness is telling us that we needn't have a real, living, breathing female with us to respond sexually. What is needed for a good old healthy erection to occur is the opportunity to objectify, fixate, and conquer.

Well, now we have some clues as to how our penis gets socialized and what it responds to, and there are endless questions to ask. But my first question is: What happened to me on those three occasions when I didn't get it up at the proper time?

Tell me how this sounds. My relationship to the woman and the woman's relationship to me were similar in all three instances. They were women I knew very well. They were people I liked very much. Liked because they were decent, liked because they were loving, liked because they were involved in the struggle (at great risk and cost) to make this world a better place. But with them, though I find them very attractive, I didn't automatically play stud the way I had been socialized to do. Because I knew them as whole beings, I couldn't objectify them, and consequently couldn't fixate on (though I tried) or conquer them. And they didn't put pressure on me to do that (as women can, and do, for a variety of reasons). So I didn't play my role and they didn't play theirs. No roles; no seduction, no Objectification/Fixation/Conquest— ergo, no erection (except at those odd, un-propitious times when I was probably unconsciously fixating on a part of their body or fantasizing and got the penis into gear).

We spent, I think, very intimate and sensuous moments together. And since those evenings, we've talked about what happened. And about this essay (each of the women has read it). And we'll spend other evenings together, trying to learn about the damage, the terrible damage, that has been done to all of us. And stopping its continuance. And trying to undo as much of it as we can. Well, that's one possible explanation for the "no erection at the right time" mystery. And I come off looking pretty good. Looking pretty damn egalitarian. At least I did until I talked to a friend who, given the same information, had an entirely different interpretation of what happened. Her version follows.

I have, to a certain degree, re-socialized myself and become liberated because I was able to accept these women on all levels as

26

equals. Except for one level: I was not capable of accepting females as sexual equals. I held onto this last bastion of male supremacy with a death-grip. I was willing to deal with these women on a human (rather than male-to-female) basis, except in relating to them sexually, where I still had to deal with them on an objectify, fixate, and conquer basis. But since I couldn't objectify them, I rejected these women rather than give up my last heirloom of maleness. I totally refused to allow them to sexually stimulate or arouse me. By preventing my penis from getting into gear, I ironically preserved my male superiority in the situation. This is because the women, who also need to be re-socialized, would not understand that my lack of erection was a result of fearing that I was going to lose touch with the last remnant of male socialization. They could not understand that I was in fact forestalling my own liberation because I lacked the courage or the knowledge necessary for the last step. What the women would feel is that I have rejected them, since they knew other women stimulated me sexually. They would feel that there is something wrong with them, some way in which they are lacking, if they cannot arouse me. So in refusing to allow myself to be stimulated by them, I have in fact turned the tables and made them feel inadequate in relation to me. In making them feel inadequate, I made them doubt the very thing in themselves that I was doubting in myself— sexuality. And while they are pretty liberated, it is the area of their own sexuality which they still have to deal with more.

Well, there's another explanation for the syndrome. And I don't come off looking so good. In fact, I look rather bad. Even desperate. It's an interpretation that is fairly consistent and contains energy. When I first heard it, it really threw me, which gives some credence to its validity. Then I thought, although my friend's interpretation is interesting, I really think mine is more accurate. But that may be male equivocation. Also, I'm not sure that the two interpretations are mutually exclusive (to explain that would take another essay). But the important points to remember are that we still have much to learn and that there are alternatives to avoiding, fearing, and ignoring present sexual realities. If we nurture our blindness and cheer our resistance to change, the damage will continue and worsen.

Some of you may be thinking that because all three instances dealt with the first night of a relationship, the analyses are invalid. And some of you may be thinking that even if a relationship begins in a classical sex-role way, the couple can still grow beyond the male/female roles that they embodied when they first met. I agree, but with major qualifications. I have seen relationships that never grew beyond where

27

they began. No comment necessary. I have also seen relationships that have grown, but I think we have to ask: What is the nature of that growth? What do they grow from? I think those are important questions because when the shit hits the fan in a relationship, friends of the couple will often say things like: "After all those years . . ."; "It's hard for me to believe . . ."; "Of all the couples we knew, they seemed . . ."; "It came out of nowhere . . ."; "I just can't understand . . ." Was the couple's break-up really "unexpected"? There are surprises, I think, only if certain basic questions were never asked, existing realities not examined, and alternatives not explored.

The terrifying (to me) evidence is that we males never are dealing with the whole female being at the beginning of a relationship. We have been socialized, on behalf of our penis, to divide a woman's body up. The vernacular of males is usually a dead give-away and varies from slightly crude to incredibly crude. Phrases like "I'm an ass man" or "a breast man" or "a cunt man" or "a leg man" are common self-perceptions and self-descriptions. The street jargon of males watching females stroll by is similar: "Would I like to get my hands on those tits" or "Look at that beaver [cunt]" or "I could suck those sweet nipples for days." The refined professor in the yard gazing at a coed amongst the grass and trees might offer up "a veritable Diana with alabaster orbs" in a non-iambic mode. But the phenomenon is the same. Fixation. That is how we see. We objectify (generalize) the woman and then we fixate on a physical characteristic. And even later in a relationship, when to varying degrees we do deal with the whole female person, very often we snap back into our original sex roles (as if sleeping together for the first time?). We do it because that is how we have been socialized to act and respond. We do it because it is the path of least resistance. We do it. It is the only way we know.

During the past year I have tried to call up and reabsorb conversations I have had with various males over the years concerning females. I've also spent a lot of time talking to all kinds of males, working class and professional, young single males and males who are "happily married and have three lovely children." When sexual fantasies were discussed, I found that there are very similar fantasies among most males.

The fantasy is revealing. "The ideal turn-on would be two or three women at once, who are lesbians, and who are of different racial/cultural origins." Why is this the super-dream? Simple: it allows for magnified Objectification, Fixation, and Conquest. Two or three women are more than one. Lesbians are by definition the most difficult conquest, so they are potentially the greatest trophy, the strongest vitamin for building healthy egos and solid definitions of self as powerful male. Differing racial/cultural origins add exotic uniqueness and make one a universal image of manhood. And this, remember, is the common fantasy of what are normally regarded as sexually healthy, well-adjusted males.

So, while many relationships do grow beyond the initial sex-role encounters, I think it becomes increasingly clear that the growth is upon a diseased foundation. And as a result, there are built-in limitations (and too often, built-in tragedies) in relationships as we know them—which means perhaps all relationships we have seen, known, or been personally involved in. And that is why we can no longer feign surprise when a relationship we consider good and mature begins to crumble and the old sex roles come exploding off the blocks like sprint champions. It happens in many forms, depending on the cultural/economic backgrounds of the people involved. But it does happen. Has happened. Will continue to happen—if left unexamined.

I've spoken to a number of friends about this essay and asked them to read it and offer criticisms. They did. Some were nervous, some calm, some just smiled. But most of them agreed with the general thrust of the argument (there were disagreements over specifics). And we talked for many hours about sexuality. But our discussions didn't have an immediate or visible effect on our existing realities. Because we have all been thoroughly socialized. We are all trained actors. Character actors. Method actors. And no method actor with twenty years or more experience is going to lose his skill, forget or confuse his role, miss the lines at the right time, unless the script is re-written or eliminated, the sets changed, and the desires and expectations of the cast, stage hands, directors and audience re-socialized.

I want to ask people to do that, but I can't. Because I don't know what that kind of re-socialization entails. I have some vague ideas, but at this point I'm struggling. I can't offer any simple answers. Obviously, there are many risks involved. Some of my male and female friends, who are pretty open and enlightened people, have said that they would rather keep things the way they are if trying to change them is going to cause doubt, pain, and an awful lot of work. I suspect that those conditions will have to be a step in the transition (although easier than we think); men and women are going to have to be prepared for rough times and be ready to deal with them. But when I look around me and see the alternatives to taking risks and living with uncertainty, those alternatives are so unpalatable that the need to change becomes a command. Even though it's not going to be a rose garden. At least for a while.

***

I would like to raise a few questions. I think all of them have been asked before. And they have been answered before. But I would like to ask them again and attempt to at least partially answer them in the context of the socialized penis. I'm very aware that these questions don't have simple answers, and I don't want to discount other answers that have been offered. I have read answers to these questions that I have agreed with. But my intention isn't to definitively answer these questions by exploring all info available. My intention is much less ambitious: to see what (if any) new perspectives are available by placing the questions against the backdrop of Objectification/Fixation/Conquest. Some of the "answers" may seem old hat; others may seem substantively different; still others may strike you as foolish. What really matters is that we all understand that there's so much more to learn and so many essays and personal accounts that still need to be written.

My attempted "answers," even within their defined context, aren't sufficiently thorough and aren't intended to be the last word on anything. So consider each "answer" a question, and deal with your own shit.

Why do so many men fear women's liberation? One of the things that terrifies men about the women's movement is that women are talking to each other. About themselves. But also about men. And that as women do this, the man's game is up, his strategy is laid bare, and he feels the threat of being objectified. As his machinations, maneuvers and *modus operandi* become known, he won't be able to perpetrate the fraud that he is something special to his woman (women?), since many women are getting to know that all men do pretty much the same things in striving to empty their sacs. Now, many women have known this all along but have either kept quiet about it or repressed their knowledge of it because they have been socialized to do so and because there are pressures that bear down hard if they don't. And men didn't know, or pretended not to know, that women knew; so they thought they were always successful in convincing their women that they were special and unique (and therefore a valuable commodity). And now that men are being exposed, some of them are cowering in their nudity. As a close woman friend once wrote to me, "Men don't marry harlots; they know too much."

Why do men hate women? Not too many men will admit to this; and I'm not sure what percentage of men actually do hate women. But more than a few women believe men do. And I think a number of men do hate women but aren't aware of it.

To hate someone (because of race, religion, or political belief), you must first de-humanize them, make them sub-human. After you have done this, you can hate them (and even be righteous about it) because they aren't worthy of human regard, consideration, or treatment (e.g., "gooks"). When men objectify (generalize) women, they take the female's human-ness away, making her less than human, non-specific, sub-human. This allows men to carry out their role with women, exert their power over them. But if a man has a bit of decency lurking in his brain (and I like to think most do), he hates himself for having been evil enough to destroy the female: that is, evil enough to have taken a whole, breathing, thinking, feeling human being and to have made something less than human of it. He also dislikes himself for the crude games he plays, the strategies he develops and implements to relieve "the torment of the testicles." And he may even resent the fact that this role is demanded of him and that he is a prisoner to it.

But all this is difficult for a man to realize or admit about himself. And deal with consciously. So he transfers the hate to the woman for making him act in a less than human way and she thereby becomes responsible for his sub-human actions. So she is made sub-human a second time because the man feels she is the one who caused him to be sub-human. So he hates her. Hates her even though he is the one who is the de-humanizer. And because her existence, as a socialized woman, reminds him of this. Constantly.

Why do men get jealous? If a woman rebels (flirts, denies him sex, has an affair), it lets the man know that he has failed to de-humanize his woman, failed to make her his subject. Therefore, he is a failure, less than a whole man, with cracked ego and lost manhood. And this thought doubles back because he feels that that is why his woman prefers other men who are more manly than he. (And what if she's *right?*)

Why do men go to other women? In relationships that grow beyond the initial sex-role-playing, a time often comes when the man can no longer conquer his woman because she is willing and there. But the man has his penis socialized (and his brain along with it) to feel manly when he is fixating and conquering. And he may by now know her too well even to be able to fixate on her, since he has probably come to realize that her breasts and vagina are connected to the rest of her being. So the old excitement isn't there. "Something" has gone out of the relationship.

Another explanation for why men run to other women is that other women are closer to being whole human beings (like their loves once were). The other woman is by definition more attractive, more interesting, a potential new trophy, while his wife (or lover) is a less-than-whole human whom he has already de-humanized. When (if) he conquers this new other woman, and succeeds in de-humanizing her, the man will tire of her also and look for yet another close-to-whole female being.

Men who are not capable of running around are often considered suspect by men who do run around. Again, the crude male vernacular tells the story: "She's got him by the balls." Or: 'He's pussy-whipped."

Why is premature ejaculation a problem? There are three varieties of premature ejaculation. The first is a result of some anthropological studies which suggest that all Western men ejaculate too soon; but since this problem has been discussed elsewhere and is considered the norm, it will not be discussed here.

The second variety of premature ejaculation is described by that great teenage pre-coital phrase—"coming in your pants." Which translates as ejaculating before the reality seems to warrant it. The third variety is ejaculating before the woman has orgasm (what if she doesn't have orgasm?). Both of these latter varieties lead us back to the way the penis is socialized: it responds to Fixation and Conquest. Usually men come too soon because they are having fantasies which include Fixation and Conquest. They are not really sleeping with/involved with the woman in their arms.

When I was in my teens there was a common bit of advice provided by experienced males on the subject of premature ejaculation. It was: "Think of garbage cans" (oh, the power and beauty of language). Which was profound advice although no one knew why. What the advice means is: if you think of garbage cans, that is, if you interrupt your Fixation and Conquest syndrome, you will interrupt your sexual functioning. When the time is right, forget the garbage cans, and you'll ejaculate on schedule. So the problem of premature ejaculation is really rooted in the factors which caused the present kind of penis socialization to develop.

Why are men afraid of "nymphomaniacs"? If you're laughing at this question, you'd better figure out why the ideal turn-on for most males is a lesbian and not a "nympho."

"Nymphomaniacs," by definition, can't be conquered. In fact,

32

they may be objectifying/fixating/conquering the man. Instead of using, the man is being used. He is nothing special or unique to this woman—she's had a hundred more like him. So sleeping with her undermines the man's definition of self. Also, because a "nympho" is defined as insatiable, a man (in his heart of hearts) knows his limitations but his ego isn't likely to let him admit this easily. So the "nympho" is feared because she destroys the male role in a very basic way.

Why do some people have an aversion to homosexuality? The simple answer is that all of us have been socialized to fear/hate/scorn homosexuality. For that reason, I may not be capable of dealing with homosexuality in a non-prejudiced manner. The only non-partisan reason I can think of for my aversion to homosexuality is that most homosexuals I have known have not transcended the sexual roles we are all damaged by. They have their male and female too and are playing the same games we play except that they play them with members of their own sex. Which may explain part of our aversion: namely, we dislike homosexuals because they are the epitome of what our roles are, of how we act, as males and females. In that way, they are an insult to us. They mock us, make a joke of us, seem to caricature what we'd really look and act like if only we had the sufficient distance from ourselves to rationally observe our actions.

There is another obvious, perhaps too obvious, reason for our fear of homosexuals. A female homosexual makes a man feel unnecessary, inadequate, and un-manly because she doesn't need men. A male homosexual makes a woman feel unnecessary, inadequate and un-womanly because he doesn't need women. And nothing in our socialization has prepared us for not being needed by members of the opposite sex.

Why do men masturbate? Because it feels good and it's fun. It may be a natural outgrowth of our unnatural sexual socialization. It provides sexual release and may be the only sane choice (as opposed to abstinence or rape, for example) where there are no other alternatives.

Perhaps we should first ask: how do men successfully masturbate? First, the penis (sensitive thing that it is) responds to friction, if that friction is connected with Fixation and Conquest (that is why underpants and zippers by themselves do not constantly have all men walking around with erections all the time). And secondly, the penis has been socialized to respond to the imaginings of Fixation and Conquest.

So, when men are in a situation or society where social intercourse does not result in genital intercourse, men may masturbate for any one of (or combination of) a number of reasons. It feels good. It's amazing to see what their own body can do. They're "horny." They fear impotence, and masturbation (inadequately) alleviates that fear for a while. They played around with a woman for a few hours but they didn't make it into bed, and their balls hurt, and masturbating is an effective way of relieving that pain or pressure. They didn't want to "attack" a woman (let's say, on a first date), so they masturbate to insure their penis won't be in control of their social actions that evening. If they are impotent with women, or if they have no one to sleep with, masturbation provides sensual pleasure. And most important, ejaculation defines one as male; so if you're not "shacked up," or having an affair, or married, masturbation allows a man to continue defining himself as male, as a power, as a conqueror.

***

I wrote this essay during the summer of 1971. From the beginning I was annoyingly aware of the limitations of what I was doing. I knew it was a narrow exploration, a formulation that would help me deal with one aspect of male sexual socialization. It also had an undercurrent of behaviorism, which I don't like and didn't want; but I just wrote, and what happened is what you read. The essay isn't, and wasn't intended to be, a consistent historical tract or sociological treatise. Nor was its design political, in the worldly sense. I felt the need, and thought I saw the reasons, to stay fairly specific.

Because it's easy to escape. From self and others. It's safer to be all-inclusive in generalized "out there" ways. It's tempting to become resigned to the "realities," to let the definition of the disease become an argument that supports the disease's continuance. To say, "Yes, I'm damaged, but just look around at the whole fucking world and how messed up it is and how the hell can I change until all those things out there change, allow me to change, help me to alter my being?"

I agree: it is near-impossible for any one of us to change the world. I agree: it is difficult to change the self if the world remains a constant (especially since self is contained in the definition of world). But the world doesn't change by itself, and the one place the individual *can* begin is with self, translating self to the world in a personal, rather than grand, political way. (And maybe, at some time, in a grand, political way, too.)

Perhaps the greatest short-coming of the essay is its avoidance of political and societal questions. "Does unalienating work necessarily

34

result in unalienated sexuality?" "In what ways does patriarchy determine social-sexual roles?" "To what extent does our physiology affect our social development?" And many others. All vital questions, but ones which permit the possibility of escaping one's self. And since what I've read is largely political or scientific or psychological, and predominantly academic, I thought it might be meaningful to deal with a specific topic, from a personal and self-specific stance.

Another problem was trying to envision the audience. Males only? Males and females? Whichever individual happens to be reading the words? I didn't have an answer to that, though I tended to conceive of it as a dialogue with men. But what if the essay alienated some men who didn't share my experience of "normal" sexual socialization? I couldn't discover anything close to a perfect solution to the whole question of audience (or voice). So I wrote by feel and instinct. And if I've insulted or harmed anyone, that wasn't the intent.

During the six months I re-read and re-thought what I had written, yet another problem became apparent: the essay raised many questions (direct and indirect) which I didn't deal with. And now that I've done the final re-write, I still haven't dealt with them. Because discussion is endless and I'm just not up to writing a monstrous tome. So I avoided tangents and detours and tried to exercise self-restraint. And also because many of the questions are questions I can't answer.

Another point of information. Throughout the essay I used the word "socialized" rather than a word like "conditioned." Intentionally. A word like "conditioned" loses sight of who does what to whom. The word "socialized" never lets you forget that there are many things—males, females, cultures, societies, institutions, nations—that do it to all of us. Not the maligned mother or mythified father, but everyone and everything that embodies and fosters sexual role-playing. And I didn't want to lose sight of that larger context, even though my parameters overtly excluded it.

All this is as explanation. And premature apology. And maybe self-defense.

Copyright (c) 1972 by Jack Litewka. From *The Lamp in the Spine,* Fall/Winter 1973-74, and *Liberation,* March/April 1974. Reprinted by permission of the author.

Refusing To Be A Man

John Stoltenberg

John Stoltenberg read this statement at a meeting of the National Organization for Women in New York City, June 19, 1974, as a member of a panel on the subject of "bisexuality."

I wouldn't say I'm a bisexual. That is not a word I would use to tell you something about my life, my body, or the people with whom I make erotic commitments.

I would be angry if anyone carelessly called me a bisexual, a heterosexual, or a homosexual. Those are not merely inexact words. They are bad words. They are the words of a masculinist culture. They are the vocabulary of male domination. They come from a language devised by men in order to perpetuate a system in which men are conditioned to be the pursuer, the aggressor, the possessor, and the fucker.

I renounce being that kind of man. I reject any use of language which in any way defines me as that kind of man. And I abhore the language which indicates gender when that language would be used to objectify the bodies of the persons with whom my body has felt intimacy, sharing, mutual respect, and trust. The language which objectifies those partnerships objectifies both partners in the relationship. I am not an object; I reject anyone's erotic objectification of me. And I do not make love with objects, nor with people who clamor for objectifying attention. Not anymore. I no longer want "to be a man" in any conventional sense of the word—and here I refer specifically to masculinist genital functioning.

The truth of my body and the sexual ethics of my life have nothing in common with the lies of the culture in which I live. I would like to say of myself: I intend to live as a moral androgyne. I am genitally male, but I endeavor with my heart to rid my life of male sexual behavior programming. My body never accepted that programming in the first place. I used to think there was something wrong with me. Now I'm dead certain there's something wrong with the program.

My body doesn't lie. The truth of my body contradicts cultural masculinist expectations.

***

My body longs to be together with someone I love. We live in a rhythm of reunion and separation. Our love is recent. We plan to live together soon and for the rest of our lives. The truth of our reunions is the shared truth of our friendship, our work, our moral intelligences, and our bodies. Our bodies don't lie. I can only imagine life together. I cannot imagine life apart.

And there are a few other people in my life, whom I care about with my heart. And we are compassionate companions. And with each of them, my body has been, or could be, for the time being, intimate, if in the moment that became our mutual choice—a way of being together appropriate to the fullness of our feelings for each other.

But I could not be in the bed of a man who is masculinist—whose sexuality has the theme of prowling and pronging, whose body has internalized all the cultural expectations of exertion, tension, and performance—of getting erections and having orgasms—of making something happen. I reject encounters with such men as biologically inauthentic. They toxify me. I don't want to know them. I don't even want to hang around.

And I could not be in the bed of a woman who has internalized those expectations of male sexual behavior and response. I refuse to be her oppressor.

***

Please understand why I am about to say what I am about to say. I believe that in the so-called male bisexual, his masculinity is a constant. Whether he is "attracted" to men or "attracted" to women, he obtains his manhood as he takes his pleasure. For a man to call himself bisexual is to pride himself in the functioning of his cock: it pops up and is ready to have sex with more warm bodies than before. There is a dangerous consistency in male sexual behavior programing which makes not very difficult the shift from fucking men to fucking women or from fucking women to fucking men. The fact that male bisexuality has become trendy worries me a lot. I think for males, bisexuality is just another form of phallic imperialism—just another adventure in the quest for assistance in masturbation—and just another escalation in masculinist sexual aggression.

The man who can bang away to orgasm in the vagina of a woman is just going to bang away in my ass. The woman whose sense of herself depends on male approval is just going to expect me "to be a man to her" in a way that would be wholly dishonest for both of us.

So I don't want to talk about bisexuality. I don't like what it means when it refers to male sexual activity and response. I don't believe in bisexuality. I reject it as a word. I reject it as a way of life. And I don't want to have anything to do with it.

But I want to talk about masculinity. I agreed to be on this panel tonight because I want to say something about male sexual biology. And I want to say something about the difference between what I feel to be the truth and what I understand to be the lies in our culture— our male-dominated, female-victimizing sexual politics.

***

I want to talk about two lies. The lie of male orgasm. And second, the lie of male erection.

First: the lie of male orgasm. The lie is that male orgasm and ejaculation are the same thing. The lie is that if you're male, you first have a genital sensation of two or three seconds of "inevitability" during which you couldn't stop if you tried, and next you experience certain internal genital contractions which include squirting out of semen, and thereafter you have a "refractory period" during which your penis gets soft and rather uncomfortable if touched very much. This refractory period lasts from 15 to 30 minutes or longer, depending on age and so forth, before the man could presumably have another erection and come again.

In my experience, this is not true. In my experience, orgasm and ejaculation are not the same. In my experience there is a male orgasm separate and distinct from ejaculation, and these non-ejaculatory orgasms can be multiple. These non-ejaculatory orgasms can and will happen over and over again if stimulation continues. And the only built-in biological cause for stopping is fatigue.

There is no sensation of "inevitability" before such orgasms. My body doesn't know in advance that such an orgasm is going to happen, but my body knows that such an orgasm has happened after it has happened. There is no discomfort or extreme sensitivity afterwards, but there is a clear refractory period, which seems relatively short.

To me, these orgasms seem to occur in waves. They are without effort and tension. I do not "make them happen" nor does my partner. They seem to occur naturally in the general interflow of erotic communication. I do not internally "jack myself up" in order to function, perform, and come. In fact, since that was my conditioning, I went through a period once when I rather consciously unlearned that old way to have an ejaculation. My body still knows how. But my body doesn't like to do that anymore, and I avoid encounters where that would be expected of me.

I know for a fact in my body that there is a sensation of completeness, of being-one-with, and of wholeness during and after—if I have not strived in any way for that other fiction of sexual achievement.

Ejaculation is another phenomenon. Sometimes ejaculation happens also, but I have come to mistrust my conditioning which identifies the so-called "necessity of ejaculation" as being part of a scenario of male sexual success and satisfaction. In fact and in the truth of my body, ejaculation is something else. I have learned that if I have strived for ejaculation, or put effort into ejaculating in any way, the result is a rather uncomfortable refractory period—which I take to be the body's message that I strove inauthentically to achieve some cultural lie about "release of sexual tension."

In my experience, my body has learned and remembers that ejaculation will happen naturally, of its own accord, if in fact my body has an authentic wish to discharge an accumulation of semen. And my body will tell me if that's what's about to happen, and I can let it happen, or not let it happen—but I no longer choose to make it happen. Because I prefer the truth of my body to the lies of the culture in which I live. And if I think about ejaculation, it is in the context of the politics of birth control—and the responsibility that I take for my ejaculate in relation to the body of a woman.

So-called "premature ejaculation," by the way, I understand to be an instance of ejaculation without orgasm—a natural biological discharge mechanism similar to nocturnal emission in young males. And were it not for the fact that the culture puts such a premium on inauthentic male sexual performance, it would probably not be such a big deal.

Similarly, what's called "impotence" is another internalization of a perverse system of male-dominant cultural values. Men (and women) are taught to believe that a cock is either limp and dysfunctional or erect and functional, and anything in between doesn't have sense unless it's clearly on its way to erectness or legitimately on its way to limpness (a legitimacy which can be presumed only if ejaculation has been achieved). Which brings me to the second lie I want to talk about: the lie of male erection.

The lie is that rigidity means arousal, rigidity means power, rigidity means manhood, and rigidity means the urgency for something called "release of sexual tension." In fact, I now believe, rigidity is usually a symptom of tension artificially induced. (I say "usually" because I am discounting those rigid erections which occur naturally in males when the bladder is very full.)

The truth is that bone-hard erections aren't very comfortable. They stick out from your body and are painful if bent. And they feel a little dead. They function in fucking very well, in that they are good for rape. But the idea that they feel good—that they are sensate—is only a cultural illusion.

I believe that the culture reinforces stiff hard-ons as symbols of male aggression and power. And I believe that in order to fulfill that cultural expectation, a man growing up in this society learns how to make himself hard by certain internal muscle constrictions and by certain fantasies of penetration and violation. The culture teaches men those fantasies all over. The man learns to induce that muscle tension in his body on his own, by various pelvic thrusts and squirms. The muscled, tense, and aggressive body of the macho-male-American is the product of this conditioning. All forms of social aggression—in speech, dress, body movement, and military and economic exploitation—help men support their erections—erections which, if the truth were known, would be perceived internally as biologically inauthentic.

***

I have suffered these lies in my life. My mind has asked questions: Will it stay up? Will I get it in? Why is it getting softer? What's wrong with me? I wish I were harder. Now my mind asks: What's wrong with the society I live in? Why has this society made me keep thinking about the hardness of my cock, such that to this day my mind has been trained to wonder: What am I feeling in my genitals? Is this feeling appropriate? Am I male enough? What will my partner think? How can I manage to keep up passions and appearances? And so forth.

I realize now, finally in my thirtieth year, that the society I live in had an economic use for me and tried to groom me: for the military, the police, the government, the corporations, the universities, the professions, the religious power structure—all the positions you have to "be a man" in order to get to and in order to perform in. Somehow, in my case, society failed. Somehow I never made the connection between aggression and my sensual feelings.

My father, I suppose, was not society's accomplice. Inadvertently, and quite naturally, he never helped society to program me as a domineering, pleasure-seeking male. My father is gentle, loving, caring, and responsible. I can't recall him ever having given me another kind of message that there is any other way to be a man. He really broke the rules.

In my life I have tried to achieve phallic identity: as a married man and then as a gay man. But I never imagined or pretended I was good at it—neither in relation to the bodies of men, nor in relation to the bodies of women. So I was at liberty to learn the immorality of the politics of male-ism: The politics of genital objectification, sex role delineation, and the oppression—and profound victimization—of women throughout their lives.

Finally, I feel at liberty to say: I intend to do what I can to renounce—and to overthrow—the culture we live in with its masculinist lies. And to discover and speak, with my words and with my body, some other truths instead.

Copyright (c) 1974 by John Stoltenberg. First published in *Win*, July 11, 1974. Reprinted by permission of the author.

Lovemaking With Myself

Jamie Bevson

Masturbation has become a central, unifying experience in my daily routine. I trudge up to my room at the end of a typically frazzled, emotionally-draining day and pour out my frustrations and joys into my journal. Then, removing my clothes, I slowly begin pulling together alienated and scattered fragments. From dance and yoga I've learned to stretch out the tenseness in my head, shoulders, back, legs, hips, and toes. Flexing, extending, relaxing, breathing deeply and rhythmically, I stand, sit, lie on the carpet or pillows. I create a space for myself the way I would for a special lover. Music, candles, incense. I will perhaps find myself dancing in my nakedness in front of the mirror or rubbing all over my body with oil—belly, nipples, navel, toes, armpits, face, neck, arms, legs. My noisy mind begins to quiet as I slip into the totality of my body. In time, even though I may not have felt sexual tension earlier, my penis becomes erect. Often I sit cross-legged in front of the mirror next to my bed, singing and swaying, feeling rushes of sexual excitement all through my body. Before ever touching my penis, I will lubricate my finger or my vibrator and slowly, tenderly, penetrate my anus. Massaging my asshole or my prostate, I cover my penis with oil and softly, gently, stroke it. My favorite position for orgasm is on my back, hips above my head, ejaculating into my mouth, recycling my semen. Unfolding this foetal cocoon, one vertebra at a time, completes a meditation of self-love.

Did that embarrass you? It was scary to write. Masturbation has been a continuous sexual involvement for thirteen years of my life, yet I choke on the word. For years I would "jerk-off" under the covers, lights off, touching only my penis, not moving or breathing, deathly afraid of discovery (a still lingering fear). This guilt and fear, which most of us feel to some degree, is rooted in four thousand years of patriarchal religious, medical and social prejudice which identifies masturbation as "self-abuse" and "immature." Even my liberal friends think of it as a substitute for the real thing or an indication that "something's wrong with your sex life."

Fortunately, these attitudes are changing. Kinsey's and other studies have revealed: "Everybody masturbates! From infancy to old age, either consciously or unconsciously, everyone masturbates . . .It's quite obvious that people are happier and better adjusted when sexual excitement can be resolved by orgasm." (*Self Love* by Gordon.)

Unfortunately, however, as Kinsey also found, "*fantasies* are almost universally present as precursors to [male masturbation] . . . Men frequently have fantasies of unfulfilled or repressed desires. Fantasies . . . become so interwoven with the orgasmic experience, that the normal heterosexual *(sic)* experience fails to satisfy, and the dream is preferred to the reality." *(Self Love)*

These fantasies, in my experience, have been examples of the type of masculine sexuality which dominates our culture. The fantasies have been essentially of rape or being raped. "I feel like mostly any fantasy men have . . . about either sex is not a good thing. There may be some kinds of fantasies that are not oppressive but I've never experienced them and I can't conceive of any. I believe my fantasies are oppressive because they always use and manipulate the person being fantasized.They never take into account the person's mind or feelings—only the body. My fantasies give me complete control over sex—I don't fantasize give-and-take sexual relations. As a man, I've been taught to take control of sex, and fantasizing plays right into this shitty pattern. The fantasized lover is distorted and is used to satisfy men's sick hyper-sex-drive, which has been created and embedded in our minds." *(Brother, No. 4)*

How does a man deal with this patriarchal perversion within himself? I first began struggling with my rape fantasies, about five years ago, as feminist friends began demanding it. I began to think of masturbating as making love to myself. Around the same time, not coincidentally, I had my first positive homosexual experience. In *Brother No. 4,* Robert describes a similar experience—"After a couple of months of good experiences, I realized that what I really wanted to do was to be able to lick my own penis—but I couldn't do it. After a while I realized that if I couldn't lick my own penis, I still wanted to lick a penis—therefore someone else's. And I also wanted someone to lick my penis. So I think there is some kind of link between homosexuality and masturbation." David Gordon concurs: " . . . every [masturbatory] indulgence is in effect a homosexual act which serves as an outlet for the release of the homosexual trends which are universal and present in all." *(Self Love)*

Refusing to "jerk-off" to fantasies and struggling to "make-love-to-myself "have brought me in touch with strong homosexual feelings. Looking at myself, especially in a mirror, touching myself all over, listening to my breathing, tasting my semen, all this associated with sexual pleasure, reinforces my sexual attraction to men. At the same time, the process of making love with a real person, *myself,* is liberating me from my fantasies, making them unnecessary.

Of course, I'm not liberated from fantasizing. I still flash sexually on women and men I see (maybe I will forever), but I don't respond by jerking-off; I'm trying to diminish the sexual response associated with the flash. I'm struggling not to cop-out to the "quick-fix" of pornography or fantasies. I'm struggling with the compulsion to "get-my-rocks-off-quick," struggling against the tendency of Orgasm-As-the-Goal and the Only Worthwhile Sensation in lovemaking.

I'm struggling with the patriarchal notion that erections are powerful ("potent"), struggling to get away from the penis-focus, the frenzied jerking.

My sexual partners, first women, then men, have confronted me with these masculinist parts of me, and I've discovered them in other men. I've found that not only do they oppress women and vulnerable men, but they are very limiting. Through making love with myself I am experimenting with creating a new, unmasculine sexuality.

I take time, half an hour to an hour. I release tension through body movement and massage, not orgasm—which allows a more relaxed orgasm, an extended orgasm. I bring myself to the point of orgasm and back off. I continue to make love following orgasm. I have moved beyond my uptightness about my asshole. It's no longer smelly (the smell's erotic!), dirty, out of control or tight, or ugly. I discover new sensations—food, colors, clothes, chanting, hyperventilating, drugs, showers, and hot baths. As Betty Dodson says in *Getting to Know Me:* "Masturbation is . . . the way we discover our eroticism, the way we learn to respond sexually. Sexual skill and the ability to respond are not 'natural'—at least not in our society. Doing what 'comes naturally' for us is to be sexually inhibited." (*Ms.* Aug. 1974)

Sometimes I fear that men discovering sexual self-awareness will just perform better, and will succeed in taking but not giving love. But somehow, in my experience, self-love removes the desperate orgasm-hunger that blinds us, that pushes us to be insensitive and to oppress people. We become less horny and so become more insistent that lovemaking be something else—emotional, sharing, communicative, spontaneous. And we can see more clearly our real needs for sensual contact, trust, responsiveness, companionship, and commitment. Moving away from fantasies and orgasm-erection orientation brings me closer to making love with friends (even though they don't fit my fantasy "type"). I can trust them to be affectionate, receptive and honest, to help me transcend the burning fear of "impotence" or the explosive letdown of releasing horniness.

Bibliography
"Getting to Know Me," Betty Dodson, *Ms.*, August 1974.
"Making Love with Myself," Robert, *Brother No. 4,* 1972.
"Men and Our Bodies," *Brother No. 6,* 1973.
Self Love, David Cole Gordon, 1968.

From *A Forum for Changing Men,* January 1975. Reprinted by permission.

How Pornography Shackles Men
and Oppresses Women

Michael Betzold

Pornography is booming. What was once found only in a few sleazy blocks in big cities is now available almost everywhere. Even small towns have their massage parlors, "dirty" bookstores and skin flicks. In the cities entire blocks have been ravaged by the porn-mongers.

So far most of the vocal opposition to pornography has come from the far right. A few women's groups have spoken out against porn, but it's not a major item on any feminist agenda. And why isn't pornography an issue for anti-sexist men? After all, men produce and consume the stuff and by doing so exploit women and promote their own worst fantasies.

Skin flicks and porn reading matter market women as commodities, denying physical uniqueness; women are presented as "tits and ass" with bulging breasts and painted-on smiles. This caricature of the female body and its reduction to a few sexual essentials is presented undisguised in the "hard-core" material and covered up with sophisticated packaging in *Playboy, Penthouse,* and "soft-core" porn films like "Emmanuelle." Whether explicit or implied, the underlying message is the same: women are to be treated by the consumer (the male reader) as pieces of ass.

Besides this overt equation of "women as cunts," pornography contains hidden messages. For example, the recent surfacing of sado-masochistic material in more respectable publications like *Penthouse* illustrates how reactionary sexism gets mingled in with the turn-on photos. The material suggests that women should not only be fucked, but beaten, tortured, and enslaved—triumphed over in any way. *Penthouse* gets away with this murderous message by casting two women in the S/M roles, but it's no problem for a man to identify with the torturer—the victim is provided.

Pornography is loaded with attacks on feminism. Men are told to reassert their mastery over women. Perhaps this explains why porn is booming. Even if the consumer grows tired of the "wide-open beavers," he may continue buying for the ego-bolstering message that men are still on top, and that's where they should be.

While pornography promotes a male fantasy of continued societal power, its effect is to render men more powerless to meet their emotional needs. Besides reinforcing destructive fantasies toward women, porn promotes self-destructive attitudes in men. By providing substitute gratification, it provides an excuse for men to avoid relating to women as people. It encourages unrealistic expectations: that all women will look and act like Playboy bunnies, that "good sex" can be obtained anywhere, quickly, easily, and without the hassle of expending energy on a relationship. When men view women as sex objects, they are also objectifying themselves, a point not often appreciated

Pornography contains an implied image of men. The porn reader imagines himself to be either a "Playboy"—with all the status that implies—a "Hustler" (a working-class version of the Playboy), a "Dude," a "Scamp," a "Stud," etc. Commercial messages about clothing, food, appearance and behavior accompany these projected images.

Crucial to all these variations of the macho image is the demand for sexual performance. Pornography promotes our insecurities by picturing sex as a field of combat and conquest. Sex is portrayed as man's finest sporting event. The pressure is on for the man to perform flawlessly—how else could he possibly satisfy the voracious sexual appetites of the women presented to him.

Emotions get in the way of performance, so they must be controlled. Emotions are messy, so pornography attempts to render them superfluous. If casual sex is as available as porn implies, and all those women out there are just waiting to be taken, it's merely a matter of the male demonstrating his technical expertise in manipulating sexual response.

The obvious result is that the male consumer of pornography becomes deadened to his feelings. Emotional needs are denied altogether or telescoped mercilessly into the search to obtain exclusively genital satisfaction. Although what most men want is physical affection from another human being, what they end up thinking they want is to be laid by a Playboy bunny.

Coming to rely on pornographic materials to service sexual/emotional needs, men become ripe objects for manipulation. Powerful, suggestive advertising can exploit basic needs by inserting a commercial image between feelings and their resolution. So that more products can be sold and more profits made, superfluous artificial needs are created. Thus we are trained to consume TV dinners and other synthetic non-foods which subvert our need for genuine nourishment. In a similar way porn sellers give us a need for artificial sex that diminishes our capacities to enjoy genuine sexual interaction. The sex of pornography in unreal, featuring ridiculously oversized sexual organs, a complete absence of emotional involvement, little kissing and no hugging, limitless capacities for orgasm, and superhuman erotic calisthenics. Porn presents sexual Olympics where the goal is to set new records of size, frequency, and capacity.

Substituting a supervised, manipulated, pseudo-sexual experience for the real enjoyment of sex is porn's way of coopting sexual liberation. The unbinding of Puritanical morality in the '60s unleashed potentially disruptive forces and uncovered the whole interlocking network of repressions that keep business going as usual. A freed sexuality directly threatens the system because people begin to realize how grossly the workplace and established social relationships distort their needs for sensual enjoyment and playful activity. Sensing this, the commercial entrepreneurs were one step ahead of the game. While "revolutionary" became a Madison Avenue catchword, sexual liberation was channeled into marketable sex.

Porn does not eroticize work or social relationships. On the contrary, it provides a cheap and non-time-consuming method of "servicing" freed sexual energies so that the worker can return contentedly to a job that is anything but satisfying.

Completing its subversion of sexual liberation, porn eventually compels a return to Puritanism. By its unlimited excesses, it provokes a reaction from the forces of repression. Because most porn is degrading, it justifies the Puritan's disgust with all sexuality. In its consumers, porn promotes a hatred for sex. By limiting sexuality through its standardization, sex becomes greatly narrowed and ultimately boring. By reducing sensuality to genital orgasm, porn contracts a large, varied and hard-to-control human need into a small, quick, controlled jerk-off. By unlimited exposure of breasts and cunts detached from real people, over-saturation eventually reduces to near-nothing the porn consumers' capacities to be genuinely stimulated by human beings.

Ultimately, pornography is anti-sex. While exploiting them, it maintains all the Puritan taboos. Special sections of bookstores are hidden from public view, require an admission price, and enforce an age requirement; advertisements for skin flicks leave out letters (S_X) or sport suggestive titles ("Behind the Green Door") to emphasize the once-forbidden nature of the subject material. Sex is sold as dirty and evil to attract those who are fascinated by the forbidden. What is presented is generally so mindless and impersonal that any but the most hardened are soon turned off. The lesson is that turn-ons are really turn-offs, so why bother with sex? This sort of "liberation" is a dead-end for everyone except those who profit from our inadequacies and powerlessness.

There may be several reasons why opponents of sexism have not acted more openly against pornography. We may fear being accused of harboring vestiges of Puritanism, of being anti-sex or "unliberated." We may fear being aligned with right-wingers. Probably we are most immobilized by a libertarian confusion.

The rallying cry of porn dealers is freedom of speech and the press, that the state has no right to interfere in the private sexual tastes of consenting adults. Censorship of any sort, we all agree, is reprehensible.

Yet we would be appalled if movies showed blacks being lynched or castrated, Chicanos being systematically beaten and tortured, and we would quickly protest. If whole blocks of a city were given over to the sale of material directly oppressing black people, we would run the merchants out of town with little thought about their First Amendment rights. But we say nothing when the same activity goes on with women as the victims.

The solution is certainly not to call upon the government to impose censorship. But anti-sexist men should be staging protests against the sale of pornography and trying to raise the consciousness of their brothers who consume it. The goal should be to put Hugh Hefner and all his imitators permanently out of business, to make the marketing of women as sex objects as impossible as the selling of blacks as slaves.

Reprinted from *Male Bag,* March 1976.

Learning from Women

Bob Lamm

The following article represents excerpts from a speech delivered to the the Queens College Women's Student Union on October 28, 1975.

I want to begin by stating how much of a pleasure and an honor it is for me to be speaking here at the invitation of the Women's Student Union. Sometimes, when speakers make these declarations, it's a matter of form and courtesy. But it's a very special honor for me to be here, because I owe a very great debt to the women I've known at Queens College—many of whom have worked with the Women's Student Union, with Queens Women Against Rape, and on the Women's Festivals. Officially, in many cases, I was the teacher for these women. But in reality they were *my* teachers, and I come here today to try to express a little of what I've learned from them. Despite all my male and professorial resistance, they taught me quite a bit about their lives and oppression as women, about feminism, and about my own sexism.

When I started teaching at Queens in the summer of 1974, I was very much impressed with my own qualifications for teaching. I thought I knew a whole lot about men's lives and about masculinity. And (although I was too clever to say this out loud) I thought I knew a whole lot about women's lives.

The truth is that I knew virtually nothing about the reality of women's lives. The truth is that I came here with no serious background in feminist literature. The truth is that I had no understanding of how absurd and sexist it was for a man to teach a course on men and masculinity without a good grasp of feminist literature. The truth is that I had no idea of how much I didn't know.

And the most *glaring* truth is this one: there's nothing unusual about what I've just said. It's quite common. This afternoon, once two o'clock comes and classes begin again, a whole lot of male professors are going to start telling women students about their lives as women. Some male professors may call this teaching process biology or psychology or history or literature or anthropology. I would call this teaching process what many feminists have called it—*male supremacy*. This so-called educating goes on in every part of this college, and in every part of the world—except for the few small bits of turf that feminists have managed to fight for and win.

Thus, there was nothing very unique about Bob Lamm coming in to teach a course about sexism without much understanding of women's lives or feminism. But something unique did happen to me after I started teaching here. Unlike many male professors at Queens College, I didn't get away with my act so easily. Lo and behold—there were a lot of strong, eloquent, angry women in my classes who weren't awed by my professorial power or by my male left politics. And these women changed my life.

***

My course on men and masculinity in the summer of 1974 was intense and explosive. It lasted six weeks—three nights a week—but it felt like a year. The students in the class—both women and men—were among the most honest people I've ever met in my life. As a result, the class included moments of risky and revealing self-disclosure. It was also the scene of bitter and shattering political fights. Women in the course, speaking out of their anger as victims of a sexist society, wouldn't sit by quietly and be insulted and patronized. Men in the course, speaking out of their fear and hostility to feminist challenge, wouldn't sit by quietly and listen to attacks on their patriarchal privileges.

One thing I learned was the importance of men *listening* to women, *listening* to women's feelings and anger, and fighting off our potential for serious backlash. I had repeated conferences with a few male students, and found myself telling them again and again to listen to the women in the class. Not to freak out, not to strike back in anger, but to work hard at hearing what the women were saying.

The more I found myself in that role, the more I realized how little I myself listened to what women were saying. The more I observed the backlash and misogyny of male students, the more I had to notice my own backlash and misogyny. And, as I moved increasingly away from a mediating teacher role to active personal involvement in the class, some of my own woman-hating anger began to emerge right in front of me. By the end of the course it was clear, as one male student wrote, that I was just another fucked-up, insecure man—only with more power than the male students.

50

During the first week of the class a woman student asked me if she could present a special session on rape—a subject that my course syllabus did not cover. I reacted favorably and we set up the class for the next week. Now, at first, my consent may seem like an enlightened act, but it wasn't. It was an act of uninformed male liberalism. I had no idea of the political and educational importance of having a class on rape in a course on men and masculinity. I was simply being amiable or cooptive, depending on your point of view.

My misunderstanding of rape went something like this. I perceived rape to be a serious crime, somewhere between mugging and murder. I was vaguely aware that men were the perpetrators—and women the victims—of this particular crime. But I never considered the political implications of these obvious facts, or the connection between rape and our norms of masculinity.

My mental image of rape was of a sex crime, of what men continue to call a "crime of passion." My image of rape victims contained a lot of subconscious suspicion—what kind of women would *get themselves* into that kind of position? Thus, I had in my head every vicious, woman-hating stereotype that this society promotes about rape—right down to blaming the rape victim rather than the rapist for the crime. I had no understanding of the politics of rape—or of how my own power and privilege as a man might have some bearing on the continual rape of women by men in our society.

Women students changed all that. The class on rape and the discussions which followed shattered all of my traditional male prejudices about rape. Women students taught me that rapists are not peculiar, abnormal men. Rapists are very normal masculine men. There is no exact profile of a "typical rapist" because rapists come in all sizes and shapes, all races and nationalities, all ages and social classes. Many are white middle-class husbands and fathers.

Women students taught me that rape is neither a sex crime nor a crime of passion. Rape is often premeditated. And rape is a crime of *violence* rather than sex. It is a crime of violence against women. It is an attack by men on women's bodies, on women's feelings, on women's very existence. Women students taught me that rape is not an isolated brutal crime against women. It is only one small part of a systematic pattern of male violence against women in America. Some women are raped in their homes or in the streets by men whom we call "strangers." Some women are raped in their homes or in the streets by men we call psychiatrists, doctors, college professors, friends, lovers, husbands, and fathers. And some women are raped in the streets or in offices by men who merely stand there and commit rape with looks, with smirks, with insults, and with threats.

Women students taught me that rape can involve psychological as well as physical coercion. Many men, if asked "Have you ever raped a woman?" would quickly respond in the negative. But what if the question were, "Have you ever, at any time, in any way, through direct physical attack or subtle psychological manipulation, coerced a woman into close physical contact?" How many men could easily answer *no* to that question?

Thus, women students taught me that rape is something in which I myself am deeply implicated—directly in my relationships with women, and indirectly since I benefit from the male privilege that legitimizes rape. For rape is one of the most savage, and yet one of the most accurate, metaphors for how men relate to women in this society. It is a political crime committed by men as a class against women as a class. Rape is an attempt by men to keep all women in line. It is a clear expression of the hatred of women that so pervades our society and our visions of masculinity.

One final thing that I learned about rape was about rape jokes and warnings. Every time that a man calls a woman a "bitch," the threat of rape lies behind his hostility. Every time a man calls a woman a "witch," he reminds her of the slaughter of millions of women whose independence and medical knowledge threatened male dominance. And every time a man makes a joke about rape or wife-beating, he issues a warning to women. But, if I learned anything at all from women students, I learned this: rape is no joke.

***

The second course I taught on men and masculinity took place in the spring of 1975. It was as intense as the first but in a very different way. In the first class, when women spoke out, men responded out of self-righteous indignation and all hell broke loose. In the second class, when women spoke out, men evaded the issue and pretended to be sympathetic. This made honest interactions impossible. The eventual result was that the six women students in the class decided to split. They came in one afternoon and announced that they were holding their own separate class for women for the last six weeks of the semester.

The women spent those weeks meeting on their own without students or a male teacher. Their final papers unanimously proclaimed what a valuable experience the all-women's class had been. As one student wrote, "Our common bonds as women enabled us to discuss topics with our feelings. We can express our thoughts openly because of the oppression we share. We don't have to *prove* what we say is valid. We trust each woman's words and respect her feelings." Every woman wrote about this class in similarly glowing terms, including the women who had been most hesitant at the time of the split.

Now, as a male teacher whose women students all left his class, what did I learn from this experience? Before the course I already had some understanding of why women wanted their own space to control as they saw fit. Because of this, I accepted and supported the women's split and didn't try to stop it. But talking to the women students at the end of the term, and reading their final papers, taught me some vital lessons about the value and necessity of women's space. And when I say women's space, I mean this in a very general way. I mean space and time that women exist in and control without male presence or dominance. I mean women's classes, women's studies programs, women's centers, women's self-help clinics, women's consciousness-raising groups, women's coffeehouses, women's bookstores, women's newspapers, women's music, women's communes, women's farms, and, of course, women loving other women. When I speak of the importance of women's space, I'm speaking of all of these things and a whole lot more.

I don't need to dwell too long on an obvious point: men in this society have *no concept* of the importance and beauty and necessity of women controlling their own space, their own bodies, their own lives. Every bit of our socialization as men tells us that we're indispensable, that women simply can't get along without us. We're told that women can only find love from a man. We're told that women have nothing to say or give to each other.

But here's what I learned as a male teacher. The best college course I've ever been formally responsible for—the very best—was the one where I wasn't there, where I gave no professorial direction, where women controlled their own classroom time.

And that says something very crucial to me—something that men had better start to learn. The notion that men are indispensable to women is the worst kind of lie. Not only can women function and grow quite well without us being there—women in many situations can function and grow *much more easily* without us being there. So if men *really* want to help women—as we always claim—one concrete step is often to get out of the way. Women students in my class learned more

53

from each other than they ever could have if I was there. That fact crashes rather heavily into my male ego and my professorial conceit—but it's true and it won't go away. And it helps me to understand a little better that word that frightens and angers men so much—*separatism*.

Which brings me to a final point about the split. I *did* have ultimate power; I could have stopped it but chose not to. I could have threatened those six women with no credit or with flunking grades or other academic hassles. As long as male teachers have that kind of power over women's lives, it doesn't matter all that much whether they choose to use it or not. It doesn't matter if male teachers are overt pigs or benevolent paternalists or sincere allies of the women's movement. Things will be different only when women in the academic world—and in the rest of society—don't have to answer to *any* man, even one that is supposedly sympathetic.

***

I taught a class on the politics of sports during June of 1975. There were fifty students, forty of whom were men. The atmosphere often felt like a boys' locker room, and the politics and logic of most male students was about on that level. During the first class I spoke of a mass riot that took place in Pittsburgh in 1971 after the Pirates, the local baseball team, won the World Series. When I spoke about the fact that many women had been raped during this so-called "celebration," most of the male students laughed. And that was only the beginning.

Women students in the sports class taught me a very valuable lesson about male bonding. If a man in the class mentioned football halfback O.J. Simpson or baseball catcher Johnny Bench, it was presumed that everyone knew who they were. Meaning that everyone who *really counted* (men) knew who they were. In this class, the language and trivia of sports became an easy and subtle form of male bonding, just as the language and trivia of physics or psychology or Marxism can be the same.

Here's an example. Many of you may not know that the outstanding play in baseball's 1955 World Series was a long running catch by the Brooklyn Dodgers' Cuban left fielder, Sandy Amoros. Many of you may not even *care* about that catch. But, in the dynamics of sexual politics, that bit of trivial, stupid knowledge gives me status and privilege. The male students in the class couldn't relate to my sexual politics or my unorthodox teaching style, but they could immediately develop bonds with me—or me with them—based on checking each other out over such trivia.

The mentality works like this. "I know about Sandy Amoros—therefore, I'm OK, I must be a real man, I must really have a penis. And since you, another man, have one too, then we're OK. We're on top of 53 per cent of the world that doesn't have penises. And we're also on top of the men who don't know about Sandy Amoros. They probably don't have penises, either." This may seem crude, but it is the psychology and power politics of male bonding. And that particular class was full of male bonding.

Trivia may seem very *trivial*. But actually it's a wonderful example of the mystification of knowledge. And the mystification of knowledge is a prime trick of every oppressor—in this case, men. Men don't want to explain obscure trivia; men don't want to share our useless or useful knowledge with women because it's one of our advantages over women. It's part of our power over women; it's an essential ingredient in male supremacy. We keep women feeling un-intelligent and incapable of learning. And every once in a while, we condescend to teach women some bit of knowledge or skill out of the goodness of our male hearts.

The trivia of sports, like the pseudo-complexity of academic language, makes the out-group, the oppressed group, feel awed and powerless. And that's just how men want women to feel about sports and about life. Sports trivia is only one of a million subtle and blatant ways in which men bond together to oppress women. And I did it all the time—and never thought about it—until women students in my class raised the issue.

***

I've tried to touch on some of what I've learned from women and from feminism. Needless to say, I'm still very much at the beginning, and the same is true of every man in this society. Each of us, if we're serious about learning from women and dealing with our sexism, has a lifetime project ahead. If we sincerely want to learn and change, we've got to start reading every available bit of women's writing and feminist literature. This includes women's novels, poetry, herstory, political literature, autobiographies, biographies, newspapers, journals, and the like.

Also, if we sincerely want to learn and change, we've got to try to shut up and listen to women. This is still the hardest thing for me to do, and yet it is the most essential. In a conversation, men rarely let women get a word in; and if a woman talks, a man usually interrupts; and even if a man doesn't interrupt, men don't listen anyway. We're too busy mentally formulating our next bit of oratory. If we want to learn and change, we've got to begin by listening to women and trying to really hear them.

Beyond that, I'm not sure what to say. I know it may seem bizarre or suspicious for a man to speak this way. I know that every time a man says anything halfway reasonable about sexism, it can simply be one more male game—one more way of trying to manipulate women and control women's lives.

But I honestly wish that things were different. I wish I could live in a society where women *truly* were free, where male supremacy seemed so perverse as to be totally unimaginable, where the kind of masculine sickness that still shapes my personality didn't exist. I wish I could live in a society where all of us here really could be friends, and respect one another, and be apart or together as any of us saw fit. I wish that I could live in a society where a Women's Student Union wasn't under pressure to include a male speaker on its program, where a speaking program *of women only* and *for women only* was considered fully legitimate and appropriate and beautiful.

I know all of these things are very far off, but I hope that they're possible someday. Too many men have ruined too many women's lives already. I've seen more than enough, and I've done more than enough, and I want it to stop.

From *Morning Due: A Journal of Men Against Sexism,* Vol. 2, No. 2, 1976. Reprinted by permission of the author.

MALE SUPREMACY

Section Introduction

The first article in this section, "Patriarchy, GUS and I," by Marty Jezer, provides a brief introduction to male supremacy in non-conformist sub-cultures in the United States. GUS, an acronym for Great Underground Subculture, refers collectively to the various protest movements of the post-World War II era: bohemianism, hipsterism, the beat generation and the modern counter-culture. "Within this tradition," Jezer wrote in a prefatory note, "are many men and women who live beyond the bounds of traditional stereotyped sex roles. But a strict patriarchy that mirrors the patriarchy of . . . mainstream American society has been an essential characteristic of this self-proclaimed alternative life-style." Originally written as part of the *Win* "Special Issue: Men" in April, 1974, the article concludes by questioning whether the men's liberation movement is not another attempt to consolidate male power under the impact of the women's liberation movement. (These observations are elaborated by other authors in the section "Men's Liberation [Criticisms]".) Jezer's writing teaches us how much we have in common with previous generations of men. The oppression of women has historically been an intrinsic part of men's training and integral to their identities.

The remaining four articles in this section are analyses of male supremacy written by men who adopt the perspective of radical feminism. The authors accept the basic premise of radical feminist theory, that the division between men and women is the oldest and most universal form of oppression, and that it is the root of *all* other forms of oppression. In this view, sex caste is the primary hierarchy in human history; it precedes and is a prerequisite for the development of classes. Women's oppression originates in, and is determined by, patriarchy, not the class system. Consequently, these men are committed to the struggle against sexism as their major form of political activity.

In "All Men are Misogynists," Leonard Schein concentrates on the male psyche in a sexist society. He believes that woman-hating is at the core of men's consciousness under patriarchy. Drawing heavily on Shulamith Firestone's powerful interpretation of the Oedipus complex, Schein attempts to explain how misogyny is produced by masculine sex role socialization. In a second part, he argues that rape is the behavioral expression of woman-hating. Both rape and masculinity maintain men in power. Schein concludes by calling upon men to redirect their anger against women toward the institutions of patriarchy.

In the first part of his essay, "Toward Gender Justice," John Stoltenberg reviews some of the main features of heterosexual male domination. This is followed by a discussion of sexism among gay males and in the gay liberation movement. He argues that men have an investment in patriarchy, regardless of sexual orientation. Like Schein's, this perspective raises the question of men's role in opposing sexism. Whereas Schein supports men's consciousness raising while recognizing its dangers (see "Dangers of Men's Consciousness-Raising Groups" in the next section, "Anti-Sexist Practice."), Stoltenberg criticizes it for being an organizational form which unites males, reinforces masculinity, and perpetuates women's oppression. He outlines a plan whereby men can individually begin to struggle against sexism by reading feminist texts and repudiating masculine solidarity. Eventually, he believes, men may be able to work with women. He concludes by providing a list of feminist readings.

Gary Mitchell Wandachild's condemnation of the left's reaction to the feminist movement is summarized in the title of the next article, "Complacency in the Face of Patriarchy." He believes that male domination persists in the left and that the left continues to ignore women's oppression. Failing to recognize and oppose patriarchal rule, leftist males are attempting to preserve their privileges in a sexist society. Without a specific struggle against male supremacy, Wandachild believes, socialist movements generally fail or at best reproduce hierarchies of domination. He concludes by emphasizing the primacy of a feminist revolution.

In the final article, John Stoltenberg asserts that "Eroticism and Violence in the Father-Son Relationship" is crucial in the oppression of women. Beginning with "The Context" of the father-son relationship, he defines patriarchy as the legal ownership, maintained by physical force, of women and children by adult men. In "The Content," he outlines the process by which the idea of ownership of the lives of other human beings is implanted in the consciousness of males. Fathers use the power of their patriarchal position in the family to intervene in what they imagine to be the erotic relationship between mothers and male children. The father's aggression coerces the son to escape from the father's rage by abandoning his relationship with his mother, identifying with his father, and, following this model, becoming the oppressor of women. In thus becoming a "man," he acquires the right to own human property and a position within the dominant caste. Stoltenberg argues that through this process, oppressive masculine consciousness is the psychological inheritance of each succeeding generation of males under patriarchy.

Patriarchy, GUS and I

Marty Jezer

It was in high school during the late fifties that I read Jack Kerouac's *On The Road* and decided to become a beatnik. I wasn't sure what that entailed; all I knew was that my upper-middle-class suburban environment bored me and the future offered no signs of release. It took me about five years to navigate my uncertain journey to a beat pad on the Lower East Side (actually, at first, it was a 1½ room modern studio apartment with air conditioning). By this time, in 1962, I was living in sin with a woman, smoking dope, hanging out with poets, writers, artists, musicians and other hip types, and congratulating myself for being so cool.

For more than a decade I've lived within this ever-evolving subculture in a variety of ways: in the city and on a farm, with friends, in a commune, with a wife, a lover, and sometimes alone. During this period, I've gone through many personal changes and experienced how the subculture as a whole has changed. At times, I've self-consciously viewed my life as a political statement and as an example of a viable, radical alternative to the way of life that I left behind. It felt good altering the way I lived to meet the challenge of US militarism and imperial expansion and the consumer demands of corporate capitalism.

Through it all, though my awareness of women has changed, as has the image I hold of myself as a man, the patriarchal structure of my culture has remained intact.

This has shaken my confidence in the meaning of GUS and, hence, the direction of my own life. (GUS—the Great Underground Subculture—is the acronym Gary Snyder used in *Earth Household* for the historical "tradition that runs without break from Paleo-Siberian Shamanism . . . right down to the first tribal gathering/be-in at Golden Gate Park.") I believe that the people within this tradition are among the most sensitive and socially aware people on the earth. My friends have been my teachers and we've explored and learned much together. I expect a lot from them/us and from myself; more than I do from people who inhabit the mainstream—though living in a small rural town in Vermont has shown me that there is much to learn from them. Still, I look to people within the tradition of GUS (and this includes political people as well) for guidance. If we don't adjust our lives to meet our expanding awareness of human needs and set this kind of example, who will? I don't think this is elitist, and it is not a substitute for grass-roots political activity. But, change, after all, has to start somewhere and why not with ourselves. Barbara Deming, describing Karl Marx's insights about feminism, says that "Even when an extraordinary man, like Marx, sees that there is need for such a step, the privilege he enjoys dulls that vision, and also causes him to forget what he has seen." How true! What I want to describe is how the built-in patriarchy of GUS dulls the vision of so-called "radical" men, makes us forget even our occasional insights about how we dominate our own small slice of society, leads us to ignore our usually overbearing rhetoric about the necessity of change, and causes us to reinforce this patriarchal structure despite good intentions.

The seed-bed for the counter-culture of the 1960's was the bohemia of the postwar years and the 1950's. This was a small isolated subculture of working artists centered mainly in New York and San Francisco. This bohemia, though it liked to stick its tongue out at the bourgeoisie, made no pretense of being a radicalizing force or of proselytizing beyond its own embattled bounds. That came later. Nevertheless, its existence was correctly perceived by middle-class America as a threat to its young. One of the best-selling novels of the fifties, Herman Wouk's *Marjorie Morningstar* described the lure of bohemia to middle-class youth. The parents of middle-America heaved a collective sigh of relief when Marjorie resisted the hedonistic temptations of bohemian life and settled for the virtuous security of the middle class. But a lot of teenagers who read the book when it first came out figured that Wouk had given her a raw deal.

If *On The Road* inspired a generation of young men to abandon the promised security of affluent American life to seek out experience, *Marjorie Morningstar* accurately reflected the experience of a generation of young women who were pressured into giving up the quest. During the 1950's, there were few well-known women artists, though there were, I am sure, a lot working in the closet. This, of course, has changed. Today, the feminist movement has encouraged a renaissance of women's art, which leads one to wonder where all these creative women were back in the fifties. There is a cruel irony in this. When I was in school, poetry, etc. was considered sissy stuff. Only women read it. But it was the men who became the "serious" poets and who created a self-serving image of the holy wildman artist so that they could retain their machismo style and still do woman's work. I know that what got me interested in poetry was not good writing. Instead, it was the hip way the beat poets carried themselves, the way they defied convention, and made it possible to be intellectual and also cool and tough.

Fifties' bohemia, in the way it related to women, reflected the culture of the society it prided itself in rebelling against. Though this pattern has remained, it was not always so. The bohemia that developed around the time of the First World War was politically developed and had a powerful feminist orientation. The Red Scare of the 1920's did this movement in and when the left emerged again during the Depression, its focus was on the economic crisis, with "the woman question" only a peripheral concern. Then came the war, and women were called to *man* the assembly lines of industry as their men marched off to battle. The hard-hat image of Rosie the Riveter replaced the contented housewife ideal. Soap operas began to emphasize strong women who pursued professional careers—*Dr. Kate; Her Honor, Nancy James; Hilda Hope, MD; Joyce Jordan, Girl Interne; Portia Faces Life* (the heroine was a lawyer); *Mary Marlin* (she was a U.S. Senator); and of course the venerable *Ma Perkins,* who operated a lumberyard. The war also saw the creation of *Wonder Woman* comics and also *Mary Marvel* and *Nyoka the Jungle Girl,* who was a feminist Tarzan. World War II forced society to abandon its traditional sex-role stereotypes and acknowledge, as did the Office of War Information in 1945, that the work of women in war production "disproved the old bugaboos that women have no mechanical ability and that they are a distracting influence in industry."

The economic needs of American capitalism in the postwar world forced women back into the home and the popular image of women was arbitrarily reversed. The overwhelming concern after the war was averting another depression. The industrial system had to absorb 11 million returning veterans or face mass unemployment, a second depression, and a domestic upheaval that probably would have toppled capitalism. Working women (and blacks, etc.) were expendable and, with the collaboration of labor unions, they were laid off *en masse*. The media picked up on this cue. Movies, radio, books, television, and advertising drove the message home. The role of women in peacetime was to consume the plethora of useless and useful goods coming from industry, raise children, and keep husbands happy. The hit record of 1946, crooned by Perry Como, underlined the new cultural line:

> *Surrender, why don't you surrender?*
> *How long can your lips live without a kiss?*
> *Surrender, I beg you, surrender*
> *How long can your heart resist?*
> *I'll bring you a love you can cling to*
> *A love that won't be untrue*
> *So please be tender, and darling surrender.*

Given the intensity and ubiquity of sexist propaganda, it took an exceptionally stubborn woman to break through the socialization process and remain committed to her art.

Sanctions against creative women were pervasive within bohemia as well. The bohemian lifestyle functioned as a necessity of creative work; there was nothing escapist or dropped-out about it. Bohemians lived cheaply because their only asset was the time they had to devote to their art. For this reason, they shunned time-consuming careers and favored, as part-time work, menial or physical labor that left their minds free for thought. Creative work is also solitary work. After a day alone at a typewriter or in front of a canvas, there is a need to unwind and relax with convivial company. Hence, the famous bar scenes of the 1950's and the incessant party-going. (During the 1960's, political demonstrations served this purpose.)

But these were predominantly male scenes; a place for men to hold court, discuss their work, exchange ideas, and argue politics, a subject taboo in mainstream American life. As Michael Harrington described the bar scene of the 1950's (his new book *Fragments of a Century* says much about this period): "The late night was a gregarious, potentially erotic release from a disciplined existence." And of the in-group quality of these scenes: "Pretty girls could enter it rather easily, men much less so, and the faces changed slowly." Women were welcome, but not for their ideas, or for what they could add to the conversation.

Bohemian men, like men everywhere, share many intimacies. But in general (among close friends this often is not so) men do not let their emotions down or talk about their personal problems and doubts. Yet, creative people, especially young artists struggling for acceptance, usually poor and unrecognized, often lose confidence in their talent, and need a tremendous amount of ego support. Creative people will share ideas, but hoard emotional energy for their own work. Women artists attempt to cope with this problem by meeting together to discuss and support each others' work. Men have never done this, and have relied on women to provide necessary ego support. Besides, the macho image that bohemian men so carefully cultivated made it impossible for them to admit to such "weakness." Out of this had evolved the typical female role in bohemian life—the chick.

Women usually came to bohemia with the same creative ambitions as men. But there were few women role-models to provide support and few men took them seriously enough to provide encouragement. The only niche available to women in the bohemian subculture, as in the dominant culture, was the nurturing or supportive role. Besides ego support, women also provided male artists with income (often with the kind of compromising office job—in corporations, for instance—that no principled male bohemian would ever accept—and a male bohemian, by definition, was "principled"), and cooked, cleaned house, and raised babies. In bohemia, the male artist was the dominant figure and the functions of the society were geared to his needs. Here is Paul Goodman, in his novel *Making Do,* describing typical bohemian life (the italics are mine):

To exist in decent poverty a man had to meet strict requirements. He had to have a refined taste for the highest things, which alone do not cost money. He had to be doing something so worthwhile that he did not need extrinsic rewards. He had to choose his vices very carefully and healthfully. His wife had to respect their way of life so highly that she did not need to keep up with the Joneses. *They had to be able, in a pinch, to live on bread and water.*

Why was there no feminist resistance to this overwhelming oppression, an oppression that virtually destroyed an entire generation of creative women? During the fifties, being a bohemian was the most daring and radical life a person could lead. Women, especially, risked being disowned by their families and condemned by society on moral grounds. And bohemia, being small, isolated and poor, existed on the defensive. Understandably, the trauma of fifties' life was sufficiently risky to discourage a more far-reaching rebellion against male domination which would have ultimately threatened the well-being of the entire community. Besides, feminist ideology, like all radical ideology, was suppressed. Family, schools, the media, even the respectable intelligentsia of the time, all demanded adherence to the orthodox line of woman as happy homemaker. In the 1950's there was no political awareness or encouragement from within the bohemian community to sustain such a challenge.

Not surprisingly, I first learned of feminism from a man. My best friend (and most influential teacher in the mores of bohemian life) spent his days at home working on a novel, and hanging out with his friends. This was a typical arrangement, and his wife worked in advertising to support their growing family so he could have the time to write. The afternoons I killed at his house were an important time for me, like going to school, only better. One day my friend told me that he was a feminist. I was very impressed with this bit of confidence (I don't think any of us were ready to admit to being socialists quite yet) and filed the idea in my brain for future reference.

It didn't take me long, after giving it much thought, to conclude that I, too, was a feminist. What this meant, if I would have articulated it then, was that women had the right to be free and independent and to do everything that men did. But there was a hitch. Not seeing any women writers, poets, intellectuals, or artists (they were there, but I didn't *see* them, i.e., take them seriously) meant that it never occurred to me that women had such ambitions. So I could hardly prevent them from doing what I refused to acknowledge that they wanted to do. Hence, feminism involved only what was apparent; and by my limited and self-serving definition, it was a means of advocating what was then the bohemian status quo.

One thing I did notice in my explorations of this new underground world was that there were smart, sexy, beautiful women everywhere. If women were to be as free as men, I concluded, then I'd have to believe in what the press then described (in shock and horror) as FREE LOVE. Well, we tend to take what used to be called free love as pretty routine, but at the time the idea that women had the right to sexual pleasure, and could choose and discard lovers with the same freedom as men was pretty advanced and, to listen to the way the middle class reacted to it, the most dangerous, subversive idea that bohemians had. Only the bravest couples then lived openly together.

(I lived with my woman friend for about eight months in 1963. As fear mounted that we'd be discovered by our parents—who probably knew but couldn't ask because that kind of thing was never talked about—the pressure of our secret led us to get married.) Though this aspect of sexual equality did strike a blow at Puritan morality and was an important advance in social relationships, it also served to deflect a potential feminist challenge against the dominant patriarchy. Feminism, as my male friends and I defined it, was kept in the bedroom, and limited to what we could comfortably accept and use to advantage.

Men took the role of defining the limits of feminist ideology very seriously. Indeed, men took the role of defining everything seriously. And basic to their worldview was the image of themselves as holymen artists, in touch with some life-giving spiritual force. I want to be careful here, because in a certain respect this is a valid assumption. An inspired artist is, I believe, connected to a kind of power. In religious terms, an inspired artist (and, for that matter, any inspired person who does work with the kind of concentrated energy that makes what they do a statement of their life) is in touch with a Godhead. But what happens with male artists (and this is a role that is sanctioned and encouraged by the patriarchal expectations of male-defined bohemia) is that they take this aspect of their public or working life and turn it into a private conceit. That is, not willing to let their art speak for itself, they adopt as a style the message of their art.

Inspired art often expresses the deepest human emotions. When a person says that he or she likes this poem, or that painting, or this piece of music, what he or she is often saying is that it speaks in some way to his or her own life and provides insight and meaning. The art of the postwar era, with its attack on formalism, structure, objectivity and reality, and its emphasis on an internalized subjective free-flowing prophetic voice, fit this role perfectly. And, increasingly, male artists took their role as prophets, shamans, wisemen, wildmen in touch with essential truths, etc., to heart. Given the strict sexual categorization of bohemian life, the men became religious figures—"holy artists," while the women were left to take satisfaction as liberated chicks.

To expand this further: In the postwar a new ideology began to pervade bohemia and further inflate the male ego. Hipsters took their cue from the intense, angry and alienated jazz world of bop. Jazz has always been a masculine art. Except for female singers, the number of working women jazz musicians, until recently, could be counted on the strings of one guitar.

The essence of bop was a rebellion against the commercial values that white musicians had brought to jazz. As such, it represented a frontal attack on the values of white America. White bohemians articulated this alienation in social/political terms. Hipsters saw World War II as a sham. The holocaust of Hiroshima and Nagasaki was the equivalent of the gas ovens of Nazi Germany. The Cold War, McCarthyism, and the materialism of the affluent fifties fed on this disillusionment. Hipster alienation became so total that it could not even acknowledge the reality of American life. In effect, the hipster pulled the plug and cut himself off; he was the first American drop-out.

Hipsters prefaced everything they said with the word "like" so as to declare at the onset that what they were about to say was merely illusion. In this moral vacuum (which was actually a moral response to an immoral situation) the only quality that had meaning was style, i.e., not what one did, but the way one did it. (Hipster ideology had its aesthetic parallels in modern music, abstract expressionism and the literature of the beats, and other fifties' poets and writers.) Norman Mailer, who suggested in *The Naked and The Dead* that fascism had triumphed in World War II, became the hipsters' most articulate ideologue. In a column in the *Village Voice* he hashed out the meaning of hip.

> To a square, a rapist is a rapist. Punish the rapist, imprison him, be horrified by him and/or disinterested in him and that is the end of the matter. But the hipster knows that the act of rape is a part of life, too, and that even in the most brutal and unforgivable rape, there is artistry or the lack of it, real desire or cold compassion, and no two rapes are ever the same.

The essence of hip is style; living one's life as if it were art, a jazz solo, a poem, a cascading flow of color. Everything else has failed, and art alone remains real and holy. To the hipster, the public role of an artist as creator is merged with the private role of one's personal life as art. The world becomes a canvas, a woman a typewriter on which the holy man pounds out his story. Rape, in the hipster sense, becomes an aesthetic experience, at least for the rapist. The victim just does not count.

The hipster was a transitional figure between bohemian and beat. Or, to put it another way, the beats were hipsters as perceived by the mass media. In the mid-fifties, public life in America began to open up. There were stirrings in the peace movement and in civil rights, and the many isolated groups of artists were coming together in bohemia around a common aesthetic that would come to be identified by the media as "beat" but which encompassed a wide diversity of ideas.

The catalyst for this emerging movement was a karass consisting of Jack Kerouac, Neal Cassady, Allen Ginsberg and others who, during the late 40's and early 50's, were careening around the continent energizing different bohemian scenes wherever they went. (Karass—as bokoninism: "If you see your life tangled up with somebody else's life for no very logical reason, that person may be a member of your karass. Humanity is organized into teams, teams that do God's Will without ever discovering what they were doing." See Kurt Vonnegut, Jr. *Cat's Cradle.*) But it was not until 1957, when Ginsberg's poem "Howl" was beginning to attract attention and Kerouac's *On The Road* was published, that the media began to take notice.

At the same time, a new generation that was too young to remember the depression (and so was not uptight about economic security) and only faintly remembered the war (so did not have its idealism shattered) was becoming socially conscious. Unprecedented affluence and tight employment sanctioned student life (it postponed the entry of young people into the job market) and made the bohemian lifestyle possible for the children of at least the upper middle class no matter what their creative potentials. The mass media, reacting to the beats with characteristic overkill, publicized it all across the land (by the very act of attacking it) and inspired the growth of beat communities wherever young people were sufficient in force.

This is where I came in; at first, like so many, spending Saturday nights in the Village and Sundays hanging out in Washington Square Park, getting a feel for the way of life, eventually discovering that I wanted to stay. Though I would later make friends with older creative people who would take me under their wing, teach me the values of their tradition and respect for the world of the mind, my first cues about how to be in bohemia came from Kerouac's novels. And what attracted me most was his vision of community (indeed, bohemia was always an oasis of community in a country that was destroying its every remnant), his Whitmanesque celebration of the wonder of America (an innocence that was probably an illusion even then), and his characterization of Neal Cassady (Dean Moriarity in *On The Road*) whom I recognized as the first great American hero in literature since Huck Finn.

Of the sexual patterns of beat life, I noticed nothing and learned nothing. The image-role I had settled into in my suburban life seemed to fit this new world of bohemia quite well—which is to say that the way Kerouac dehumanized women in his novels (which, remember, are fairly accurate descriptions of a period in his life) did not strike me as extraordinary. I was impressed, of course, by the way women chased after Cassady and by what I took to be his open-hearted and innocent treatment of them (which from a women's perspective was outright brutality) and figured that if I could learn to be as hip as Cassady, I, too, would score. But that every woman in Kerouac's books—except his Chicano lover in *On The Road* and his high school sweetheart Maggie Cassady—is there to be fucked or is having a nervous breakdown or committing suicide, did not strike me as odd.

There is, I discovered later, a dimension of the beat scene that Kerouac left out of all of his novels. This was the fact that bisexuality was the prevalent mode in bohemia and that homosexuality was fairly open and accepted. Kerouac and Ginsberg were attracted to Cassady not only because of his incredible energy, but because they were his lovers. The only book that explores this facet of beat life and brings out the human (that is, the non-heroic) aspects of their lives is a porno novel, *Memoirs of A Beatnik,* by the poet Diane di Prima.

Slowly, in the sixties, as the New Left encouraged political awareness and the beat lifestyle began to attract more and more people, we began to see our way of life as a political movement that represented a positive alternative to the death-culture, a self-consciously revolutionary lifestyle that was to form the basis of a new society coming to life within the decaying shell of the old. The counter-culture was no longer an elitist haven for working artists, but an embryonic place where the best people of the sixties generation had come to create life anew. The public spokesmen, the prophets, the writers (and I was one), the leaders, the wisemen and gurus who laid out this dream were, without exception, men. And the vision of the new society kept the patriarchy of bohemia intact. In the male utopian vision, women were still chicks.

There is much to be said about the gains the counter-culture made, especially in those areas that were not media shucks. The concept of the flower children, for instance, despite much that is superficial and trendy, made an effective break with machismo and encouraged men to be gentle and to express a fuller range of feelings and emotions. But male dominance and institutionalized patriarchy remains solid.

Consider the drug culture, for instance, where men heads mystified the drug experience so that dealing became a priestly calling and dealers became a class apart who distributed psychedelics as if they were administering a sacrament. And did we really need Tim Leary to tell us that an acid trip could be a religious experience? And what should we make of all the professional gurus attempting to channel mysticism into their own patriarchal churches and who have perverted a healthy resurgence of spiritual awareness into yet another male dominated religious trap? Male dominance appears under many disguises. Is the men's movement yet another patriarchal trap?

Men have always thrived in movements, have delighted in laying out heavy cosmic raps, and have usually ignored emotions and feelings in favor of abstract political analyses. Men have always used movements and controlled the language of movements to sustain their power. Building a movement around men's liberation would seem to legitimize this patriarchy all over again. It would say that men have to struggle together against some outside oppressive force when what we need to do is to struggle with ourselves.

Certainly, it is good that men are starting to relate to each other in ways that differ from traditional male fraternity. Men, after all, have always been brothers, happily bopping about on one historic mission after another. So it is good that we are becoming more open and learning to be unashamed of expressing emotions and vulnerability. But a society in which men and women can live together as equals would seem to call for something more than personal psychosocial adjustment. It would call also for dismantling the patriarchy. For this we need support from other men, from friends, and lovers. But do we also need a movement?

From *Win,* April 11, 1974. Reprinted by permission.

All Men Are Misogynists

Leonard Schein

(Most of my understanding of misogyny is due to Shulamith Firestone's book, *The Dialectic of Sex).*

For men to become fully human, to liberate ourselves from forced sex roles, and to really understand ourselves, one of the first things we must deal with is our hatred of women. We have to understand the origin of our misogyny and the full significance of the fact that we live in a patriarchal society. Patriarchy's foundation is the oppression of women. The cement of this foundation is the socialization of men to hate women.

Looking at our development as males, it is easy to see how misogyny originates. As young children, our first attraction is to our mother, a woman. As we grow older, we learn to transfer our love for our mother to an identification with our father. Freud refers to this as the Oedipus Complex. The male child's fear of his father's power makes him repress both his love towards his mother and his hatred towards his father.

In her monumental work, *The Dialectic of Sex,* Firestone analyzes this transference in terms of power. The patriarchal nuclear family makes all its members dependent upon the male (father-husband). It is in this oppressive atmosphere that we grow up, and we are extremely sensitive to this hierarchy of power even as children. We realize, more than adults know, that our father (and society in his image, from policeman to doctor to president) is powerful, and that our mother is powerless. She has to scheme and manipulate through sympathy to get what she wants.

As the male child develops, he knows his mother's love for him and her powerlessness. The father has the real power and is the avenue to success, excitement and the world. Consequently, the male child is faced with a difficult choice. As Eric Fromm writes, "But while father does not represent the natural world, he represents the other pole of human existence; the world of thought, of man-made things, of law and order, of discipline, of travel and adventure. Father is the one who teaches the child, who shows him the road into the world." The boy must choose between continuing his identification and love for his mother, which is much more rewarding emotionally, or transfering his identification to his father and becoming male-identified. This power-based transference is the critical beginning of our misogyny.

First, we have to justify this betrayal of our mother (women). We also have to deal with our anger, resentment, frustration, and ambivalence during this "difficult transitional phase." We find it impossible to vent this anger at its true source (patriarchal society) because that is where the power rests. The safest place to express this anger is toward our powerless mother—woman. We rationalize her position of powerlessness, think that she is, in fact, inferior, and see this as the natural order of things (rather than seeing that she is forced into a position of powerlessness by patriarchal power). As our consciousness develops its picture of women as inferior, we then objectify our dominant position and their subordination. Psychologically, we objectify the people we hate and consider our inferiors (another example of this process is its extension into racism).

A second situation which feeds on, deepens, and solidifies our hatred of women developes a little later in time. We begin to realize our privileged position in society as males. The Orthodox Jew prays to God every morning thanking "Him" that he was not born a woman. Subconsciously we intuit that our privilege can only be maintained if women are kept "in their place." So we live in constant fear, as the threat to our power is everywhere (even, and especially, in our bedroom). This fear of the challenge to our power explains our paranoid hatred toward the "Uppity Woman." And psychologically, we hate those we fear; we hate those who threaten our egos and our economic and cultural power.

A third factor contributing to our hatred of women is our jealousy of their powers of creation. Fromm and Jung in excellent studies have shown through patriarchal myths, symbols, folklore, and religion that there is one universal theme—man's jealousy of women's power to procreate. In fact, in some cultures, men are so envious they experience "labor pains" when their wife delivers a baby. Zilboorg in *Psychoanalysis and Women,* edited by Jean Baker Miller, mentions that, "It is not penis envy on the part of the women, but woman envy on the part of man, that is psychogenetically older and therefore more powerful." And psychologically, we know that jealousy turns into envy which turns into hatred.

Another result of the transference of our identification is the double, ambivalent (good/bad) image of women. We have to find some way of continuing our loving feelings for our mother without losing our access to power. We perform this balancing act by putting our mother (and a select few other women like wives, relatives, and friends) on a pedestal and mythicizing her as the mother/virgin. This is what romantic love is all about—seeing one woman as somehow special (not "just like a woman"), and raising her above the class/caste of inferior, powerless women. This mother/virgin image of some women allows us to justify our granting of power and protection to them as a result of their dependency upon us.

For the rest of the class/caste of women we create the whore/seductress myth. This degradation is expressed best in the often-heard male saying, "Put a paper bag over her head and fuck her."

We create this image for many reasons. First, we have to deal with our sexual feelings which patriarchal society represses. Patriarchal society cannot allow free or natural or equal sexuality because that would strike at the basic core of patriarchy, its sexual politics, i.e., the oppression of women, separation of emotionality from sexuality, role division at birth, the nuclear family, and the violating, alienating "reality principle." Second, we can blame women as scapegoats for our faults and failures (Adam and Eve myth, where the Fall of Man is blamed on Woman, so we are then reasonable in controlling these "devilish" creatures). Third, we can use this good/bad dichotomy to keep "our" women in line (in fact permitting us to raise some onto the pedestal). This split creates a class/caste of women we can "protect," and justifies our possession and power over them "in their own interest." Fourth, this image makes it possible for even the lowest, most horribly degenerate man to feel some self-worth, as he is always superior to women. Fifth, the image permits free rein to our misogyny.

Rape must be understood in terms of being the logical, concrete expression of our misogyny. The popular newspaper image of rape, a man (or men) taking out his physical violence for the class/caste of women on one particular woman, portrays the rapist as abnormal or insane (some demented person other than ourselves). This image protects us from the real facts of rape—that all men in patriarchal society have a rapist consciousness, are potential rapists and gain from the constant state of intimidation that rape imposes on *all* women. The classic study of rapists, Susan Brownmiller's *Against Our Will: Men, Women and Rape* shows this: "Studies indicate that sex offenders do not constitute a unique or psychopathological type; nor are they as a group invariably more disturbed than the control groups to which they are compared." Criminologists have written that rapists are the "most normal of men having normal sexual personalities." The existence of this type of rape (forcible physical violence "on the street") serves many useful functions for our male consciousness/power and, therefore, is tolerated and even subtly encouraged in our society.

We enjoy the existence of forcible rape (even if we ourselves would not do it) because it verifies our power over women and our enormous "sexual potency." Rape has always been a turn-on in pornography and popular culture (for example, the frequency of the coverage and detail of rape in the *New York Daily News, The National Enquirer,* and other best-selling media). We rationalize that women even secretly harbor rape fantasies and enjoy our "super-cock machismo" behavior. Forcible rape perpetuates the myth system of male dominance and female passivity. As Susan Griffin states in her article in *Ramparts* magazine, "Rape: The All-American Crime": "In the system of chivalry, men protect women against men. This is not unlike the protection relationship which the Mafia established with small business-es in the early part of this century. Indeed, chivalry is an age-old protection racket which depends for its existence on rape."

The fullest expression of men's misogyny through rape is in war. All armies, regardless of race, nationality, class, religion, or culture, engage in rape, torture, and mutilation of women. During warfare, women no longer have the protection of their men and are seen in their "true" position as free game, powerless objects to be exploited. War destroys the "illusion" of women's claims to be human beings because the mother/virgin image is stripped away. What remains is brute force and hatred, in which women are seen by the inner core of our consciousness as whores, objects, cunts.

Forcible rape is used to terrorize women, to keep them in a state of constant fear, and to let them know where the real power lies. Any woman, no matter how rich or poor, intelligent or dumb, attractive or unattractive, regardless of race or age, can be and will be raped. This indiscriminate terrorism is used to limit women's freedom of movement and to continue her dependence on men. It is the raw edge of sexual politics. Rape cannot be eliminated until we deal with its basic cause—misogyny as a result of patriarchy.

Our culturally ingrained hatred of women is also expressed when challenged by women in the feminist movement who are demanding their equality as human beings. The most liberal-pacifistic men, who have felt "liberated" and supportive of the women's movement, when *personally* threatened by the consequences of the feminist revolution, have used vile abuse and power games to maintain a dominant position. The woman becomes a "castrating bitch," a "hard woman," and she is blamed as though it is her fault for demanding what is rightfully hers.

We must understand that our anger (and hatred) is something that comes from within us. It is not women's fault. It is the attitude that patriarchal society has encouraged us to feel toward all women. When finally confronted with the reality of feminism, which threatens our power and privileges, our defenses cannot hide our true anger and we turn to incredible violence.

We have to accept that this anger belongs to us and stems from our hatred of women. I know men say that they really do not hate women, they have just treated them unfairly because of socialization ("Those other men are rapists, not me."). This can be a cop-out and untruth. All men do hate women, and until we take responsibility for our personal hatred, we will not be able to seriously explore our emotionality nor treat women as equal human beings. Men's consciousness-raising groups should not make the mistake of trying to comfort and smooth over our anger and violence toward women. Fundamental to our consciousness is misogyny, and it will not disappear until dealt with honestly. We must understand that the privileges we enjoy as males in our society come directly from our hatred/violence toward women.

Our anger must be redirected toward the true enemy—patriarchal society. We are in the peculiar position of being the enemy we are trying to destroy. We are limited, in terms of our growth as full human beings, and we are the oppressor at the same time. *As long as patriarchal society exists, no matter how liberated we become, we will still be the oppressors of women.* We have to turn our individual awareness and energies into an active, collective political struggle to destroy sexism and patriarchal society which makes all men misogynists, all men rapists, and all men emotionally crippled.

For more thought and insight into misogyny, I highly recommend the following: *Feminist Revolution* by the Redstockings, *The Dialectic of Sex* by Shulamith Firestone, *Against Our Will: Men, Women and Rape* by Susan Brownmiller, *Women and Madness* by Phyllis Chesler, and *Woman Hating* by Andrea Dworkin.

Toward Gender Justice

(This article is adapted from a statement read by the author at a conference of the Gay Academic Union in New York City, November 29, 1974.)

The Heterosexual Model

I want to begin by describing certain features of the patriarchal society in which we live, certain features I will call *the heterosexual model.*

In this model, men are the arbiters of human identity. From the time they are boys, men are programed by the culture to refer exclusively to other men for validation of their self-worth. A man's comfort and well-being are contingent upon the labor and nurture of women, but his identity—his "knowledge of who he is"—can only be conferred and confirmed by other men.

Under patriarchy, women are not reliable witnesses to a man's worthiness, except in bed—and there as a class, not as individuals. Thus if a particular women does not esteem a man's genital functioning, he has the right to turn to another woman who does, without loss of phallic worth.

Women are programed to refer to men for their identities as well, but the program is seriously stacked against them. In the heterosexual model, a woman's "knowledge of who she is" cannot be separate from her relation to an individual man. The only validation of her self-worth to which she is entitled is whatever identity she gets from being supportive to, and the property of, a man.

Under patriarchy, men are the arbiters of identity for both males and females, because the cultural norm of human identity is, by definition, male identity—*masculinity*. And, under patriarchy, the cultural norm of male identity consists in power, prestige, privilege, and prerogative *as over and against* the gender class women. That's what masculinity is. It isn't something else.

Attempts have been made to defend this norm of masculinity as having a natural basis in male sexual biology. It has been said, for example, that male power in the culture is a natural expression of a biological tendency in human males toward sexual aggression. But I believe that what is true is the reverse. I believe that masculinist genital functioning is an expression of male power in the culture. I believe that male sexual aggression is entirely learned behavior, taught by a culture which men entirely control. I believe, as I will explain, that there is a *social process* by which patriarchy confers power, prestige, privilege, and prerogative on people who are born with cocks, and that there is a *sexual program* promoted by the patriarchy (not Mother Nature) for how those cocks are supposed to function.

The social process whereby people born with cocks attain and maintain masculinity takes place in *male bonding*. Male bonding is institutionalized learned behavior whereby men recognize and reinforce one another's bona fide membership in the male gender class and whereby men remind one another that they were not born women. Male bonding is political and pervasive. It occurs whenever two males meet. It is not restricted to larger all-male groupings. It is the form and content of each and every encounter between two males. Boys learn very early that they had better be able to bond. What they learn in order to bond is an elaborate behavioral code of gestures, speech, habits and attitudes, which effectively exclude women from the society of men. Male bonding is how men learn from each other that they are entitled under patriarchy to power in the culture. Male bonding is how men get that power, and male bonding is how it is kept. Therefore, men enforce a taboo against unbonding—a taboo which is fundamental to patriarchal society.

The subsequent program for male sexual behavior, patriarchy's prototype for male genital functioning, is, of course, *the fuck:* the hard cock, the vaginal penetration, the tense pelvic thrusting, and the three-second ejaculation. Authentic sensations get unlearned. What gets learned, and therefore what gets felt, is genital operability.

But men learn that they have power, prestige, and privilege in the culture long before they ever learn how to fuck. And then, I believe, what each man learns on his own is that in order for his genitalia to work this way reliably—that is, to operate in intimacy in the way that is commensurate with what the man knows of his power and prerogative in the culture—he must claim over his partner a corresponding advantage. There must be for him, in the erotic encounter itself, some real or imagined disparity of power and prerogative between himself and whomever he fucks. Otherwise he can't do it. He can't accomplish the program—the sexual program for expressing his cultural attributes—his attributes obtained by belonging to a gender class which has defined itself as supreme.

Men who fuck differ only in the form of that power disparity which they require between themselves and whomever they would choose to fuck. Some men rape, some men marry, and so forth.

At the slightest hint that there could be between the partners a common dignity, a reciprocity of moral concern, or any justice whatsoever—in that moment prototypical male genital functioning fails; in that moment, it goes numb.

Men who are programed to make genital assertions of their masculinity in erotic encounters with women know privately but well what an unreliable gauge of masculinity their genital programing really is. Far more reliable are their non-erotic bonds with other men—where power, prestige, privilege, and pride are actually gauged and exchanged; and where the culture's norm of masculinity originates and prospers.

The Sexual Politics of Gay Male Liberation
Patriarchy, then, is grounded in a cultural norm of masculinity

perpetuated by the sexual politics of heterosexual men. Their sexual politics—how they affect the gender class of women—are quite clearly to keep women oppressed. And their masculinity—their power in the culture as over and against those women they oppress—derives from their bonds with other men, not from their erotic activities. Whatever men do in the name of their so-called heterosexual orientation is an assertion of that power, not how they obtain it. The only way a genital male could be disenfranchised from that power, which under patriarchy is his birthright, is by failing to bond well enough with other men—not through any failure on his part to exercise some heterosexual standard of genital functioning.

Why, then, has *homosexuality* in men been grounds for denying some males full access to the birthright of their gender class? In the Judeo-Christian tradition of patriarchy, there is a stricture on male-male assfucking. Historically, the prohibition has been against that act, not against men who behave together with affection which reinforces their affinity. An early version of this injunction is written in Leviticus 18:22 *(The Jerusalem Bible)*: "You must not lie with a man as with a woman. This is a hateful thing." Significantly, this dictum occurs in the context of a catalogue of conjugal rules which ritualize and institutionalize two main themes: the property rights of men over the bodies of women, and an absolute loathing of female carnality. Similarly, wherever else there have been laws on the books against male-male assfucking, those laws are tucked in among legislation, enacted and enforced by men, to execute their purpose of maintaining the powerlessness of women. The law against sodomy between males is not a discrete phenomenon. It is a thread in a legal fabric which systematically oppresses women. And in this context, patriarchy's aversion to sodomy between males is a necessary expression of the taboo against unbonding, since to assfuck a genital male is to "lie with" him "as with a woman," and since under patriarchy, the way to lie with a woman is to make a genital assertion of male power in the culture, over and against her body in particular. A man violates the taboo against unbonding if he asserts that power disparity genitally *between himself and another male.* I believe therefore that the cultural bias against male homosexuality stems directly from these two facts: That patriarchy requires that men maintain their brotherhood through a common contempt of women; and that the male homosexual act is construed as a threat to the male-male bond, since there is the implication that one of the partners gets fucked as a woman.

Recently, in the history of patriarchy's relentless advance, there has occurred a movement for homosexual liberation. The main argument for this movement, as adduced by genital males, seems to me to be this: That laws against the male homosexual act should be repealed; that males who engage in it should be free to do so without fear of censure or economic liability; that the male homosexual act, if performed between two consenting genital males, ought to be construed by both partners *and by the culture* as a valid form of male bonding; and that all the rights, privileges, and powers belonging to genital males by virtue of their membership in the male gender class should belong as well to men who assfuck other men and to those men whose asses get fucked. In other words, the claim that male homosexuals are fully entitled to male civil liberties is based on the presumption that the male assfuck is a special expression of a co-equal power bond between men; that the male assfuck is not an assertion of a power disparity between the partners, since neither partner, prior to the act, is as powerless in the culture as a woman, and since each partner, after the act, can take his place in the culture with his masculinity intact.

To summarize, the relationship between cultural "homophobia" and male "gay pride" is as follows: Under patriarchy, both the basic prohibition against male homosexuality and the basic argument for male homosexual liberation are expressions of the same sexual politics—namely, the accreditation of men by contracting to vilify women.

These same sexual politics are evinced in certain factions of the male homosexual movement which have solicited the support of lesbian women. The Gay Academic Union and the National Gay Task Force are two such organizations, initiated by men and enlisting lesbian participation on the pretext of a novel ruse: that the predicaments of gay men and lesbian women in society are analogous; that gay men and lesbian women are disenfranchised from power in the culture for the same reason and in the same way. This is conspicuously not the case. The struggle of lesbian women is against the whole of institutionalized misogyny. The dilemma of gay men is merely to prove that they are not women. The struggle of lesbian women is against all forms of male power over their lives: the male capitalists who decide when women are needed in the labor force and when they are not; the male courts who decree lesbian women are not fit to rear their children; the male professors who would teach them reverence for great men; male rapists, male pornographers, male psychiatrists, male gynecologists; and all of the laws, customs, and habits which define women as the carnal chattel of men, which deny women absolute control of their own bodies and lives. The dilemma of gay men, on the other hand, is how to get cultural confirmation of their masculinity, how to come out and be one of the guys, how to have full access to all the powers, prestige, prerogatives, and privileges that other men have over and against women.

It is no accident that certain gay males are promoting the notion of a lesbian and gay male coalition. Such a notion is absolutely in the best interests of gay males, especially gay males in the professions, who have an economic stake in male supremacy and who persist in believing that the only real issue is homosexual liberation. Gay males consistently make no commitment to the struggle of women against male power over their lives. Such a commitment would contradict the objective of male homosexual liberation, which is to secure for gay males their birthright to power in the culture over women. Gay males may pay lip service to the issues of discrimination against women, or gay males may make token adjustments within their organizations to grant women "more equality," but these are solicitous and reactionary stratagems, intended to let women know they are "welcome," or intended to keep women from leaving, because the fact is that these men have a specific political need to belong to an organization in which women are present. An all-male organization merely serves the personal needs of gay men within it to acknowledge and esteem one another's masculinity. Patriarchy permits gay men to obtain masculinist power in this way, by bonding with other men, organizationally, professionally, and personally. But patriarchy prohibits gay men from exercising that power over other genital males. Masculinist power is for use against women. Men are not supposed to treat men the way they treat women. That is at the center of the gay male appeal to straight men for acceptance, and that is at the center of the gay male need to have women in their organizations. Because if the truth were revealed that the impulse of most gay men *is* to treat selected genital males as if they were women, then the entire credibility of the movement for male homosexual liberation would be impugned. Under patriarchy, the acceptable exercise of masculinist power requires the presence of the gender class which by definition is powerless—women. Thus, an organization in which women are present provides exactly the form gay men require in order to assert their masculinist power, and by asserting it, to demonstrate to the culture that they are not in fact faggots, that they are not in fact women, but that clearly they are the men and they have power over and against the women.

In order to end the system of patriarchy, the very sexual identities of males will have to change. A male is no less complicitous in that system by being homosexual than by being heterosexual, or vice versa. A male is complicitous in that system by reason of his investment in *masculinity,* a norm of human identity which is consistent with and derived from his privileged irresponsibility to women. Under patriarchy, a commitment to the maintenance of masculinity *in any form* is a commitment to sexist injustice.

The form of men's consciousness raising is but a new manifestation of male bonding. Whether composed of straight men or gay men, these groups are defined in every detail by the culturally programed urgency of men to bond, in order to confer and confirm their masculinity, which is their power in the culture over and against women. The patriarchal taboo against unbonding circumscribes the "consciousness" of all-male groups in a very political way, since effective male bonding requires that a genital male not respect the life of a woman so much as he respects his own and that of his fellows. In the context of men's consciousness-raising groups, therefore, it is formally taboo to comprehend and take seriously women's emerging political analysis, except in a self-interested or reactionary way. To take seriously in one's "consciousness" the fact of sexist injustice would have to mean for men, as it does already for many women, *a total repudiation of masculinity*. All "men's liberation," which in form and content is masculinity-*confirming,* is thus an escalation and permutation of masculinist aggression. And its victims, ultimately, are women, whether or not they are taken to bed.

Masculinity is not, as some have said, a vague set of "qualities" (such as "ambition," "strength," "courage," or "competitiveness"). Nor is masculinity an abstract "role," which can be "played" or "not played," or which any two people can take turns at. What is denoted by the word masculinity derives from the objective reality, the fact of our lives under patriarchy, that all members of the gender class of males are entitled to obtain their sense of self by postulating the selflessness of the gender class of women, their sense of worth by asserting female worthlessness, and their power in the culture by maintaining the powerlessness of women. Masculinity is that sense of self, that sense of worth, that right to power which accrues to every male on account of the global subjugation of women. Thus masculinity, that cultural construct of human identity, is antithetical to gender justice. And, in short: masculinity is immoral.

What is required is moral commitment to struggle for gender justice. That means that genital males must find a form for taking responsibility to the lives of women.

There are many apparently "sensitive," "compassionate," and "sympathetic" men around—men who present themselves as being in favor of social justice but who act in their lives as if they would sooner die than relinquish the prerogative that they got by being born male. It has been men like these who, through the political left, have given us their masculinist visions for social change and who, through the arts, psychiatry, and philosophy, have described for us the great male themes of modern life: alienation, estrangement, anguish, and dread—all out of that typical man's sensibility which holds his male self to be at the center of the knowable universe. Many such men have said that their male hurt and their male pain would be tempered if only men would learn to cry more, or feel more, or trust other men more, or have better sex. Many such men would prefer to make self-interested emotional accommodations rather than moral commitment. I think the grim reality at this point in human history is that not very many genital males have access to a moral conscience which has not been gender-linked along with the rest of their sexual and social programing.

But I believe that there are a few genital males who are persuaded that what is wrong with the culture is its sexist injustice and that what is wrong with their lives is their complicity in it. And I imagine that those few genital males might commit themselves to these two projects:

One. I imagine that a genital male could begin, with a kind of humility, to read and study feminist texts, a study which if full-time could take a year or longer. I think it is not possible to take seriously women's lives if one is ignorant of what it means to bear the real brunt of masculinist aggression. And there is much information which women have written which absolutely gives the lie to all those catchphrases of men's liberation, such as "Men are victims, too." It is time genital males understood that the road to gender justice is not paved with self-indulgent aphorisms about "the essential personhood of men and women." The fact is that men's lives and women's lives are different because, from birth, men and women live under absolutely different cultural conditions. And genital males cannot presume to understand the conditions under which women are forced to live their lives by imaginary analogies to the privileged woes of men. (See "Suggested Beginning Reading List for Genital Males" below.)

Two. At the same time, I imagine that a genital male could begin to live as a conscientious objector to all the scenarios of male bonding—to refuse to cooperate with all the patterns of expectation that, whenever two males meet, they are to respect one another's masculinity and condone one another's power over women. And I imagine that during this period of conscientious bond-breaking a genital male might discover to what an appalling extent male friendships and alliances are based on the private understanding that "we are men, not women, and therefore we are preferred." I don't underestimate the shock that will come with this recognition: when a genital male discovers that seemingly innocuous exchanges between himself and another genital male can turn in an instant into a tacit pact against women, and that all he was ever programed to long for in relationships with men connects at its very center to a process that keeps women oppressed. What is necessary is for genital males to betray the presumptions of their own gender class—conspicuously, tactically, and uncompromisingly. The alternative, as I see it, is to betray every woman who has ever said she is not free.

I think these are two ways a genital male could begin to live differently: by studying feminist texts and by resisting masculinist bonds. And I think that these two ways are merely a beginning.

Eventually, perhaps, some genital males could share in the struggle against sexist injustice as honest allies of feminist women. But at this point in time, this much is clear: None of us can presume that we have yet done enough in our own lives to eradicate our allegiance to masculinity. Unless we change, we cannot claim to be comrades with women. Until we change, the oppressor is us.

SUGGESTED BEGINNING READING LIST FOR GENITAL MALES

1. Women, the Law, Medicine, Money.

De Crow, Karen. *Sexist Justice.* Random House, 1974.

New York Radical Feminists. *Rape: The First Sourcebook for Women.* New American Library, 1974.

Brownmiller, Susan. *Against Our Will: Men, Women and Rape.* Simon and Schuster, 1975.

Schulder, Diane and Florynce Kennedy. *Abortion Rap,* McGraw-Hill, 1971.

Frankfort, Ellen. *Vaginal Politics.* Bantam, 1973.

Chesler, Phyllis and Emily Jane Goodman. *Women, Money & Power.* William Morrow and Company, Inc., 1976.

2. Theory and Herstory (in order of original publication)

Flexner, Eleanor. *Century of Struggle: The Woman's Rights Movement in the United States.* Atheneum, 1973.

Solanis, Valerie. *SCUM Manifesto.* Olympia, 1970.

Morgan, Robin (editor). *Sisterhood is Powerful.* Random House, 1970.

Millet, Kate. *Sexual Politics.* Avon, 1970.

Davis, Elizabeth Gould. *The First Sex.* Penguin, 1971.

Firestone, Shulamith. *The Dialectic of Sex.* Bantam, 1972.

Chesler, Phyllis. *Women and Madness.* Avon, 1972.

Rossi, Alice S. (editor). *The Feminist Papers: From Adams to de Beauvoir.* Bantam, 1973.

Rowbotham, Sheila. *Women, Resistance and Revolution: A History of Women and Revolution in the Modern World.* Vintage, 1974.

Dworkin, Andrea. *Woman Hating.* Dutton, 1974.

Atkinson, Ti-Grace. *Amazon Odyssey.* Links, 1974.

Dworkin, Andrea. *Our Blood: Prophecies and Discourses on Sexual Politics.* Harper & Row, 1976.

Copyright (c) 1975 by John Stoltenberg. First published in *Win,* March 20, 1975, and in *Social Policy,* May/June 1975. Reprinted by permission of the author.

Complacency in the Face of Patriarchy

Gary Mitchell Wandachild

If radicals would hope to build a movement capable of sustaining the kind of commitment from large numbers of regular folk necessary to create fundamental structural change in American society, then we will have to recognize that serving the people doesn't mean serving the needs of men. Any authentic and serious American Left must mark its political birth by a fundamental challenge to patriarchy. Radical analysis without such a commitment is not rooted in material reality but rather in a level of abstraction that has lost a true sense of the material (of the *mater,* which in Latin, German and Greek refers to the Mother, the source of reality).

These suggestions are made in light of recent events that indicate a growing retrenchment on the left in opposition to feminist priorities and a particular hostility to feminism that has once again prominently risen to the surface amongst male radicals. Over the past year in the pages of *WIN* and other left-to-liberal publications (*Seven Days, Liberation, Ramparts, The Village Voice, The Nation, Commonweal*) the interests of women have increasingly been betrayed. Voices are raised which oppose women's rights over their own bodies, denounce Jane Alpert through the use of innuendo, lies and double standards, ignore women's demands and struggle in "revolutionary" Portugal, dismiss the ERA as "middle class," support a misogynist Supreme Court nominee and belittle or ignore criticism from feminists, deride as exaggerated feminists' concern and outrage on the issue of rape, ridicule concern over pornography, rationalize layoffs of women and minorities for lack of seniority when that lack is due to past discrimination, and in general criticize feminism as being a deflection from "serious" radical struggle. A series of articles by David McReynolds in *WIN* that argue radicals need to "regroup for much more fundamental change than we had thought necessary" reflects the general attacks on feminism from the left by charging that feminism detracts from the principal attention that radicals must pay to the issue of class.

But how are we to regroup? Who determines what is necessary? What is *more* fundamental? I ask these questions because McReynolds' articles begin with an important supposition: that the Left has not been speaking to, or in language comprehensible by, those people it has sought as its constituency. Unfortunately, David continues this tendency. He raises issues of which there is already general awareness. It is surely not unexpected to hear that the class origins of radicals' lives impede the building of an authentic and effective revolutionary movement. This is but a reaffirmation of concerns which occupied radicals prior to the rise of the second wave of feminism in the late 1960's. McReynolds' articles are one more defense of what some refer to as the "dying male left." An "old boy" of The Movement is calling for a regrouping.

During the heyday of movement activity evils of the System abounded, or so it seemed. Through analysis and feeling we *knew* what had to be changed. David continues in this belief, as does most of the male left. The problem, it is said, is not seeing the problem, but finding ways of dealing with it. On the contrary, feminists argued then that radical politics suffered from the more basic failure of vision, from a myopic fixation of theory and program as it proceeded from masculine consciousness, demonstrating a lack of concern and an ignorance of the actual material base of society—the material reality of patriarchy and its effects upon the lives of women and vision of men. For radical men the problem still seems to be seeing the problem. The word patriarchy connotes ever so little to male radicals, as little as the word capitalism likely did to most of us when we attended public schools in our capitalist nation. But while radicals have since made the effort to comprehend the evils of capitalism, few male radicals have made a comparable effort to comprehend the iniquitous reality of patriarchy.

While lack of attention to the class origins of "our" lives has compounded the analysis radicals make of prospects and programs for change, ignored have been the material effects that patriarchy has had upon the indicators of complex social and economic phenomena. Who is a "worker," or of the working class? Does income, education or job classification indicate "class" position? For example, do office workers and nurses fit into traditional working class models—or is class a function of a husband's position when one is a woman and a worker? Which parent do children use to derive their class origins? Where does the unpaid labor of a housewife and mother fit into the model? Is the traditional left model of the working class merely an analysis of political economy in terms of fathers? What sensitivity is there to past, extant and new sexual segregation and stratification of employment opportunities and work roles in the determinants of class in left analysis? A serious American Left must at the very least know of and to whom it speaks when it purports to offer an analysis based upon some sense of the daily life of its constituency. But in taking McReynolds' articles as somewhat representative of the tendency to ignore the material reality of patriarchy as it affects over half of "the people's" lives, the willingness of the male left to use myth and propaganda to blind us further to patriarchy emerges.

As Lucy Komisar notes, the left fails to see the relation between imperialism and patriarchal rule: "It has been part of American tradition from the time of the frontier, through the phallic big stick of Theodore Roosevelt to the foreign policy of the present. And yet, the antiwar critics of American foreign policy have never raised the issue in quite these terms. They have decried imperialism, or militarism, but their criticism has sometimes been flawed by the very machismo that provokes the policies they deplore . . . The machismo factor is the key to an understanding of the Mayaguez incident, the Vietnam war, and, until it is altered as it should be, of US foreign policy for years to come.

Radical men treat such feminist analysis glibly, like McReynolds who condescendingly trivializes and reduces such analysis to a point at which it is dismissed. Feminism is charged with failing to touch *the basic problem.* What is meant is that feminist analysis has challenged what male radicals have heretofore put forth as the basic problem.

Rather than deal with the issues raised—rather than responsibly discuss contending perspectives on "moving towards revolution"—the tendency among radical men has been to guilt-trip those with whom they disagree. But a "serious American Left" will not be drawn together by this tactic, which even assumes its own palpably false conclusion, as when McReynolds writes: "We were not born into a class of oppressed people." This undifferentiated view of reality from a male perspective plagues male radicals. Underlying this view is a hidden agenda of a patriarchal Left. It is contained in arguments of male radicals, like McReynolds, that pass over the substance of feminist analysis by refusing to acknowledge the male perspective from which they—as men—envision revolution. A patronizing and gross dismissal of feminist theory pertaining to misogyny and sex-based oppression in patriarchy inevitably follows, as false as it is facile. It is apparent that something else is going on: analysis is not being offered anew, but dissidents from the male left line are being put in "their" places.

McReynolds, for instance, suggests that women view the police as "employees" or as "protectors." His words betray a deafness to the voices of women who describe police*men* as utterly allied with the misogynist reality against which women contend, as allied with men's interests—specifically with the rapist, the "john," the pimp, the husband who violently assaults his wife, the husband who refuses (between 62 and 87% of the time) to comply with support payments ordered by the courts. In patriarchy, police protect men's property and men's law, as a function of class of course—but not the rights of women. McReynolds and most male radicals don't see they speak with the voice of a man—one who may be versed in history but who is ignorant of herstory. What else explains such a statement as "the Bill of Rights was written for *us*" and means the "us" to be inclusive of women. Radicals know the Bill of Rights (and the Constitution) were never intended for blacks, but it is not clear whether radicals like David know or care that such documents were neither written nor intended for women. A struggle against this constitutional reality is somehow not within the reach of "revolutionary" priorities often outlined by male radicals.

But a similar struggle of Blacks, i.e., predominantly as it affects

86

black men, often merits the radical stamp of approval, as when McReynolds cites the struggles of Southern Blacks for certain rights (voting, public accommodations)—rights which he explains "were automatically enjoyed by the rest of us." He forgets though what has come *automatically* in the lives of women under patriarchy. It is clear that radical men need a crash course in feminist history to remind them of what women have had to struggle for in over two centuries of this nation—and of how much yet remains to be gained.

The assumptions that underlie the "phallacies" in much of what passes for analysis by male radicals are rooted in this plain ignorance. It becomes more than merely grating to see this ignorance displayed, for it distorts analysis: as when McReynolds argues "we fought to extend to others the rights we ourselves already had." The use of "we" is analytically duplicitous and opportunistic for it puts the gloss on the invidiousness of patriarchy. What was meant as analysis becomes instead mindless propaganda for a gratuitous myopic vision blind to patriarchy and uninterested in the misogynist consequences of presumably "revolutionary" schemes. For in the present, as has been true historically, women fight to extend to others rights that they, as women, are denied—even by those on whose behalf they have struggled.

Women in the anti-war movement opposed the violence of the State directed against boys of draft age sent to kill or be killed in a war not of their making and rallied against the violence of U.S. imperialism seeking control of Vietnamese lives, while the violence of the patriarchy continued to war upon women in numbers which *yearly* exceeded the entire total of American boys wounded or killed in ten years of Vietnam, and while the imperialism of patriarchy continued control over women's bodies, relegating women to a colonized status as breeders, as low-or-unpaid menial workers, as chattel of men. Feminists in Portugal today struggle alongside their "brother" socialists, but their "brothers" in no political party will endorse the struggle or demands feminists make for the rights of women.

Consider the women of the abolitionist movement, black and white, who were sold out by their radical brothers, black and white, with the campaign for and passage of the 14th Amendment to the Constitution that made the possession of a penis a constitutional *sine qua non* for personhood. Even Frederick Douglass, a leading black abolitionist and originally a partisan of some feminist causes, sold out to the political fraternity willing to admit blacks (if they were penis possessors) but lined up to keep *all* women the chattel of men. In a speech to the annual meeting of the American Equal Rights Association in 1869, Douglass tried to contrast the predicament of Blacks and women—though he neglected to consider black women. To the gathered delegates he declared: "I do not see how anyone can pretend that there is the same urgency in giving the ballot to women as to the negro." Of course, what Douglass meant was to black males.

Women were more than merely invisible in the language male radicals used—male radicals could not see the plain reality of women's lives, such that someone like Douglass could argue: "With us, the matter is a question of life and death, at least in 15 states of the Union. When women, because they are women, are hunted down through the cities of New York and New Orleans; when they are dragged from their houses and hung upon lamp-posts; when their children are torn from their arms, and their brains dashed out upon the pavement; when they are objects of insult and outrage at every turn; when they are in danger of having their homes burnt down over their heads; when their children are not allowed to enter schools; then they will have an urgency to obtain the ballot equal to our own."

Conveniently, the urgency of black women to obtain the ballot, by Douglass' own reasoning, escaped note by him. But moreover, in denying all women's struggles an urgency equal to the struggle of black men, or in relegating feminism to some "secondary" status, male "radicals" evidence a blindness that recurs whenever women seek but simple justice from their "brothers." It didn't seem evident to Douglass nor is it seemingly relevant to McReynolds and his contemporaries that women, solely because they are women, were and continue to be hunted down through the streets and dragged from their homes. And though not hung upon lamp-posts (or any longer burned or hung as witches *per se*), being terrorized and imprisoned in backwoods camps, kidnapped to be slaves to the lusts of lumbering men, left brutalized and assaulted or dead in marshes, or dismembered (emotionally or physically) in some back alley, rooftop or yard seem grisly and horrible enough fates to equate with lynching. Of course, we have no *history* of this sort of misogynist terrorism, but a herstory of the reality of women's lives is emerging.

Nineteenth century feminist journals contain a wealth of information that is only now coming to light. Historians are discovering organized movements of women waging struggles against such terrorism—movements that were previously ignored, misinterpreted or dismissed. A recent book by David Pivar, *Purity Crusade: Sexual Morality and Social Control 1868-1900* (Greenwood, 1974), details the struggle of women in what has been conventionally called the Social Purity

Movement. While the book is not written from a feminist perspective, it tells of a struggle against patriarchy, giving a new interpretation to what historians have traditionally concluded was a conservative movement. While Pivar uses the language of patriarchal reference, for example describing the patterns of organized kidnapping of women and mass rape as merely "commercialized vice," he provides the context in which such misogynist terrorism can be perceived for what it was. Our history books never told us of massive "camps" in Michigan, Wisconsin, and throughout the middle-and-northwest in which women were "guarded in a virtual prison and used to satisfy the lusts of lumbermen from surrounding camps . . . Vicious dogs were kept to discourage [escape] attempts and to track girls *(sic)* who tried." Pivar recounts how nineteenth-century women fought laws which resulted in higher sentences for the stealing of a purse than for rape, too.

Patriarchal accounts discuss such organized struggles of women as efforts to thwart prostitution or the misnomer of "white slavery," but the women Pivar tells us about were consciously in an inchoate stage of struggle against patriarchal rule and misogynist practices of men that, among other things, included the hunting down of women—a reality that radical men whether in the nineteenth or twentieth century have difficulty in seeing. Other works in women's history have documented similarly ignored examples of misogynist terrorism, both physical and emotional, and the incipient struggles of women to battle such patriarchal violence.

One can look also to the rampant patterns of rape and violence in pornographic literature of any period (e.g., *My Secret Life,* the works of Henry Miller, or contemporary cinema) that males define as a commonplace, a norm, and for which males have developed numerous euphemisms. The daily newspaper gives some idea, through reporting of sensational cases that excite the editors of the male press, of the misogynist terrorism with which men attack women, too.

In Douglass' day, women, solely because they were women, were consistently denied custody of their children; today, women continue to fear that their children, particularly female children, will have their lives snuffed out by males on misogynist rampages. Women were and continue to be objects of insult and outrage at every turn, whether on the street, on television, upon theater marquees and advertisements, and even in some "movement" circles. Neither women nor their daughters were allowed access to education in the period of which Douglass spoke. Subsequently, we've seen the development of tracking according to sex spread throughout all levels of education to further constrict educational opportunity.

Also consider how radicals have been in the vanguard of the struggle against racial segregation in education, whether in Arkansas or Boston. But where are the protests and demonstrations and agit-prop radical press coverage to support Susan Lynne Vorcheimer and her sisters who are struggling to enter Philadelphia's most prestigious public high school, Central High, which for two hundred years has been a bastion of male exclusivity. Her efforts were recently set back when a Federal Court stayed a lower court's ruling which had held in her favor. Her struggle, and those of other girls, do not seem to merit the attention of male "radicals." One does not read about it in the "radical" press, but only in feminist media, or sometimes even in the "establishment" press.

When will "radical" men join the struggle against segregation operating along sex lines in education with a fervor comparable to the struggle for racial equality, whether that means pointing up the obviousness of the applicable principle in *Brown v. Bd. of Education* that "separate but equal" is "inherently unequal," or challenging the subtler sexist schemes in admissions, in guises of divergent tracking, or in curricular materials.

It is also illustrative to look at the condemnation of the Supreme Court nominations of Carswell and Haynesworth, on charges of racism, that came from liberal, civil rights and left groups across the country — juxtaposed against the silence of those groups upon the recent nomination of Judge Stevens by President Ford. Feminists fought a lonely battle to have their charges against Stevens even heard and received no aid from their "brothers" in those groups that had attacked the earlier nominations of Carswell and Haynesworth, even though feminists had also joined the fight against those nominations.

Furthermore, what is so often attributed to the "massive blind spots" of middle class radicals turns on not class, but the male nature of movement leadership. While class perceptions may have impaired the vision of some radicals, what Robin Morgan has called the "ejaculatory nature" of leftist politics seems a more accurate characterization of the movement's failings. Confrontation substituted for commitment, not because of class but because radical men were indeed more a part of the problem than they were of the solution. The tactics and strategies of the movement were less a class reaction against revolutionary change, as McReynolds would have it, then a male reaction against making basic and long-term commitments, to people and struggle.

Moreover, radical men have trivialized the very issues upon which women of the left structured an analysis that sex, in a more fundamental way than class, was at the root of oppressive and exploitive societal relations. Feminists are accused of attacking men, of betrayals, of turning upon "brothers"—as if to suggest a motive of vengence and not one of justice, as if to disparage feminist theory as being narrow and reactionary rather than being concerned with the profound investigation of a dialectic of sexual stratification that could empower extensive progressive structural change in society and humanize (read: feminize) culture. For instance, the slogan "emasculate the law" has not fired the imagination of radical men who somehow feel threatened by the various meanings conveyed therein, when the slogan merely shows that the struggle against repressive authority is the struggle to excise what has been erected by patriarchal law givers. The slogan reverses the misogynist meaning of "emasculate" (a meaning that I have yet to see disturb "radical" male authors when the word is employed to just mean weaken) and seeks to connote the idea that to weaken the law is to struggle for justice when weakening the law removes the masculine. That which patriarchy views negatively becomes the positive value, and there emerges the goal of strengthening the feminine, the power of women. Radical men need not have qualms about the struggle to emasculate the law unless their identification is with the patriarchy.

If there is to be a serious struggle against repressive and illegitimate authority by radicals, it must be at root a struggle against patriarchal rule. But male radicals have not rushed to support feminists in an analysis which demands such a fundamental revolution, preferring instead to suggest that some women merely want a bigger piece of the bourgeois pie. This latter suggestion is what has been divisive amongst radicals, not the critique of sexism and revolution offered by feminists. Male radicals, like McReynolds, who accuse feminists of attacking men, of creating divisions and deflections, have either let an unneeded defensiveness substitute for analytic comprehension or have meant to indicate that we and they are not of the same movement, that they have not broken with the patriarchy, that they intend to be "good brothers" in the tradition of "good Germans."

Radical men must seriously join the dialogue on the depths of sexism, specifically in the Left and radical movements, and more generally on the issues raised by feminists in analyses of patriarchy. It is absurd to hear someone like David McReynolds baldly declare that the real problem lies in "the basic social structure" (what wonderous precision of language!), and that feminism is a deflection from the struggle to overturn that structure. For the basic disagreement over what constitutes that basic social structure is passed right over. Implicit in McReynolds' argument is his refusal, similar to that of many male radicals, to even acknowledge the presence of contending analysis. Such is an example of the male left's failure to discuss radical feminist analysis with a seriousness equal to that with which male radicals demand that women take any number of male-centered preoccupations: whether those be men's personal dilemmas, "men's liberation," or male socialist perspectives and sexist social revolutions.

To put it bluntly, feminism is a movement that "radical" men and "the Left" seem only too willing to trash, to ridicule, to put in its "place," or to destroy if *they* can't control it. Consider what kind of commitments radical men have made to feminism. Token articles are allowed to appear in radical journals, conveniently followed by a flurry of letters from men who ask why such "extremist" women must be allowed to clutter the pages with their rantings. Moreover, the "token" articles that do appear have no influence on the perspectives of men who write on "radical" themes. (A fine exception to this trend has been in the editorial policy and content of articles in *Social Policy*.) A patently androcentric perspective is the norm preserved. For example, reportage on Portugal has all but ignored the struggle of feminists there to overthrow patriarchal rule and the reaction which met organized feminism. This has been the trend from *Ramparts* to *Liberation* to *WIN* and recently to *Seven Days*.

But further, check what else *hasn't* happened!

When white and black radicals struggle for "civil rights" there is no indignant characterization of that struggle as "reformist." But male radicals have so characterized and denigrated the struggle for the ERA, perhaps to rationalize their refusal to make any commitment to the struggles of women. Radical men have let their penises proselytize their minds. It becomes apparent that there is a real need to ask according to whose agenda—women's or men's—the transformation of society will progress. On whose terms will we struggle—and according to what ethic—that of feminism or an androcentric left's?

Consider that some leftist men now look approvingly on electoral politics. Has this anything to do with the campaigns of Tom Hayden and other former male radicals running for office? Is it because such men are leaving once prominent women in the shadows? Moreover, where was movement support and publicity when feminists like Elaine Noble, Bella Abzug, Pat Schroder, Elizabeth Holtzman, Lt. Gov. Krupsak of New York and others ran for office? Additionally, why have radical men only shown interest in the Senate campaign of Hayden and not in Bella Abzug's in New York?

Consider how stone silent male radicals have been in regard to the terrorism of and guerilla war waged against women by patriarchal vigilantes in which nearly half a million women (a number projected from FBI statistics) are yearly attacked, maimed or murdered. Consider if a half a million Blacks, Jews, or any national minority, or group of political radicals, were *yearly* the victims of politically inspired terrorist assaults solely because of being Black, Jewish, etc.? What would radicals do? The struggle of Blacks in Boston was joined to halt intimidation and terror minor in comparison. Compare how we struggled for the Vietnamese, for draft-resisters and for boys sent to kill or be killed. But I've yet to see a word in the press dominated by male radicals about the terrorist attacks that are an integral element in the oppressive reality of patriarchy, which struck at 500,000 women last year. Moreover, more than words are needed where the issue calls for a sustained commitment to struggle.

Clearly, the elimination of rape has not been a priority in the eyes of male "radicals." In ignoring the misogynist violence of men and the imperialism of patriarchy, male "radicals" and pacifists manifest a malevolence similar to that which characterizes the very violence of men, which makes rape the common, not-so-metaphoric, expression of male behavior towards women. There is little concern among male radicals to challenge any misogynist malice—any *male*violence—any male violence directed at women—whether of arm-chair rapists as they ogle on the street, in offices, at demonstrations, of workers similarly allowed to erect fantasies of power, or of ruling class patriarchs who pursue the enigma of conquest through sexual and economic objectification.

There is little understanding that pornography is not about sex but rather is a fundamentally misogynist expression of patriarchal rites—and is correlative in civil liberties terms not to free speech rights of segregationists which some ACLU types would defend but rather to the purveying of racist and anti-semitic Nazi ideology at the time of Hitler's Germany, propaganda forms which even the ACLU would likely deem unworthy of defense. Racist propaganda like the film *Coonskin* has recently drawn radical ire for its outrageous attempt to market racism as art or entertainment. But where are radicals who would denounce, picket and demonstrate against the glut of misogynist and sexist propaganda that patriarchy markets as "sex" films or pornography? Where were male radicals when such films as *Deep Throat* were being shown? Not in the streets demonstrating against such propaganda, but most likely in the theaters drooling alongside their "brothers."

To have any kind of credibility as radicals, men must begin establishing serious commitments to feminist programs, rather than presuming to suggest there is a "basic" problem that makes feminism a "secondary" concern or a deflection from the real, necessary struggle. Male radicals need to open their eyes to the material reality that their gender class origins obfuscate: the systematic hunting down of women who presume equal access to public space, the daily training and propaganda that foments rapist ideology, the laws that sanction gynocidal terror and judicial intimidation of women who would resist such terrorism. Male radicals must begin to see aspects of male behavior that turn men's lives into instruments by which the patriarchy stultifies the lives of women, either with whom they live, with whom they work, whom they pass on the street, or whom they exploit and oppress with a glance at the covers of the sexist rags that preponderate on magazine racks everywhere. For if the subject is to be revolution, as in David McReynolds' recent articles, and a monologue masquerades as dialogue, with feminism relegated to the periphery, what we are hearing is merely leftist patriarchal reaction. If the struggle is not against the patriarchy, then what occurs is but a mere power play among the boys.

In a 1973 article, Adrienne Rich suggests there may be a greater alliance between "the men of the worldwide left and the men of the most powerful patriarchy in history, than between the men of the Left and the feminist movement." An article by Fran Moira in *Off Our Backs* (Dec. 1975) illustrates the tendency for patriarchal retrenchment in progressive and revolutionary movements worldwide. Rather than attempting a synthesis of such analysis, an understanding of the dialectic evidenced by the emergence of feminism as a challenge to patriarchy, male radicals confine their vision of revolution to one in which rule by the minority—by men—is preserved. This cannot be tolerated as "radical" if the word is to have its meaning preserved. Radicals must reject arguments that would propound to revitalize "the boys' movement," aptly labeled as such by Robin Morgan, the priorities of which were and are—as Jane Alpert courageously argued in "Mother Right"—irrelevant to moving masses of people to embrace political perspectives that would radically restructure their lives and the society.

Neither can opportunism be tolerated; an authentic commitment is not one which "allows" for discussion of "male chauvinism" or *tolerates* an autonomous women's movement, yet continues to view

94

feminism as ancillary to revolutionary struggle. Patriarchy is not a sin, something to be confessed, forgiven and forgotten. It is a method of organization and rule at the base of the social structure, it is a value system that must be uprooted and replaced. Authentic social revolution will only progress with a societal extensive rise of gynocratic authority. When the material reality of patriarchy becomes visible, the challenge of revolution becomes a challenge to the egregious rule of men.

Because "brotherhood" and fraternity are suspect as expressions of male bonding, particularly when a commitment to struggle against patriarchy is not clearly present, male radicals must learn to comprehend Sisterhood as the encompassing relation upon which a commitment to struggle must be based. The tension will be great, as when Mary Daly used the phrase "Sisterhood of Man" in *Beyond God the Father* to invigorate imagination for a leap beyond the patriarchal consciousness of the brotherhood of man. But male radicals must begin to look beyond themselves, beyond "brothers," beyond all other men to the lives of women and the experience of patriarchy. A myopic masculine vision, unaided by the agency of Sisterhood, can't adequately conceive of revolution, of change grounded in a radical understanding of material reality. Until men of the Left are willing to break with patriarchy, they will be imprisoned within the limitations of mere seminal thinking. The most striking aspects of arguments by male radicals, as in the McReynolds' articles, will continue to be the general acceptance of the "phallacies" proffered by patriarchy—of the tyrannical hold that patriarchal consciousness exercises upon the revolutionary imagination of men through the privileges the gender class of men enjoy.

There is though a curious and terrible irony in all of this, in the defensive posture that male radicals take in opposition to the sweep of feminist analysis, in accusations of betrayal and charges that feminism threatens to undermine movement towards revolution. For it is patriarchy which in reality has men "by the balls" so to speak. And it is capitulation to this grip out of fear—of emasculation, of the loss of privilege, of being likened to women, of having to know powerlessness without any illusions of supremacy—that causes the revolutionary agency of the traditional left, working class men, to be whipped into line, bought off, seemingly by the forces of capital. Moreover, the tragedy in the Left's blindness to patriarchy and the defensiveness of male radicals in response to the revolutionary dialectic suggested by feminism is evinced in the lack of success that socialism has had against the forces of capital or, where "successful," its general failure to be held true to its promises and its degeneration into oppressive tyranny. For capitulation to tyranny, whether it be capitalist or socialist, is what complacency in the face of patriarchy promises.

To struggle against such complacency is thus to struggle against capitulation to the grip patriarchy has upon revolution. To cut away at the misogynist system that accompanied recognition of paternity, and elevated the father (or the fatherland) to a position of supremacy is to build a movement that reaches to the root of both women's and men's lives, for it reaches—and affirms—what is material, the *mater,* the actual source of change in the organization of human society long obfuscated by the myths, rites and rules of patriarchy. With the passing away of patriarchy, with its defeat, with the eradication of misogyny, a revolution will have been accomplished to supplant the incomplete or partial alterations in the economic base of society with a more radical conception of material change than any *man* has yet imagined.

SUGGESTED READINGS

Phyllis Chesler, *Women and Madness* (Avon, 1973).

Mary Daly, *Beyond God the Father: Towards a Philosophy of Women's Liberation,* (Beacon Press, 1973).

Barbara Deming, *We Cannot Live Without Our Lives,* (Viking, 1974), particularly, Letter to Arthur Kinoy: Women and the People's Party (pp. 153-168) which also appeared in *Liberation* (Dec. 1973) under a different title.

Andrea Dworkin, *Woman Hating* (Dutton, 1974).

Marge Piercy, *Small Changes* (Doubleday, 1974). A novel which presents feminism and left politics in illustrative contexts, and a delight to read.

David Pivar, *Purity Crusade: Sexual Morality and Social Control 1868-1890* (Greenwood, 1973). Particularly, see chapters 3-5.

Elizabeth Reid, "Patriarchy is another form of colonizing people," *Majority Report* (August 9, 1975), p. 12.

Adrienne· Rich, "Caryatid, A Column: War, Rape and Masculinity," *American Poetry Review* (May-June 1973), p. 10-11.

Florence Rush, "Sexism in the Male Left: A Double Standard for 'Informers formers'," *Know News* Vol. 6, No. 5 (August-September, 1975).

Diane E.H. Russel, *The Politics of Rape: The Victim's Perspective* (Stein and Dav, 1975).

Susan Brownmiller, *Against Our Will: Men, Women and Rape* (Simon and Schuster, 1975).

G.J. Barker-Benfield, *The Horrors of the Half-Known Life* (Harper and Row, 1975).

Gina Covina and Laurel Galana, *The Lesbian Reader* (Amazon Press, 1975). Available from Amazon Press, 395 60th Street, Oakland, CA, 94618.

Joanna Russ, *The Female Man* (Bantam, 1975). Sci-fi that is insightful and visionary.

Mary Hartman and Lois Banner, *Clio's Consciousness Raised—New Perspectives on the History of Women* (Harper Torchbooks, 1974).

Ann Forfreedom, *Women Out of History: a Herstory Anthology* (1975). Available for $4.50 from Ann Forfreedom, 1947 Bell Street, Number 26, Sacramento, CA 95825.

Also the following important journals:

Feminist Studies ($8/yr), 417 Riverside Drive, NY, NY 10025.

Women's Rights Law Reporter ($12/yr), 180 University Ave., Newark, NJ .

Signs ($12/yr), University of Chicago Press, 11030 Langley Avenue Chicago, Illinois 60628.

Quest ($7/yr), P.O. Box 8843, Washington, DC 20003.

From *Win,* January 22, 1976. Reprinted by permission.

Eroticism and Violence in the Father-Son Relationship

John Stoltenberg

This article is adapted from a speech delivered in Woodstock, New York, October 10, 1975, co-sponsored by the Woodstock Women's Center and the Woodstock Self-Defense Committee. Many of the values and insights in this article are based on the theoretical work of Shulamith Firestone (*The Dialectic of Sex,* Bantam, 1971), and Andrea Dworkin (*Woman Hating,* Dutton, 1974).

I believe that the father-son relationship is a fundamental force in the global oppression of women. In this article, I analyze that relationship, both from the perspective of radical feminism and from the perspective of one who has grown up as a son.

The Context

The sexual political context of the father-son relationship is the form of social organization called patriarchy, or father right. Father right is not a morally neutral form of social organization, but it is the only form there is, anywhere on the planet. The *Random House Dictionary* defines patriarchy as "a form of social organization in which

97

the father is the supreme authority in the family, clan, or tribe and descent is reckoned in the male line, with the children belonging to the father's clan or tribe." All children under father right belong to fathers, not to mothers, because the father possesses the mother, legally and carnally; the verb "to possess" indicates literally what he does to her.

One remarkable aspect of father right is the quantity of violence required to enforce it, the quantity of violence required to perpetuate it, to keep it the form in which humans live out their lives.

Many would like to believe that father right is simply an ingenious and equitable human invention of kinship which is necessary because of the composition of zygotes—so that a person who contributes a sperm cell and a person who contributes an egg cell might know with equal certainty who is related to whom genetically. But father right is not so simple. Father right is not so scientific. Nor is father right a function of gender justice in any way.

Fundamentally, father right is a system of ownership, literal ownership of other human lives—ownership of the labor, will, body and consciousness of whole other people, of whole human beings. And that ownership begins with ownership by adult men, ownership of the only means of producing those lives, the flesh and blood of women.

Patriarchal law *legalizes* that ownership. Normal phallic eroticism *embodies* that ownership. Patriarchal culture also romanticizes, spiritualizes, emotionalizes and psychologizes the right of men to own women and children as property. Patriarchal culture tends to obscure the violence in those structures of human relationship which are essentially structures of possession, as of inanimate objects. But it is in patriarchal law and phallic eroticism that father right is fixed and father right is felt. The law and the phallus are both primary instruments of owning.

The reality of male ownership in all human relationships under father right can be seen immediately and most clearly as it affects the lives of humans defined by culture as female—all humans, that is, who were born without a penis.

At no time in a woman's life is she not defined by culture as the actual or potential property of someone who is male, someone born with a penis. First, as a child, she is owned by a father, the man who owns the flesh of her mother in marriage. That man owns her as a daughter, according to law, until such time as her body is contracted into marriage, that is until she is possessed carnally and legally by a husband.

The modern western marriage custom of a father "giving away the bride" is a cultural remnant from the time in history when the father sold his daughter for money. This commodity exchange, the bride price paid by a husband to a father, continued in Europe until shortly after the Crusades, when a lot of men had died and the bottom dropped out of the market for brides. According to the economics of supply and demand, the bride price was abandoned and fathers began to give their daughters away for free. To this day, the marriage ceremony is a ritual reminder that title to a woman's body has been transferred from one male owner to another.

Legally, a husband cannot rape his wife; she is his property; he can do to his property whatever he pleases. And whatever he does, the law will not charge him with rape. Historically, rape was recognized as a crime only against the male owner of property. If the woman who was raped was still the virgin daughter of a father, the law recognized the rape as a crime against the father whose property was devalued. If the woman who was raped was the married wife of a husband, the law recognized the rape as a crime against the husband whose property was stolen. Rape exposes the reality that female flesh is never her own. If at some time in her life it is not the carnal property of a father or husband, she still has no claim to it; it belongs to any man who wants it. To this day, in any court of law, a woman who is not married, who is also no longer the virgin daughter of a father, faces cruel societal censure if she claims that a man committed a sexual act against her body and will. The presumption is that such a sex act is not a real crime against any man, since no particular man owns her, and therefore she has no valid reason to complain. And to this day, any woman who is raped also faces hysterical rejection and abuse by any man who regularly fucks her. Though he may or may not legally own her body in marriage, he has felt that he owns it while fucking, and he no longer can function with the same feeling since his personal property was defiled.

Patriarchal law both protects and expresses a cultural norm of phallic eroticism. Normally phallic eroticism responds best and basically to bodies as objects, to human flesh as property. Phallic eroticism is inherently proprietary; it is an eroticism cultivated for owning; and it is dysfunctional and insensate except in relation to human flesh perceived and treated as personal property. Phallic eroticism is inherently alienating; it is an eroticism cultivated for defending the barrier between subject and object, active and passive, owner and property, master and slave. Phallic eroticism is inherently hostile, for violence is necessary to sustain such an unnatural relationship to other human life. By defining men's property rights to the bodies of women, patriarchal law licenses and reinforces each man's private eroticized estranging, each man's private eroticized violence. And patriarchal law seeks to protect each man's erotic privacy from usurpation by other men.

According to human biology, only a woman can bear a child; a child not borne by a mother does not, in nature, exist. According to patriarchal law, however, a child not owned by a man is deemed a legal nonentity and is called "illegitimate" or "bastard," because the law grants men exclusively the right to ownership of children. A woman who is not properly owned by a man when she gives birth to a child is scorned, shamed, humiliated and castigated, and an unwed mother who persists in bearing children which are not a father's property may be forced against her will to be sterilized. There is at present no law which prohibits that punishment. In order to make certain that men will own every child that women bear, all the forces of law and culture are allied to keep every women's body the legal and carnal property of men throughout her life.

Male ownership of children has always been separate and distinct from the labor of human custodianship. If a woman is properly owned by a man when she gives birth to a child, among her duties to the man is to act as custodian of his child. That means feeding it and cleaning up after it, disposing of the enormous quantity of shit, for instance, that an infant produces in the first three years of its life. That shit-work is custodial. It is not an owner's duty. A properly owned mother literally takes care of children which are legally, always, the human property of a father.

Historically, it was a dead father's legal right to bequeath his children to another man, irrespective of the fact that his wife might still be alive. Elizabeth Cady Stanton, in an address to the Joint Judiciary Committee of the New York State Legislature in 1854, described the legal prerogative of fathers at that time:

> The father may apprentice his child, bind him out to a trade, without the mother's consent — yea, in direct opposition to her most earnest entreaties, prayers and tears . . . Moreover, the father, about to die, may bind out all his children wherever and to whomsoever he may see fit, and thus, in fact, will away the guardianship of all his children from the mother . . . Thus, by your laws, the child is the absolute property of the father, wholly at his disposal in life or at death.[1]

Four years later, as a direct consequence of action by the first U.S.

Women's Rights Movement, the New York State Legislature passed a law which declared every married woman to be "the joint guardian of her children, with her husband, with equal powers, rights and duties in regard to them, with the husband."[2] This law was called the Married Women's Property Act of 1860, and it applied significantly to mothers who were widowed for it guaranteed that they could continue custodianship of a dead father's children. This statute was the first legal challenge to a precept upon which all of patriarchal culture stands, the principle that human lives can be controlled by a father who is dead. The power of male ownership from the grave is still alive and well, of course, not only in patriarchal law and the Judeo-Christian religious tradition, but also in personal psychological identity. As Juliet Mitchell has observed:

> . . . Whether or not the actual father is there does not affect the perpetuation of the patriarchal culture within the psychology of the individual; present or absent, "the father" always has his place. His actual absence may cause confusion, or, on another level, relief, but the only difference it makes is within the terms of the over-all patriarchal assumption of his presence. In our culture he is just as present in his absence.[3]

So-called child custody disputes are a rather recent historical phenomenon. In that same speech to the New York State Legislature, Elizabeth Cady Stanton described this situation of mothers:

> In case of separation, the law gives the children to the father; no matter what his character or condition. At this very time we can point you to noble, virtuous, well-educated mothers in this State, who have abandoned their husbands for their profligacy and confirmed drunkenness. All these have been robbed of their children, who are in the custody of the husband, under the care of his relatives, whilst the mothers are permitted to see them but at stated intervals . . . [4]

The laws on divorce, as to what are its proper grounds for instance, were framed then as now in the interests of fathers. But those interests have shifted somewhat. Only within the last several decades did it become in the father's interest to allow an extension of the mother's custodial responsibilities to his children after terminating, in divorce, her domestic and coital responsibilities to him. The father's ownership of his children could thus be maintained at a comfortable and convenient distance, without the burden on him of finding someone to do the shit-work. This recent history is reflected in the few current state laws which automatically continue custodianship of children by divorced mothers, but only those children who are yet very young.

A pendulum of paternal pride has swung, however, and fathers are again rejecting divorced mothers as suitable custodians for their children. Custodianship is not ownership. Custodianship is service, shit-work, and daily care. Ownership is the legal relationship of a father to his child, a relationship of owner to human property that is immutable, even in death. Modern child custody disputes reveal how all mother-child relationships under father right become distorted and deformed according to the model of the property relationship which obtains between father and child. In a child custody dispute, the mother must now haggle on the father's turf (the court) and in the father's terms (children as personal property). And the unnatural question to be resolved is who shall "own" this child's time and company, this child's affection and allegiance—discounting the custodial labor the mother performed for that child's life, since that labor was a function of the father's former ownership of her.

Phallic eroticism entirely informs these disputes. In order to be permitted to continue her custodial relationship to a father's children, the divorced mother must pass a peculiar test as to whether or not she is "fit." That test, essentially, is celibacy, a test supported by much contemporary legal opinion. In order to continue her labor of custodianship toward a father's children, the divorced mother must demonstrate to the court that she has not improperly become the carnal possession of another man. If she must return to court years later, in the likely event, for instance, that the father has stopped sending her money to support the child, she may again be required to pass the celibacy test of "fitness." The use of money by fathers to control the lives of ex-wives and children is a custom protected by law. And the celibacy test for divorced mothers assures the father in his imagination that his ex-wife, like a daughter, will stay carnally owned by him until such time as another man legally marries her. The courts recognize the prerogative of that father's imagination not to be perturbed. Even more perturbing than carnal possession of the mother by another man is the case of a divorced mother who would share her eroticism with a woman. In a child custody dispute, a mother's lesbianism is deemed worse than adultery. The hysteria of a father whose private property has been violated by the penis of another man is exceeded by the hysteria of a father whose former private property has renounced phallic possession altogether. The courts, needless to say, protect a father from all such hysteria under the camouflage of what is best for the "welfare" of his child.

Just as father right is predicated on the right of absent and dead fathers to own and control the living, so also is father right predicated on the right of living fathers to own and control the unborn. Nowhere in America is abortion available to women free and on demand; in many states where abortion has been decriminalized, the consent of the nearest male relative must be obtained, or there must be a second attending physician to try to save the fetus. That law expresses the erotic relationship between a man and his phallus. Fathers fantasize all fetuses as male, and, in effect, as repositories of phallic life. Phallic eroticism is genital-centric; all sense of life is centered in the phallus; the rest of the body is armored and kept relatively dead. The phallus thus seems to have an independent life and will of its own, autonomous and unpredictable, and the man is at pains to control it, to make it do what he wants. Least of all does he want it to be cut off. As father right serves dead fathers, so also does father right serve men whose bodies are dead while their penises are alive.

Under father right, the first fact of every human life is that one is born of human flesh which belongs to someone barren. Every human life comes forth from a woman whose body at no moment in her life is not defined as the actual or potential personal property of men. These are the real "facts of life" under father right, the economic realities concerning the labors of mothers. Adult men own every body that has given birth and every body that gives birth. Every economic system devised by men—whether capitalism or communism or socialism—is designed to defend male ownership of the bodies and labor of women. Every religious belief system instituted by men—including Judaism which deifies the father and Christianity which deifies the son—is designed to dehumanize the person of the mother. Every psychological system theorized by men—whether the Freudian tradition with its notion of "penis envy" or the modern behaviorist view with its babies in boxes—is designed to validate male ownership of birth itself. Every agency of culture—including the state, the university, medicine, marriage, the nuclear family—is an instrumentality of male ownership of other human lives.

Father right circumscribes how we see, how we feel, and most devastatingly how we imagine. We are so accustomed to definitions of love, justice and human community which are predicated upon male ownership of other human lives that we can scarcely imagine a future in which people are not property. We are so accustomed to the traumatizing reality that in this civilization the most violent, debilitating, exploitative and ostensibly intimate relationships between humans are precisely those relations between owner and owned that we cannot imagine being related in any other way. We are so accustomed to to imagining that father right merits our respect—because we dare not

103

provoke the father's wrath, because we know in our hearts that he loves only those whom he controls, that he provides, if at all, only for those lives which he owns, that his approval is bestowed conditionally only upon persons who are his compliant personal property and that he knows no other connection to any other human life—we are so beholden to the father that we have sacrificed and betrayed all mothers in his name.

The Content

The historical origins of father right are lost in the prehistory of civilization. But socially and psychologically, father right re-originates, over and over again, in the lifetime of every male. How does it happen that a human infant, accidentally born with external genitalia, learns the bizarre propensity to own the lives of other human beings?

One explanation is that this society systematizes and institutionalizes male supremacy and father right and that this society entitles genital males to ownership of female flesh. That is certainly the fact, and the institutions of this society must certainly be abolished. But it is quite another thing to perceive that in every male lifetime a process is effected, more or less successfully, which produces in the male the character of a father, the behavior of a supremacist and the capability of owning lives—a capability realized not simply because he is socially entitled to own lives but more profoundly because he is constitutionally dysfunctional otherwise, because, in other words, only owning is erotic. Somehow, every male in his lifetime learns to adjust his entire erotic, emotional and volitional sensibility in order to become an owner, in contrast to women, who are to be owned.

Even in our present culture, there exist mythic renderings of the damage mothers do to sons, wildly inconsistent myths, from the myth of "too much affection" to the myth of "not enough." These myths have enormous power in enforcing the cultural assumption that among the mother's duties to father right is her duty to produce a son who is capable of owning a life like hers. But that is a duty which is fraught with contradictions. On the one hand, the mother's duty to the father is to remain his carnal possession and to reassure him in his imagination that his son, this little phallic presence, is not a threat to his coital privileges. On the other hand, the mother's duty to the future father in the son is always to present herself as one whom he might like someday to marry, by reassuring him, for instance, that unending quantities of her labor are his for the asking. The essential erotic contradiction in all mother-child relationships under father right is described in these words by Alice S. Rossi:

<blockquote>
. . . It is to men's sexual advantage to restrict women's sexual gratification to heterosexual coitus, though the price for the woman and a child may be a less psychologically and physically rewarding relationship.[5]
</blockquote>

That erotic contradiction exists whether the child is a son or a daughter, but if the child is a son, the father imagines that the infantile sexuality of his little boy is somehow centered on fucking his wife. Only a father could have imagined that that is what a child wants to do, but that indeed is the fantasy fear of fathers, a fear which requires much coital consolation.

Fathers fantasize all fetuses as male, as repositories of phallic life. This fantasy contradicts not only birth statistics but also the fact of gestation that until the seventh week of fetal development, all fetuses have identical genitalia. This fantasy of fathers, that all fetal life is phallic, only makes sense if it is understood to be an expression of a fundamental characteristic of phallic eroticism: that the feelings which become isolated in an adult man's phallus are experienced as disembodied and seem to be left behind in a vagina if his phallus ejaculates and shrinks there. These phallic feelings seem to have been stolen, as accords with his proprietary world-view and his contempt for women, and he imagines that in a fetus those lost phallic feelings are contained and he can somehow have them back. If the baby is born without external genitalia, the father's projection of phallic life in the fetus stops. But if the baby is born a boy, the father's projection of phallic life in the infant continues and the father perceives the infant as a rival for his wife.

The father's attitudes and actions toward his baby boy are ambivalent at best. The father desired a baby boy in order to retrieve from his wife's body all the erections that disappeared there, to re-possess in the form of infant male flesh all the sensations she drained and confiscated from the form of his erect penis. And now what does he do with it? How does he touch it? Or does he not touch it at all? While the father in his ambivalence is waiting for the boy to grow up big and strong, the son is learning the difference between mother and not-mother, his first crucial lesson in gender polarity. The child is learning that distinction from information which is tactile, information which is erotic. The child is learning how his own eroticism is in harmony with the eroticism of mother but that it is in discord with his sensory experience of the body of not-mother. The child is learning this distinction not on account of anatomy, not on account of lactation in one and the absence of lactation in the other. Babies will suckle a male's nipple just as readily as a female's, though few men will permit it. And even babies who were never breastfed learn the two concepts just as quickly. Rather, the baby is learning the concepts of mother and not-mother from a peculiar fact of culture—the fact that phallic eroticism in not-mothers is inimical to communion with other human life. Something in not-mother is alien. Something in not-mother is dead. Not-mother pets but does not touch. Not-mother fondles but does not feel. Not-mother grabs but does not hold. There is no sensory resonance of pulse and breath and motion between not-mother and the child. And the child perceives together with mother that they are different from not-mother.

By the time this distinction is fixed in the child's consciousness, the father is enraged. From the father's perspective the child, who is the corporeal projection of his phallic eroticism, is in the clutches of a woman, seemingly subsumed within her body, humiliatingly limp and soft. Now begins the arduous process by which the father will seek again to retrieve from the mother the phallic life which he seems to keep losing. He begins in earnest to repossess his son, for now what is at stake is the father's personal hold on existence, a rather tenuous hold which seems to stand or collapse with engorgement in his penis and aggression in his son.

The father's struggle to repossess the son will be played out in front of the boy's uncomprehending eyes and upon the bodies of both the boy and the mother. To be sure, the father will be aided and abetted by schools, television and other cultural accessories to the theft of sons from mothers. But the father figure in the flesh will succeed in dividing the boy's eroticism against the mother only by physical or emotional brutality. The boy will be a witness as the father abuses his wife—once or a hundred times, it only needs to happen once, and the boy will be filled with fear and helpless to intercede. Then the father will visit his anger upon the boy himself, uncontrollable rage, wrath that seems to come from nowhere, punishment out of proportion to any infraction of rules the boy knew existed—once or a hundred times, it only needs to happen once, and the boy will wonder in agony why the mother did not prevent it. From that point onward, the boy's trust in the mother decays, and the son will belong to the father for the rest of his natural life.

The authority of the anger of the father is interpreted by the son as follows: (1) Not-mother hates mother and not-mother hates me; not-mother hates us. (2) It is because I am like mother that not-mother hates me so. (3) I should be different from mother; the more different

I am from mother, the safer I will be. Those are the cardinal principles of logic in male maturation under father right. They are so simple, even a child can understand. They are backed up by the constant threat of the father's anger, so the child will remember them, and the child will never forget.

The son, in order to become as different from mother as he possibly can be, now begins to rid his body of the eroticism of the mother. He withdraws from it. He purges it with aggression. He refuses to feel it any more. In his memory, their sensory identification had been complete. In his whole body, their eroticism had been the same. Now it must be abandoned, negated, cancelled, denied; he must no longer feel with her feeling, feel how he feels with her, feel her feeling with him. Every nerve in his body is on guard against her, against continuity with her, against the erotic continuum between them, for fear of the father who might mistake the son for her. And every nerve in his body is on guard against the father, the father who hates the son who cannot get rid of the mother in his body. All the boy's sensibilities for erotic communion with other life become anesthetized in terror of ever again feeling one with mother. The boy learns he has a penis and the boy learns the mother does not. If he cannot feel his penis, he will be the same as her for sure. So begins the disembodiment of sensation in that small organ.

Later in his life, the boy's eroticism will inhabit his penis exclusively, the part of him that is not mother, the one place in his body where he can feel for sure that he is different from her, separate and discrete. He will discover to his frustration that the organ is anatomically incapable of sustaining that obsession. He will not be pleased after ejaculation, when the eroticism in his penis stops, and when he feels a kind of deadness, the death of his phallic life. The more he has purged the memory of the mother from his body, the more and more his phallic eroticism must embody his whole sense of self. This is male identity, defined by the father, defined against the mother. This is male identity, in need of constant verification, in desperate struggle not to identify with the body and eroticism of the mother. The sexual-political content of the relationship of father to son is essentially to divide the son against the mother so that the son will never stop trying to conform to the cultural specifications of phallic identity.

The Consequences and The Conclusion

We live in a two-gender system, in service to the father. There is no justice. There is no peace. That system is inappropriate to the memory of erotic communion with other life.

In fear and in honor of the father, sons learn to deny that memory, to rid their bodies of it. In fear and in honor of the father, sons learn phallic identity.

The father-son relationship is a monument to phallic identity, to the dying of the disembodied penis inside the vagina of a woman. A son must live on to avenge that death. A son must live on to repudiate the mother. A son must be withdrawn from the influence of the mother which is perceived by the father as dangerous to virility. The son must be terrorized to mistrust her, to stop feeling with her, in order that his identity should reside in his penis. This is an insane inheritance. It is passed on and on and on.

We live in a two-gender system, in service to the father's rage. Sons learn to dissociate, to be immune from the mother. Sons learn the father's rage against the flesh which gave birth to them, as a condition of escape from the father's condemnation.

That rage is the rage against flesh which is "other"; that rage is the rage against dissolution of self. That rage is the rage of the self which is a fiction, the self which is conditioned in annihilation and denial of another, inherently estranged by cultural definition, identity contingent on nonidentification, the self which must be divided against the mother or it does not exist, it is a nonentity.

Sons can fuck with that rage. Sons can kill with that rage. They can and they do. Still the father is not appeased.

We live in a two-gender system, in service to father right. Fathers, not mothers, invented and control the state. Fathers, not mothers, invented and control the military. Fathers, not mothers, wage war against other peoples. And fathers, not mothers, send sons to war.

Who are the fathers who want sons so much? Who are the fathers and the sons who can only be reconciled in sharing disdain for the life of the mother? And who are the sons who have become fathers to turn sons against mothers again?

This fathering must cease. This inheritance must be refused. This system of owning must be destroyed.

NOTES

1. Elizabeth Cady Stanton, "Address to the New York State Legislature, 1874," *Feminism: The Essential Historical Writings,* Miriam Schneir, editor (Vintage, 1972), p. 114.

2. "Married Women's Property Act, New York, 1860," *Ibid.* p. 123.

3. Juliet Mitchell, "On Freud and the Distinction Between the Sexes,"

Women and Analysis, Jean Strouse, editor (Grossman, 1974), pp. 35-36.

4. Elizabeth Cady Stanton, *loc. cit.*

5. Alice S. Rossi, "Maternalism, Sexuality, and the New Feminism," *Contemporary Sexual Behavior: Critical Issues in the 1970's,* Joseph Zubin and John Money, editors (Johns Hopkins University Press, 1973), pp. 167-168, cited in Adrienne Rich, "The Theft of Childbirth," *The New York Review of Books,* XXII (October 2, 1975), p. 29.

Copyright (c) 1976 by John Stoltenberg.

ANTI-SEXIST PRACTICE

Section Introduction

In the early 1970's, as a result of the impact of the women's movement, several kinds of male anti-sexist groups began to develop. Three publications were influential at this early stage: *Unbecoming Men,* a pamphlet produced by Times Change Press, and two periodicals, *Brother: A Forum for Men Against Sexism,* and *Double F: A Magazine of Effeminism.* What follows is a brief discussion of the three, as a way of putting into perspective the activities that are written about in this section of the anthology.

Unbecoming Men is a pamphlet first published in 1971. It contains the writings of a New York consciousness-raising group established in 1969. The more obvious meaning of the title, men transcending masculinity, was undercut by a second, implying unattractive or even repulsive men. This revulsion was described by one of the authors in a short introduction to the first article. "This article reflects a period of dejection and self-pity that didn't last very long," he explained. "Written about a year ago before I got into this present men's group, it does accurately describe a significant development in my "unbecoming' a man." The article—and the book—are excellent illustrations of the feelings of self-degradation and hopelessness about personal change that men often experience as they begin to discover deeper layers of sexism in their consciousness. An acknowledgment of the depths of one's sexism seems to operate as a prelude to change.

The unbecoming men were all young, white, mostly middle class, heterosexual, movement activists. They drew together out of a sense of isolation accentuated by the new meaning that women found in the enthusiasm and affection of sisterhood. The men were jealous of "women together and me alone," and had to learn to deal with their sexism and feelings of abandonment on their own. Women refused to nurture them or take responsibility for "their problem." Fearing that they were permanently deformed creatures, they agonized over "whether we men can ever in our lifetime regain our humanity." The attempt at a solution was to follow the model of the women's movement, forming a consciousness-raising group. The group was "occasionally used to support some of our oppressive tendencies," they wrote. The men sensed a failure with the group and the booklet, for they closed with typical self-beratement, ". . . what we've produced is only as good as we are."

Brother: A Male Liberation Newspaper began in the summer of 1971. The third issue, fall 1971, changed the title to *Brother: A Forum for Men Against Sexism.* The change in title became necessary because "when the words 'male liberation' were invented, the newspapers took these words and opposed them to women's liberation." In the beginning, *Brother* was a mixed group of gay and non-gay men, one of the few places in the country where men of different sexual orientations tried to work together collectively. Nevertheless, *Brother* was primarily straight-identified through Number VI, a thematic issue on "Men and Our Bodies," April 1973. While remaining open to heterosexuals, *Brother* became primarily a gay collective with the publication of the next thematic issue, "Men and the Family" in the fall of 1973.

Brother has appeared irregularly along with disclosures of internal conflicts which have made its publication difficult. An understanding of the differences was afforded in the summer of 1974 with the publication of "Men in Love: A Dialogue on Bisexual, Straight and Gay Male Sexual Politics." The issue was put out by two separate caucuses, bisexual and gay, within the paper. The controversy between caucuses is the subject of the issue and reflects splits between gay, straight and bisexual men in various men's organizations. *Brother* subsequently became an all-gay collective and produced an anthology of its previous writings. The first article in this section, "Stop Playboying," is the cover story of *Brother* Number II. It reports on a demonstration by men from consciousness-raising groups, together with a few women, against the San Francisco Playboy Club in 1971.

Double F: A Magazine of Effeminism, the publication of the Revolutionary Effeminists—Steven Dansky, John Knoebel and Kenneth Pitchford—began in New York City in response to sexism within the gay male liberation movement. In 1970, the three men formulated their concept of "flaming faggots," effeminate men fighting patriarchy with revolutionary means. Four issues of their journal have appeared. Pitchford, a recognized poet, introduces the effeminist movement in the first issue by urging the use of the word "faggot," a term derived from homosexual persecution in the Middle Ages. The effeminists are critical of the word "gay," stating, "We're not gay, we're angry;" they see "gay" as a trivialism and adopt the militant term "flaming faggots," playing on the double "f" in effeminism. "Just as black liberation emerged to the left of the civil rights movement," they write, "and radical feminism has emerged to the left of women's liberation, so our movement of faggot militants is beginning to be heard to the left of gay liberation."

Adopting the perspective of radical feminism, the effeminists declare that all men are sexist and that "sexism is a product of male supremacy, which produces all the other forms of oppression that patriarchal societies exhibit: racism, classism, ageism, economic exploitation, ecological imbalance." As effeminate men, they are oppressed by the masculinist standards of patriarchy and urge *all men* "to become traitors to the class of men, attacking those aspects of the patriarchal system that most directly oppress us." They consider the male left, men's liberation, and gay male liberation to be sexist male movements, "tactics for preserving power in men's hands by pretending to struggle for change." The effeminists seek to follow women's leadership in seizing power from patriarchy and re-establishing a "gynarchy," an

111

approach which seems to replace a male dominated order with a female one. They also advocate "any means except those inherently male supremacist," but repudiate a connection between violence and masculinity.

The effeminists have reported that the *Effeminist Manifesto,* the second piece in this section, "condensed itself in our minds as the best expression of our own committed politics." Susan Rennie and Kirsten Grimstad, editors of *The New Woman's Survival Sourcebook,* believe *"Double F* enunciates the most imaginative, profound, and persuasive political analysis of gender developed by *any men anywhere"* (emphasis theirs), and selected the Manifesto for their Sourcebook's section on men (see also the Rennie-Grimstad article "Men" in the section "Men's Liberation [Criticisms]" in this book).

"Drudgery and Childcare," the Manifesto's thirteenth principle, seems to sum up the ultimate paradox of Revolutionary Effeminism. In contrast with the violence-prone twelfth principle, "Tactics," there is an ironic emphasis on childcare as a "paramount concern." In order to free women for feminism, they declare caring for children to be a "duty, a right and a privilege." Steven Dansky seems to have something of this fundamental contradiction in mind when he refers to "the anomaly of effeminate men." "I stubbornly believe," he writes, "that faggots are a paradox of men, oscillating between the fury and rage that results from our victimization by the patriarchy's standards and the acquiescence we give to being the agents of sexism." In general, I personally appreciated and learned enormously from *Double F*'s early writings. I believe that the first principle of Revolutionary Effeminism, that "all women are oppressed by all men," is entirely valid, but I am critical of their violent methods of social change and their matriarchal goal.

In an "Open Letter," Karla Jay and June Rook responded to Volume II of *Double F,* the number which contained the *Manifesto.* While they agree that the ideas of the effeminists are particularly important to women's liberation, they are also very critical of the "dangerous male chauvinism" they identify in the effeminist's perspective. Jay's and Rook's letter is reprinted as the third article in this section.

In the fourth article, "Anti-Sexist Consciousness-Raising Groups for Men," Paul Hornacek begins by addressing John Stoltenberg's assertion in "Toward Gender Justice" that "men's consciousness-raising is but a new manifestation of male bonding." While Hornacek agrees with the misuses of consciousness-raising by male liberationists, he maintains it is a useful and important medium for the development of anti-sexism among men. Men's consciousness-raising can resist traditional male bonding by making the challenge to masculine solidarity, in the group and in society, the central purpose of the group. Hornacek outlines a structure which he believes consciousness-raising groups for men must follow to insure their commitment to eradicate, rather than perpetuate, male domination. He continues by providing the practical information necessary to organize an anti-sexist men's consciousness-raising group, and concludes with a list of ten essential topics for group discussion.

In "Dangers with Men's Consciousness-Raising Groups," Leonard Schein does not directly address the contradiction between the organization of men against sexism and the tradition of male supremacy. However, he begins his essay with the statement that "Men's consciousness-raising is a positive step in the struggle against sexism." Schein outlines several fundamental principles for the foundation of men's consciousness-raising groups, the first of which is the acceptance of patriarchy as the primary contradiction in society. He goes on to describe basic reasons for men's consciousness-raising and potential dangers.

In addition to consciousness-raising, a very limited number of men have attempted to fight sexism by developing a practice which demonstrates genuine support for the women's liberation movement. In this development, whether men's actions are anti-sexist or not is open to the scrutiny and judgment of feminists. Two of the most common types of support have been provision of childcare for feminist functions and participation in efforts to reduce rape. But the fact that men have a choice in opposing sexism and can elect the issue around which to organize must be recognized as another function of male privilege—for women, childcare and rape are matters of daily survival.

"Men Doing Childcare for Feminists," the next article in this section, is an example of one kind of male anti-sexist activity. Denys Howard describes his experiences and reasons for becoming coordinator of Men Doing Childcare for Feminist Functions, a small group associated with the Portland Men's Resource Center. He believes that his practice facilitates the organization of feminists, breaks down stereotypes about the interest of gay men in children, provides a non-sexist model for children, and immensely enriches his own experience.

Another support for the women's movement is the "Statement on Rape," written by the Men and Politics Group of the East Bay Men's Center and presented to a press conference in Berkeley, California, in

May of 1975. They announce that "rape is the logical extension of power relationships" between men and women under patriarchy. Acknowledging the preliminary quality of their statement and the provisional basis of their group, they provide the rationale for their organization, which is their understanding that male supremacy is the fundamental condition responsible for the existence of rape. While this group did not continue, other men in the East Bay Men's Center have joined with members of a women's anti-rape organization to do political work. In an excerpt from a letter written to the editor, Stu Lord describes the joint group and its activity.

> We are four men from the East Bay Men's Center and four BAWAR women [Bay Area Women Against Rape] who are currently working on a joint outreach project around the issues of rape and sexism. We go to Bay Area high schools to speak and lead discussions of rape and sexism, e.g., rape myths, origins (personal and societal), and strategies for prevention and elimination of rape. Basically, we believe that rape is not primarily a *sexual* crime but rather an act of *violence and degradation* perpetrated primarily (though not exclusively) by men on women. And we believe rape to be an extreme, although natural, extension of sexism.

Stop Playboying

Brother

The Playboy demonstration on Wednesday, May 26, 1971, was the first action in the Bay Area to be taken by men who have been meeting for a while in small consciousness-raising groups and have begun to understand what institutions in our lives have been oppressing us. When a few of us showed up at the Playboy Club in San Francisco, water was thrown at us from the club hoping to discourage us; instead, thirty-five to forty men and several sisters showed up. I had a rush of good feelings when I saw the support from my brothers. I really felt something I had not felt in a while: a feeling of togetherness and closeness with other men. We were united against a common oppressor, one which has fucked over all our lives and now we were expressing our disgust—but there were more positive feelings than negative ideas which characterizes so many other radical demonstrations. Some men had showed up with fifteen loaves of bread they had baked to give away free as an alternative to the 'playboys' who would go into the club for lunch. Another group had planned some guerilla theater action which pointed to the illusion that *Playboy* creates to sell happiness. The playboy is lured by the capitalist to buy expensive luxury items which he cannot really afford so he winds up having to buy things on credit; finally he is lured to the playmate covergirl who is just another objectified fantasy for the playboy; he is finally made aware by the chorus of his luxury items that it is all an illusion, just paper pleasures with no real substance or worth to him as a human being. Upon his recognition of the shuck he was sold, he discards his stereotyped role as a playboy and becomes a brother.

I remember some of the discussions we had in the Men's Rap Center about how we as males had all in some way desired the role of playboy. It was a male image that in college I had strongly identified with in my close circle of male friends—to have a nice flashy car to ride around in to pick up women and take them to my cool apartment, turn on some groovy music on my expensive stereo equipment, etc. We were convinced that so much show of wealth, success, etc., would easily seduce any sophomore, junior, or even senior coed. However, we were all frustrated. None of us could really afford the car, the apartment, etc., and none of the women around could meet up to our fantasies. We were all aware of the realities but in a subtle way we were still hooked—every month *Playboy* would be there on our kitchen tables.

We've all masturbated to those fold-out fantasies of the homespun big-busted, good-looking, all-American girl. We know now what the women think—but we never would really examine the male image part because it was too close to home. But there was no doubt that all of us desired sophistication, good looks, and wealth.

So there we were on Wednesday to try and communicate to this racist, sexist society how we as men were oppressed by *Playboy*'s mind control.

The contrast between the men on the picket line and the men who went into Playboy stunned us both. There we were with our long hair, beards, glasses, acne, dirty clothes and smiles; and there they were, straight-faced, clean-shaven, neatly-groomed, expensive suits, not one sign of emotion did they express, always cool even when we hooted, "Hey playboy; what a he-man," and whistling at them; they would just give a small twitch of their mouth into a half smile or just stare disapprovingly. Sexual stereotyped men are so repressed, so out of

115

touch with their emotions and feelings. We wanted to share something with those men as we were sharing with each other—some bread, some good vibes—but their defenses were up.

It was a familiar reaction that we have experienced as men; coldness due to fear or insecurity about our own identities and self-image; we become so conditioned to be other than human we lose contact with our humanity, our sensitivity and feeling. We wanted to explain to them that they don't have to compete with each other over empty objects—that they don't have to compromise their humanity any more on jobs that are meaningless, in relationships that are dehumanizing. But it was obvious that most of these men had been conditioned for 20, 30, 40 years and were set, so our lifestyles and feelings clashed. We felt strengthened though, and unity came out of our own fears and insecurities just by willing to support each other in attacking the *Playboy* image. It was a high feeling, one not often felt with men.

'One, two, three, four—don't want Playboy any more. Two, four, six, eight—smash the image, smash the state.'

From *Brother: A Forum for Men Against Sexism,* Summer, 1971. Reprinted by permission. This article by itself should not be considered representative of the politics of the staff of *Brother.* Each issue was meant to be seen as a whole.

The Effeminist Manifesto
Steven Dansky, John Knoebel, and Kenneth Pitchford

We, the undersigned Effeminists of Double-F *hereby invite all like-minded men to join with us in making our Declaration of Independence from Gay Liberation and all other Male Ideologies by unalterably asserting our stand of revolutionary commitment to the following Thirteen Principles that form the quintessential substance of our politics:*

On the oppression of women.

1. SEXISM. All women are oppressed by all men, including ourselves. This systematic oppression is called sexism.

2. MALE SUPREMACY. Sexism itself is the product of male supremacy, which produces all the other forms of oppression that patriarchal societies exhibit: racism, classism, ageism, economic exploitation, ecological imbalance.

3. GYNARCHISM. Only that revolution that strikes at the root of all oppression can end any and all of its forms. That is why we are

116

gynarchists; that is, we are among those who believe that women will seize power from the patriarchy and, thereby, totally change life on this planet as we know it.

4. WOMEN'S LEADERSHIP. Exactly how women will go about seizing power is no business of ours, being men. But as effeminate men oppressed by masculinist standards, we ourselves have a stake in the destruction of the patriarchy, and thus we *must* struggle with the dilemma of being partisans—as effeminists—of a revolution opposed to us—as men. To conceal our partisanship and remain inactive for fear of offending would be despicable; to act independently of women's leadership or to tamper with questions which women will decide would be no less despicable. Therefore, we have a duty to take sides, to struggle to change ourselves—but also, necessarily, to act.

On the oppression of effeminate men.

5. MASCULINISM. Faggots and all effeminate men are oppressed by the patriarchy's systematic enforcement of masculinist standards, whether these standards are expressed as physical, mental, emotional, or sexual stereotypes of what is desirable in a man.

6. EFFEMINISM. Our purpose is to urge all such men as ourselves (whether celibate, homosexual, or heterosexual) to become traitors to the class of men by uniting in a movement of Revolutionary Effeminism so that collectively we can struggle to change ourselves from non-masculinists into anti-masculinists and begin attacking those aspects of the patriarchal system that most directly oppress us.

7. PREVIOUS MALE IDEOLOGIES. Three previous attempts by men to create a politics for fighting oppression have failed because of their incomplete analysis: The Male Left, Male Liberation, and Gay Liberation. These and other formulations, such as sexual libertarianism and the counter-culture, are all tactics for preserving power in men's hands by pretending to struggle for change. We specifically reject a carry-over from one or more of these earlier ideologies—the damaging combination of ultra-egalitarianism, anti-leadership, anti-technology, and downward mobility. All are based on a politics of guilt and a hypocritical attitude toward power which prevents us from developing skills urgently needed in our struggle and which confuses the competence needed for revolutionary work with the careerism of those who seek personal accommodation within the patriarchal system.

8. COLLABORATORS AND CAMP-FOLLOWERS. Even we effeminate men are given an option by the patriarchy: to become collaborators in the task of keeping women in their place. Faggots, especially, are

117

offered a subculture by the patriarchy which is designed to keep us oppressed and also increase the oppression of women. This subculture includes a combination of anti-woman mimicry and self-mockery known as camp which, with its trivializing effect, would deny us any chance of awakening to our own suffering, the expression of which is called madness by the patriarchy, but which can be recognized as revolutionary sanity by the oppressed.

9. SADO-MASCULINITY: ROLE PLAYING AND OBJECTIFICATION. The Male Principle, as exhibited in the last ten thousand years, is chiefly characterized by an appetite for objectification, role-playing, and sadism. First, the masculine preference for thinking as opposed to feeling encourages men to regard other people as things, and to use them accordingly. Second, inflicting pain upon people and animals has come to be deemed a mark of manhood, thereby explaining the well-known proclivity for rape and torture. Finally, a lust for power-dominance is rewarded in the playing out of that ultimate role, The Man, whose rapacity is amply displayed in witch-hunts, lynchings, pogroms, and episodes of genocide, not to mention the day-to-day (often life-long) subservience that he exacts from those closest to him.

Masculine bias, thus, appears in our behavior whenever we act out the following categories, regardless of which element in each pair we are most drawn to at any given moment: subject/object; dominant/submissive; master/slave; butch/femme. All of these false dichotomies are inherently sexist, since they express the desire to be masculine or to possess the masculine in someone else. The racism of white faggots often reveals the same set of polarities, regardless of whether they choose to act out the dominant or submissive role with black or third-world men. In all cases, only by rejecting the very terms of these categories can we become effeminists. This means explicitly rejecting, as well, the objectification of people based on such things as age; body; build; color; size or shape of facial features, eyes, hair, genitals; ethnicity or race; physical or mental handicap; life-style; sex. We must therefore strive to detect and expose every embodiment of The Male Principle, no matter how and where it may be enshrined and glorified, including those arenas of faggot objectification (baths, bars, docks, parks) where power-dominance, as it operates in the selecting of roles and objects, is known as "cruising."

10. MASOCH-EONISM. Among those aspects of our oppression which The Man has foisted upon us, two male heterosexual perversions, in particular, are popularly thought of as being "acceptable" behavior for effeminate men: eonism (that is, male transvestitism) and masochism.

Just as sadism and masculinism, by merging into one identity, tend to become indistinguishable one from the other, so masochism and eonism are born of an identical impulse toward mock subservience in men, as a way to project intense anti-women feelings and also to pressure women into conformity by providing those degrading stereotypes most appealing to the sado-masculinist. Certainly, sado-masoch-eonism in all its forms is the very antithesis of effeminism. Both the masochist and the eonist are particularly an insult to women since they overtly parody female oppression and pose as object lessons in servility.

11. LIFE-STYLE: APPEARANCE AND REALITY. We must learn to discover and value The Female Principle in men as something inherent, beyond roles or superficial decoration, and thus beyond definition by any one particular life-style (such as the recent androgyny fad, trans-sexuality, or other purely personal solutions). Therefore, we do not automatically support or condemn faggots or effeminists who live alone, who live together as couples, who live together in all-male collectives, who live with women, or who live in any other way—since all of these modes of living in and of themselves can be sexist but can also conceivably come to function as bases for anti-sexist struggle. Even as we learn to affirm in ourselves the cooperative impulse and to admire in each other what is tender and gentle, what is aesthetic, considerate, affectionate, lyrical, sweet, we should not confuse our own time with that post-revolutionary world when our effeminist natures will be free to express themselves openly without fear of punishment or danger of oppressing others. Above all, we must remember that it is not merely a change of appearance that we seek, but a change in reality.

12. TACTICS. We mean to support, defend and promote effeminism in all men everywhere by any means except those inherently male supremacist or those in conflict with the goals of feminists intent on seizing power. We hope to find militant ways for fighting our oppression that will meet these requirements. Obviously, we do not seek the legalization of faggotry, quotas, or civil-rights for faggots or other measures designed to reform the patriarchy. Practically, we see three phases of activity: naming our enemies to start with, next confronting them, and ultimately divesting them of their power. This means both the Cock Rocker and the Drag Rocker among counter-cultist heroes, both the Radical Therapist and the Faggot-Torturer among effemiphobic psychiatrists, both the creators of beefcake pornography and of eonistic travesties. It also means all branches of the patriarchy that institutionalize the persecution of faggots (school, church, army, prison, asylum, old-age home).

119

But whatever the immediate target, we would be wise to prepare for all forms of sabotage and rebellion which women might ask of us, since it is not as pacifists that we can expect to serve in the emerging worldwide anti-gender revolution. We must also constantly ask ourselves and each other for a greater measure of risk and commitment than we may have dreamt was possible yesterday. Above all, our joining in this struggle must discover in us a new respect for women, a new ability to love each other as effeminists, both of which have previously been denied us by our own misogyny and effemiphobia, so that our bonding until now has been the traditional male solidarity that is always inimical to the best interests of women and pernicious to our own sense of effeminist selfhood, as well.

13. DRUDGERY AND CHILDCARE: RE-DEFINING GENDER. Our first and most important step, however, must be to take upon ourselves at least our own share of the day-to-day life-sustaining drudgery that is usually consigned to women alone. To be useful in this way can release women to do other work of their own choosing and can also begin to re-define gender for the next generation. Of paramount concern here, we ask to be included in the time-consuming work of raising and caring for children, as a duty, a right, and a privilege.

Attested to this twenty-seventh day of Teves and first day of January, in the year of our faltering Judeo-Christian patriarchy, 5733 and 1973, by Steven Dansky, John Knoebel, and Kenneth Pitchford.

Copyright (c) 1973 by Templar Press. From *Double F: A Magazine of Effeminism.* Reprinted by permission.

An Open Letter to the Revolutionary Effeminists

Karla Jay and June Rook

The following Open Letter is in response to articles which were published in Double F No. 2 *(Winter-Spring 1973), a New York male effeminist journal. These articles consisted in large part of personal attacks on various gay people deeply involved in the Gay Movement. The authors of this Open Letter, Lesbian Feminists Karla Jay and June Rook, live in*

New York City. Karla Jay is co-editor of the recent anthology, Out of the Closets: Voices of Gay Liberation.

The authors state that this Open Letter is not intended as a condemnation of Effeminism but is a "feminist viewpoint on the ravings of a certain wing of the Effeminist movement."

This open letter was rejected by the editors of Double F *for publication in their magazine.*

Dear Editors of *Double F:*

Although we feel that the magazine *Double F* contains some ideas which constitute an important step towards the liberation of humankind, and women in particular, some of the statements, particularly in Steve Dansky's article "The Gay Enemy," are riddled with contradictions and dangerous male chauvinism.

To begin with, Steve attacks various gay men including Allen Young, Perry Brass, Craig Rodwell *et al.*, and has the gall to put them in the same category as an arch-sexist pig, such as Norman Mailer. Most of the gay men mentioned, despite their failings, have at least attempted to work towards revolution and liberation; whereas Mailer has worked only towards the construction of a larger bank account and larger male ego (although not necessarily in that order).

The attack upon the gay men is both ironic and chauvinistic. Both Ken Pitchford and Steve Dansky attack Allen Young for his male chauvinism and for seeking power. Yet, we have both known Allen well and we recognize his ongoing struggle with male privilege and the power male privilege calls for. It is our experience that Allen is a sensitive and highly conscious individual in his dealings with us and with our sisters. We only hope that some of the individuals responsible for the self-righteous attacks on him in these articles can make as much progress in their struggles with male privilege. And while these individuals attack Allen so furiously, they have no scruple about quoting a statement by him to promote *Double F*—both on the back of the magazine and in a slick flyer sent to liberation people.

Another "Gay Enemy" is supposedly Perry Brass, partly for his work on *Come Out!* But as Steve Dansky himself admits, he too contributed to *Come Out!* and if Steve is entitled to beat his breast to the tune of *mea culpa* and repent, then why does he assume that other men are not as likely to change?

The final irony is that while Steve attacks Norman Mailer, Ken Pitchford [an editor of *Double F*] is having his forthcoming book of poems published by Little, Brown & Company—the same company which has a million dollar contract with Mailer! The contradiction here needs no explanation!

We could go on and on about the sophomoric way both Ken Pitchford and Steve Dansky have twisted words and hypocritically knifed everyone around them, while admitting a certain amount of guilt on their own part to give an appearance of raw honesty, but we would like to get on with our second point. This is that you define "Gay Enemies" in terms of their male chauvinism. We have already pointed out how you did this to Allen Young. Another example is Perry Brass, whom Steve defines as a "Gay Enemy" because of what he did to the women on *Come Out!*, and Craig Rodwell is an enemy because his Oscar Wilde Bookstore has a "token-lesbian-shelf." (Of course, you forgot to mention the lesbian manager and the lesbian part-time cashier, but are two-thirds of a staff a token?) Naturally you refused to let Oscar Wilde sell *Double F* and we had to buy our copy at a neighborhood bookstore which sells far more sexist books than Oscar Wilde's will ever see!

The real point, however, is that you are naming gay people as "enemies" because they are primarily women's enemies, and who are you as *men* to judge who our enemies are? You are doing in a more subtle way what male psychiatrists, male sociologists, and the entire male power structure has been doing for centuries: that is, you are telling women (or at least subtly suggesting) who their friends are, who their enemies are. You have not so subtly decided what is right for women. By pointing out the chauvinist enemy (even though your readership is purportedly male), you are being patronizing to women. Aren't we capable of finding our enemies?

Did women appoint you to be the harbingers of feminism to gay men or have you decided on your own what women will think of your efforts? As you yourself point out, "all men are the enemies," (and one of us, Karla, was one of the Redstockings who formulated that theory), so in the end you are as much of an enemy as the rest. All the male privileges you so eagerly give up are immediately handed back to you by the male power structure. You admit that you are male chauvinists, but you spend the greater part of your magazine attacking others instead of examining the ways in which you yourselves are male chauvinists. For example, your magazine reeks of violence, and what could be more macho than a bloody solution to a problem? Hasn't that always been the way of The Man?

A final point. You attack Gay Liberation as if it were a cohesive group, when in fact, Gay Liberation is no more of an ideological unity than Women's Liberation. And if you condemn the entire Gay Liberation Movement, then remember that some of those people in Gay Liberation are *women,* our sisters. It's more than a bit chauvinistic to assume that a movement is entirely male.

We think your magazine would be far more valuable if you used your pages to develop and examine your own experiences and ideologies instead of tearing down Gay Liberationists, even though we agree that some of the men you mention are more than objectionable. Instead of dumping on gay men who are, after all, as oppressed as you are, you should attack only our real enemy—white male heterosexuals. We feel that criticism of gay men is warranted only if it has some constructive point and that your frothing denunciations, which are in many cases unsubstantiated and ridiculous, tend to make one want to reject all your ideas as paranoid and irresponsible.

In Struggle
Karla Jay and June Rook

From *Gay Sunshine,* June/July, 1973. Reprinted by permission.

Anti-Sexist Consciousness-Raising Groups for Men

Paul Carlo Hornacek

Rationale

Anti-sexist men's consciousness-raising groups are beginning to appear in various parts of our country as a complement to and in support of the women's liberation (feminist) movement. These groups are not to be confused or mistakenly identified with the recent and more popular men's liberation movement. Proponents of men's liberation espouse the view that sexism is a societally pervasive institution which oppresses both women and men by prescribing stereotypical sex-role behaviors which are dehumanizing and which cause great emotional suffering. They encourage C-R sessions as a vehicle by which men can get in touch with their emotions, free themselves of sex-role assignments, learn to be more open with and caring for other men, and struggle together to fight the external (re) imposition upon themselves of the socially oppressive male role. In this manner they learn a way of relating in more rewarding ways to women and to other men.

In direct contrast to this, men who are participating in what some have called anti-sexist (or pro-feminist) men's C-R groups maintain that sexism is an institutionalized way of life in which women, gay people, and children are systematically oppressed and disempowered by heterosexual men. They agree that sexism and the external imposition of stereotypical sex-role behavior which accompanies it is dehumanizing to all people, but feel that while heterosexual men are alienated and limited by sexism, they are not oppressed by it. By definition, those who gain substantial material, psychic and other benefits by the subordination of another group are recognized as the oppressors, not as the oppressed. This distinction is not merely a semantic disagreement; it is a major difference in the purpose of the group. Anti-sexist men's C-R is designed to support women's liberation by changing men's male supremacist consciousness. Men's liberation C-R, on the other hand, supports male domination by reinforcing men's sexist consciousness. Surrendering male privilege requires a recognition of the compensatory gains for economic class differences that males are afforded by sexism. Men in our culture (and especially heterosexual men) are by birthright the benefactors of the oppressive societal institution of sexism—which was created and is maintained in their interest.

Members of anti-sexist men's C-R groups see the need for men to meet together to discuss the ways in which sexism pervades their daily lives, and how their conscious and unconscious sexist behaviors limit and alienate themselves and oppress women, gay people, and children. They recognize the inherent contradiction in men getting together and forming supportive groups in our society which is already dominated by powerful privileged male groups. The justification for men getting together in this way comes from the purpose and methods of the group which are designed to insure a commitment to the struggle against male privilege. Unity in the struggle against male supremacist consciousness is different from traditional male bonding because it is aware of the contradiction and specifically and intentionally designed to oppose male solidarity. Anti-sexist men's C-R is one of the first positive steps men can take on their own, following the example and the leadership articulated by feminists, toward a unified female and male struggle to smash sexism. In being freed from their own sex roles men can free others who are oppressed by them. Only by recognizing and struggling with this contradiction can the urge to perpetuate rather than to eradicate sexism and male privilege be overcome.

To help insure that the C-R experience does not become just one more instrument by which patriarchy further strengthens itself, anti-sexist men's C-R groups need to build the following three conditions into their structure: (1) a period of criticism and self-criticism wherein at the end of each session, group members reflect upon their own and others' sexism as was demonstrated during that meeting (this is the period when any sexist male bonding within the group is challenged), (2) a commitment to bring forth social change by personal and political activity against sexism, and (3) an acceptance of the principles and tenets of the feminist movement. (This means a recognition that sexism is an inequality between women and men in which all men benefit from the subordination of women.)

Practice

Anti-sexist consciousness-raising is an activity which permits participants to see clearly the ways in which their individual situation reflects the total social process around them. It allows people to examine and come to understand how the institutions of patriarchy foster and perpetuate the devastatingly dehumanizing effects of sexism. My experience in several anti-sexist men's C-R groups over the past five years has led me to subscribe to a structured rather than an un-structured format for C-R group conduct for men. The structure which I have found most useful is borrowed in large part from the feminist movement and its female creators to whom I am indebted for many of the ideas this paper expresses. Outlined below is a method of forming and participating in C-R groups which allows men to emerge feeling good about the fact that they are struggling with other men to give up the male-oppressor role. This format is designed to prevent competition, male dominance, the abuse of authority, and the misuse of aggression. It provides an atmosphere of trust and support wherein men can learn non-traditional ways of relating to women, to children, and to other men. Where women's groups have stressed the importance of flexibility and lack of formal structure in order to counterbalance the effects that male supremacist power structures have had upon their lives, it is important that men's C-R groups adhere to a pre-determined format which assures that anti-sexist principles and self-critical vigilance are ever-present in the process. A C-R group is qualitatively different from a rap, encounter, or therapy group because of the structure which it follows.

Men have reported a variety of different reasons for deciding to seek a C-R group, all of which have an underlying link to the feminist movement. Most are experiencing emotional pain as a result of their male sex-role and are dissatisfied with it. Some have had confrontations with radical feminists in public or private encounters and have been repeatedly criticized for being sexist. Some come as a result of their commitment to social change and their recognition that sexism and patriarchy are elements of an intolerable social system that needs to be altered. Male classmates, co-workers, relatives, friends and neighbors are all potentially good candidates for an anti-sexist men's C-R group. All men in our society have been socialized into the masculine role, all have been taught to objectify and dominate women, all have been continually exposed to a public media which teaches violence, misogyny, and the misuse of power and aggression toward women, children and other men.

The ideal size of a C-R group seems to be about six to eight people. Larger groups do not afford the degree of intimacy necessary to develop honest self-disclosure and progress toward change. Smaller groups tend to become too informal and allow little room for absence or attrition, and groups which are too small contradict the basic assumption of consciousness-raising, which is to learn by hearing the experiences of several other people.

Meetings should be conducted on a regular basis, preferably once a week, in order to facilitate continuity of thought and content. Each meeting should last for a specific pre-designated length of time, usually two and a half to three hours. This time is to be divided according to the size of the group. Most people decide to have ten or fifteen minutes for each speaker to address the topic of the session, leaving fifteen or twenty minutes for discussion and analysis, and fifteen minutes at the end of the meeting for a criticism and self-criticism period. Most groups also like to have five minutes at the beginning of the meeting for each member to say how he feels that evening and whether there are any pressing issues in his life which might interfere with his participation in the C-R session. It is important to begin and end a C-R group on time and to require full attendance at every meeting. A true commitment to fighting sexism is reflected in the fact that the C-R group meeting holds a priority in members' schedules.

Groups use members' homes as meeting places, and rotate on a weekly basis so that everyone has an opportunity to learn a little about the environment in which the other members live. Rotation of the meeting also creates an opportunity for group members to share the responsibility of hosting the sessions (perhaps providing a beverage and a snack).

While many women's C-R groups have formed and met successfully without a leader or facilitator, on the premise that all women are oppressed by sexism and therefore they themselves are best able to find their way to a liberating theory, men cannot follow the same practice. Since men are socialized into the sexual-oppressor role, it is important that when they meet to struggle against that role they have an experienced, feminist-conscious person to guide them for the first few sessions. This facilitator can be a man who has experienced anti-sexist C-R groups and who appreciates the three organizational principles of men's C-R outlined above, or a feminist who is willing to meet with a men's group for a few times to help them to get started.

During the first meeting participants introduce themselves and usually give a brief autobiographical sketch to help others to begin to know them on a personal level. After this, the real work of discovering feelings and inexpressiveness begins. To enable the sharing of emotional reactions and personal information, it is essential that group members agree to a pact of strict confidentiality. Only by this agreement can an atmosphere of trust develop. Trust is necessary for the honest sharing of personal information and for the persistent struggle against the enemy within ourselves. Members may choose to share information with outside people about the group process and structure or general topic, but not about the group content.

For successive meetings, the format is a very simple one. Topics are selected according to group preference a week in advance. During the session itself the topic is addressed by each person until it is exhausted. All topics must relate to the socialization of males and females within our society which leads to the perpetuation of sexist behaviors. The person who chooses to speak first discusses the subject by speaking in the first person, i.e., only making "I" statements based on his own experience. He expresses how the topic in question has affected his life, attempting to be honest about revealing personal information and trying to stay as close to the topic as possible. Intellectualization, a defensive maneuver by which men avoid feelings and emotional statements, is to be avoided.

The role of the members who are not speaking is very important. They are to give their full attention to the speaker and attempt to understand what is being expressed. Listeners should silently note experiences and feelings with which they too are familiar. No one is to interrupt the speaker. Questions of clarification can be raised when the

127

speaker indicates that he is finished. Speakers are not to be confronted or challenged. If a member hears sexist language or a report of sexist behavior, he is to make a mental or written note and bring it up during the criticism/self-criticism period described below.

When one person has finished speaking, another begins until all the members have addressed the topic. When the round has been accomplished, a discussion and analysis period begins. Members try to find a pattern to their experiences and draw conclusions from what has been discussed. During this period it is important to try to understand how their abstract, aggressive, unemotional masculine role has affected their lives and the lives of women and children to whom they relate. The consciousness-raising process is one in which shared personal experiences come to be seen as a consistent product of societally imposed sex-role stereotyping, rather than natural or idiosyncratic personal behaviors. Finding a pattern to shared personal experiences is easier and more meaningful when men try to relate what they reported to what they have read in feminist writings. Consequently it is important for an anti-sexist men's C-R group to simultaneously involve itself in the study of feminist theory.

The final portion of the meeting should be devoted to criticism and self-criticism, a process in which members attempt to point out the sexism in their own and others' statements. This is not a time for hostile remarks or advice giving. Criticisms are to be accepted and digested, and not responded to defensively.

After several months of meeting in this fashion, most groups begin to search for a larger purpose. Their activity may take the form of political action against sexism, formal study of feminist literature, the seeding of new C-R groups, reaching out to women's or gay groups in an attempt to meet and work together, or other specific forms of anti-sexist practice. Usually one or more of these activities begin to occur in addition to an on-going C-R group experience. Time restrictions are such that for some people, the anti-sexist political activity replaces the C-R group meeting altogether. The friendships and close ties that develop as a result of participation in an anti-sexist men's C-R group often are both profound and long-lasting. The personal insights that are gained are invaluable. The politicized views of sex-role stereotyping are enlightening, and the various actions in support of women's liberation which are the result can hasten the revolution which feminists have initiated.

Ten Essential Men's C-R Topics:
>Childhood training for sex-roles
>Marriage, monogamy, jealousy
>Work and housework
>Fathers and sons
>Rape
>Homosexuality, heterosexuality, bisexuality
>The nuclear family as a bastion of sexism
>Maleness and masculinity
>Sensuality and sexuality
>Intimacy with women; intimacy with men

References

Dreifus, Claudia. *Women's Fate: Raps From a Feminist Consciousness-Raising Group.* New York: Bantam Books, Inc., 1973.

Koedt, Anne; Levine, Ellen; Rapone, Anita, editors. *Radical Feminism.* New York: Quadrangle—The New York Times Book Co., 1973.

Pleck, Joseph H., and Sawyer, Jack. *Men and Masculinity.* New Jersey: Prentice-Hall, Inc., 1974.

Rush, Anne Kent. *Getting Clear—Body Work for Women.* New York: Random House, 1973.

Stoltenberg, John, "Toward Gender Justice," *Social Policy* (May/June, 1975): pp. 35-39.

Dangers With Men's Consciousness-Raising Groups

Leonard Schein

The formation of men's consciousness-raising groups must be seen as a positive step in the struggle against sexism. At this time it is extremely important for men to start working with other men in new ways that destroy traditional "male bonding." Men working with other men is a necessary and good direction for three main reasons.

First, men have a long history, when working with women, of cooptation, of treating women in a sexist manner, of channeling a movement's energy into male directions, and of making male issues the priorities. A few examples demonstrate this cooption process. The New Left political movement has always argued in loud and large terms about how we must fight the oppression of people throughout the world. But this same New Left was very late to recognize women's oppression. Then it developed an empty rhetoric about supporting women's liberation, but whenever priorities were set, women's issues always took last place. The New Left is only interested in the welfare of certain oppressed people. Those people are the ones who fit the traditional Marxian analysis: (male) workers, (male) third-world people, and (male) people of color in North America. The struggle of women to gain human status has never been taken seriously by people in the New Left. We have a situation in which energies are devoted to freeing oppressed males.

Not only did the New Left not work for the political benefit of women, its "Macho Marx" male consciousness perpetuated and re-inforced the worst of patriarchal role division. Male chauvinism was the New Left's "little red book;" the movement was completely authoritarian and male dominated. Men did the important work while women were stuck doing the domestic and office shit-work. The male radical "leaders" became like rock stars with their following of "groupies" to sexually nurture them after a hard day fighting imperialism.

The Gay Liberation Front is another example of a political struggle where men have co-opted the Movement away from women. In the beginning, the Gay Liberation Front was a movement of both male and female homosexuals, but after a while it was clear to lesbians that they could no longer work politically with gay males. The gay men channeled their energies and priorities into male directions and took political stances that were degrading to women (supporting pornography, sadism/masochism, and refusing to deal with butch/femme role division). Gay males were sexist toward the women and ran the movement in an authoritarian manner. The male consciousness of the gay males, in the same manner as in the New Left, prevented lesbians from being taken seriously in their own right as full human beings.

The straight world has its examples also. In the 1972 Democratic National Convention, when the crunch came, George McGovern sold women's issues down the river. Another example is that of the American Civil Liberties Union and the President's Commission on Obscenity and Pornography which, under the guise of supporting freedom of speech and press, have been the foremost champions of the legalization of pornography and prostitution. Pornography and prostitution oppress women, establish anti-female models of sexuality, and further male domination and misogyny. Male politicians and political parties have always sold "their" women supporters short because of "political reality."

The second important reason for men to work together is our need to directly confront male violence and misogyny. We can no longer take the easy way out, by relating to women and being nurtured by them and draining them emotionally, but must face directly the violence and hatred toward women which is inside ourselves. We must confront our misogyny as fundamental to our consciousness, in order to fully understand ourselves and to really understand the fears that we force women to live with every day.

The third reason is that we have similar experiences, consciousness, perceptions, and world views to share with each other. We have all been socialized in masculine roles. Together we can best explore the depth of our male consciousness—two heads are better than one. We also need each other to learn new ways of relating to people as full human beings: emotionally and caringly, without competition, aggression and power-tripping, in open, vulnerable, equal and supportive relationships. We know our experience best, and we can no longer pretend to help others with "their" oppression (especially women) because *we* are the ones who need the help; *we* are the ones who are the enemy; *we* are the ones who oppress and objectify women; and *we* are the incomplete, crippled human beings.

I believe there should be three fundamental principles as a foundation for men's consciousness-raising groups. Before any man joins a group, he should agree to these essential propositions. First, the full acceptance of radical feminism in theory and practice. By this I mean that we must agree that patriarchy is the *prime* contradiction from which all other models of oppression come—capitalism, imperialism, slavery, racism, etc. The role division that our society forces upon males and females through socialization must be actively struggled against (theory put into practice). In addition, we must see male consciousness and its concrete expressions as the main opponents of full humanism in the world, and we must realize the privilege we enjoy as a class/caste over women. We must also recognize that although both males and females suffer under patriarchal rule, our suffering is not the same, and in fact is qualitatively less than that of women. The emptiness, self-loss, powerlessness, and violations that women endure are far more insidious than our masculine role suffering. Even as incomplete, unalive human beings, we enjoy privilege and power: the world, God, and culture are all made in our own image.

131

The second principle is the acceptance of emotionality as a valid and necessary part of the new man we are trying to create. We must appreciate the limitations of logical-intellectual-rational discussion, and concentrate our energy on discovering and exploring our emotional potential.

The third principle is that we as men can never speak for women. Anti-sexist men cannot co-opt or take control of the Feminist Movement. We must realize our debt to feminism and that, for most of us, our main motivation for dealing with sexism comes from women who have forced us to, and that feminism has already provided the theory, structure, and models for us. Presently, women in the feminist movement are so far beyond men in terms of full human consciousness that we cannot bring them down to our level but must instead attempt to raise ourselves to theirs.

My experience in men's consciousness-raising groups has taught me to be aware of four dangers. The first danger is that the men's group may be used to collude against women. Since more often than not we in a men's group have common women friends, it is important that we not team up in our groups against these women. Most of us join our first consciousness-raising group because women with whom we are involved will no longer accept our sexism. In order to have fulfilling relationships and become whole, we have to deal seriously with our maleness. In entering these groups, we are coming from a place of feeling very hurt, afraid, and confused, and so we look for allies to support us emotionally. There is a tendency for us to betray women to gain sympathy and reassurance and to rebuild our deflated egos. There is also a tendency to put our own position in the best light (especially in the beginning of the group, before trust is really established) without realizing the consequences of these untruths to our female partners. There is also a tendency to play ego games with women friends: "See, I'm not as bad as John . . . See, Bill agrees with me . . . Ralph tells me that Carole does this sexually with him . . ."

The experience of the "Brother" collective in Berkeley, California, illustrates a further aspect of colluding against women. John, a bisexual, was married to Scottie for eight years and they had two children. Their relationship was monogamous until the men's group, when John "fell in love" with Bill, a gay member of the group. The following is Bill's revealing perception of Scottie's feelings:

After that (John and Bill becoming lovers) Scottie became lovers with another man. I feel that to some extent Scottie felt pressured to agree to what John wanted to do this past year—open up their marriage to other lovers, and specifically male lovers for himself . . . Yet Scottie has felt through this year less loved by John than ever before. She saw that John's love for me and other men was more emotional, more feeling—there seemed to be more loving strokes for these men than for herself. Scottie was hurt and oppressed by this inequity . . . But because she has felt less loved and because she is not bisexual, I have found myself editing my gayness for her so it would be less threatening. John has also done some editing of his gayness though less than I. I feel deceitful both to myself and to Scottie and feel this is an oppressive element for each of us in the relationship. John, Scottie and their two children are planning to leave this area. It has been projected by John and by myself that I would join them after the summer. I have talked to Scottie about this a number of times. She is being put in a very difficult position. If she says she doesn't want me to join them, she risks that John will be unhappy and resentful. If she gives her approval, she continues for herself an uncomfortable experiment from which she'd like some distance. I feel that as a man and as her partner's lover, I am unavoidably oppressive to her in this situation. I continue to be lovers with John because that is what I want and he wants and what Scottie has *agreed to* (emphasis mine).

Joel, another gay member of the group, seemed to recognize the obvious oppression of Scottie in the John-Bill-Scottie triangle. Yet he and the other members of the men's group *did nothing* to censor and stop the sexism of John and Bill. The group gave tacit approval for the continuation of men fucking over women by tolerating their relationship and being uncritical. If "Brother" were really serious about fighting sexism, it would not have been a party to such destructive sexist consciousness and behavior. Women, being typically less powerful and more vulnerable in any relationship with a man, lose (both economically and emotionally) when men bond together in their own interest. John wins everything; he holds his relationship with Bill over Scottie's head (forcing her to take another "sexual" lover). John is even oppressive to gay males (especially Bill) by not taking them seriously in an equal emotional relationship while "he gets his rocks off in a new way." It is clear that John is continuing to force Scottie into compromises and situations she does not freely choose in order for her and the two children to survive. Men's groups should attempt to prevent the recurrence of this unfortunate "Brother" experience.

The second danger we have to watch for in these groups is the misdirection of anger toward the women who have forced us to confront our sexism. Our past experience with anger has been to turn it into violence. Now, as men we are at a loss to find a new, sane method of dealing with our hostility. In opening up to our emotionality as never before, we do not quite know what to do with our anger, especially since women are no longer available to maintain our fragile egos. Groups have to be careful to direct anger towards its real source, the patriarchal society and masculinist socialization which forces every man (including "sensitive, gentle us") to have a male supremacist consciousness. Our anger is inside us. We must take responsibility for it and struggle to change. This anger cannot be smoothed over or directed towards women. It is a fundamental core of our psyche, and we have to face it squarely to become fully human.

The third danger is that we may not continue to struggle with our individual sexism. After the group meets for some period of time, we begin to develop a method of nurturing each other and having closer ties emotionally. As we become more sensitive and are more aware of our vulnerability, there is a tendency to backslide away from fighting our sexism because we do not want to hurt those we care a lot about. It is important to learn nurturing and caring, but these cannot be un-critical and unconditional. Unconditional caring is a trap for ourselves and the men we care about. The absence of criticism is not only dis-honest, it allows us to give up the struggle against sexism when it be-comes particularly painful. We develop a more hidden, sophisticated system of sexism to hide our male privileges behind false illusions.

The fourth danger is that our consciousness-raising may exist exclusively inside the group. The analysis and new consciousness that we learn in our groups must lead to political practice in order to destroy patriarchal authority, sexism, and role division. We must change the way we relate with our friends—both males and females—and we must criticize our friends' sexism. We must be willing to drop our sexist friends if the contradiction is too great. This challenge must take place at our jobs and in our social life. We must also publicly bring to the attention, especially of males, that sexism is prevalent in our society. Facing the men in the streets who are violating women (whistling, derogatory remarks, sexual objectification) is a difficult but necessary task. We cannot let the threat of male violence scare us away from our responsibility to combat sexism in other men. We need collective support because as sensitive individuals it is hard to deal with male violence alone. We must also rechannel our priorities in terms of political action into those issues which are seen by macho male consciousness as "just women's issues:" childcare, contraception, abortion, rape laws, the Equal Rights Amendment, etc. These are not women's issues or side issues, but issues that go to the very core of role division in patriarchal society. If we are really serious about our priorities, we must deal with political issues that challenge patriarchal

134

rule.

For the best understanding of consciousness-raising groups, see Kathie Sarachild's "Program for Feminist Consciousness-Raising" in *Notes from the Second Year: Women's Liberation* and "Consciousness-Raising: A Radical Weapon" in *Feminist Revolution.*

Men Doing Childcare for Feminists

Denys   Howard

Sometime in March last year I read an article in the *Scribe* about a group of men who did childcare for women's groups. I called a man I didn't know, Jamie Bevson, and told him that I would be interested in helping out. He invited me to a childcare potluck, a coming-together of other men who called themselves anti-sexist and wanted to be with little people.

I had been a "baby-sitter" for groups while I was in college. For two winters I had gone up to Menucha and spent time with five or ten little people while their parents took part in a church retreat. I had participated in Christian church school for years, sometimes as a "teacher" for very young children. But that potluck was my first exposure to other big people who tried to treat children as their equals, who sought to affirm each child's integrity and to respect their individual growth and rights.

Because I was not very active in other things, I was able to do childcare fairly frequently last spring. I remember one weekend I spent with a three-year-old named Pan, while his mother was doing a theater workshop. Pan came to my apartment and spent the day there. We went for walks to the store and over to Laurelhurst Park. I didn't have a whole lot of "toys" for him to play with and I had worried about that. But Pan taught me that anything can be an object of interest for a little person, and that in fact I had a whole houseful of toys. I really got to know him—talking to him, listening to his language, changing his diapers, sharing our food.

After I had been doing occasional childcare for about four

months, Jamie went on a month-long trip to California. We had come to be close friends ourselves, and he asked me to be the coordinator of Men Doing Childcare for Feminist Functions while he was out of town. The group had somehow stopped having potlucks, and I thought this might be a nice way to be in touch with these other men, if only for a while. Once a week I would stop by A Woman's Place on my way home from work and check the calendar for upcoming events. Then I would call the women involved in these events and find out if they needed childcare. If they did, I would call men in the group until I found someone to cover each event. This did let me talk to many men who were otherwise only names for me, and that felt good although I still missed getting to know them in a situation which was not goal-oriented. (That is, we talked on the phone only long enough to find out about the childcare; I still wasn't getting acquainted with them.)

My biggest task was arranging childcare for the feminist conference held at the YWCA last July. We had to be prepared for up-wards of twenty children, all day for two days. I was really scared that there would not be enough men, but I eventually had two men there at all times. As it turned out, there were only twelve little people there at our busiest times. I stayed during the whole event, and it was a very important experience for me.

This was the first time that I had been with a large variety of children: boys and girls, quiet and vociferous, six months to eight years old. I felt very pleased with some of the things I learned about myself that day: that I could "enforce rules" without being a strict disciplinarian; that I could hold and cuddle someone who was crying, and have them understand it. I was very excited at meeting a whole lot of women who were not freaked out at having a faggot care for the little people who lived with them. My experiences with both the women and the children made me more eager than ever to spend time with little people, although it *was* an exhausting weekend!

After Jamie came back to Portland, I did little actual childcare for groups. I was becoming more tied up in a lot of commitments. I was able to meet a community of little people who spend time at Moon Brothers, which is where Jamie lives, and this became important to me. These children are growing up in a community which consciously strives to allow them to be open, free, non-sexist people. I still find that the time I spend with them energizes me, fills me with hope on both personal and cultural levels.

In September I quit my job as an industrial first-aid medic and took a job as a big person in a day care center. My experience doing childcare for MDCCFFF, and in particular during the Women's Conference, had made me aware of the deep need I have to be with children, to spend time being myself with them and becoming friends with them. At the center I am able to be open about my faggotry with the staff, the children, and their parents. My times of doing childcare gave me that strength, and gave me a vision of how non-masculine men and non-feminine women can provide models for children that just might enable them to be real people when they grow up.

From *A Forum for Changing Men,* March 1975. Reprinted by permission.

Statement on Rape

Men and Politics Group, East Bay Men's Center

We, as a group of men, are taking a stand against rape. We feel that it's time to speak up and share the responsibility to expose and eliminate the causes of rape in our society.

We are angered by the recent court decisions in New York and Britain. These decisions legitimize the social power of men over women. They reinforce such beliefs as, sexual predatory conquest is natural for men, and, when a woman says no she really means yes. Such beliefs are wrong and are dehumanizing.

We are thinking, we are analyzing, we are raising questions. A fundamental question is, what causes rape in our society? We think that rape is the logical extension of the power relationship between people, and that a solution to rape involves changing those relationships. We cannot isolate rape from sexism, and we believe that to solve rape we must solve sexism.

Sexism is a system where one sex has power and privilege over another. In a society, such as ours, where men dominate women, this system can be called male supremacy. We believe violent rape to be the extreme form of sexism and male supremacy.

Rape can be defined as an act of aggression in which a victim is denied her self-determination. We oppose rape and believe that when a woman (or any other person) says no, she means *no*. We call for men to be more sensitive to the expressed needs and desires of women.

We believe that rape is part of a culture which rewards men for being aggressive and dominant. We think that rape is connected to the frustration produced by living in this society. Rape is anger misdirected towards a societally accepted target: women. We believe that women have the right to defend themselves against this violence and hostility.

We are just beginning to meet as a group to deal with these issues. We don't have all the answers and we're just starting to raise some essential questions. Basically, we feel that men must oppose rape. This involves personal change in struggling against the cultural and societal roles that foster rape. It also involves a struggle against this society that causes rape. We are committed to both these struggles.

"MEN'S LIBERATION" (CRITICISMS)

Section Introduction

Men's Liberation is a reaction of men to the women's movement. Often it is the reaction of non-gay or closeted gay men. Jack Sawyer and Joseph H. Pleck, co-editors of *Men and Masculinity*, a reader associated with the men's liberation movement, typify men in the movement. "Many men, including both of us," they wrote, "have been stimulated to question the masculine role through our relationship with a woman who was questioning her role." This view usually accentuates the negative aspects of the manly role, an approach which affirms the "oppressed" rather than the oppressor qualities of being a man. Men's liberation, therefore, generally denies a hierarchical structure of oppression between men and women and minimizes the role of men in the oppression of women. Thus, men's liberation can be seen as a sexist movement.

These attributes of men's liberation are criticized in a review of *Men and Masculinity* by Carol Ehrlich in the first article in this section. "Although there are a variety of perspectives represented among the 31 authors," she writes, "the basic theme is that men and women are equally incomplete, equally limited by an oppressive set of sex role behaviors." The male supremacist basis for the failure to recognize an inequality between men and women is expressed in the title, "The Reluctant Patriarchs."

In a more recent newsletter statement on "Issues for the Men's Movement: 1975," Pleck attended to Ehrlich's criticisms and addressed the issue of "the *relative* oppression of women and men" (emphasis his). He divided oppression into a personal and political sphere. In the personal, "The process is pretty similar and damaging to both [sexes] ... The suppression of 'feminine' traits in boys may be more severe than the suppression of masculine traits in girls . . ." He concludes, however, that "at the more important second level of social powerlessness, women's oppression is unique." Thus, in the political sphere he finds that "women are more oppressed than men." The conclusion, which relegates women's oppression to a selected sphere, indicates that Pleck has chosen to ignore much of the feminist critique .

Warren Farrell is another men's liberationist. His "Guidelines for Men's Consciousness-Raising" was published in *MS* in 1973, and for a time he was the NOW Task Force Leader on the Masculine Mystique. He has appeared frequently in the media and is perhaps best known as the author of *The Liberated Man,* which is promoted as the "handbook of the men's movement."

The best critique of *The Liberated Man* is Don Andersen's "Warren the Success Object," reprinted in this section. The title captures very well the cooptation of the women's movement and the commercialization of men's liberation by Farrell. Andersen's essay exposes the anti-woman, anti-gay, and anti-working class qualities of *The Liberated Man.* He concludes that Farrell communicates the needs of sensitive men "with his elitist, white, heterosexual, sexist biases intact." Farrell is the person about whom Kenneth Pitchford wrote, "Our movement (revolutionary effeminism) is not yet powerful enough to put a price on this man's head." Pitchford's statement correctly criticizes Farrell's politics with *Double F*'s typically aggressive style.

The anti-feminist qualities of men's liberation are also identified by Kirsten Grimstad and Susan Rennie in their selection, "Men," drawn from *The New Woman's Survival Sourcebook,* which they co-edited. They state, "Men's liberation is exactly *that.* It has little to do with freeing women, but much to do with increasing the well-being and furthering the self-interest of men." While they believe that men's liberation is oppressive to women's liberation, they also believe that

139

men can support the women's movement. This support, they state, must be based on an explicit recognition that sexism is the oppression of women by men. They outline four steps by which authentically anti-sexist men can contribute to building the women's movement. Their statement on "Men" is perhaps the single best review and critique of the entire men's liberation development.

Men's liberationists have organized the "Men's Awareness Network" (MAN), a "Men's Resource Guide and Newsletter" that is put out periodically on a rotational basis by various men's centers. The publications and the movement they represent are criticized by Bob Lamm in the fourth article, "Men's Movement Hype." Lamm was one of the contributors to the *Win* "Special Issue: Men." There he stated that "unless the men's movement is ready to deal seriously with *class* and *racial* oppression as well as sexism, it will never speak to the vast majority of men." In "Men's Movement Hype," however, Lamm no longer believes in the validity of a men's movement. Its composition (white, middle-class, heterosexual, male) and its politics (classist, sexist, and racist) are essentially similar to men's groups already in power. Thus, he finds the male bonding in men's liberation to be inherently reactionary to women's liberation. In a letter to the publisher, Lamm underscored his point that "my attack is on the entire fabric and existence of the men's liberation movement and, indeed, on *all* men's movements."

The final selection is my own review of "Men's Lives," the film expression of men's liberation. In it, I try to point out the four least conscious areas of the men's movement: women, gay men, racial minorities, and the working class. The review has been criticized by a radical feminist for using sexism as a concept which includes the oppression of homosexual men. It has also been criticized by men for its harsh tone and its failure to emphasize sufficiently the positive aspects of the film and men's liberation. As a result, I would like to clarify that I think the examination of the male role which characterizes a great deal of men's liberationist activity and which is the central focus of the film, is a definite improvement over the traditional, unquestioned adoption of masculinity which still distinguishes the vast majority of men today. At the same time, however, I am critical of the failure to acknowledge that the energy with which men now question masculinity is a direct result of the women's liberation movement. Further, I am extremely critical of the persistent sexism inherent in men's liberationists' failure to appreciate the inequalities in the masculine and feminine roles. Men's liberation must take responsibility for the oppressor, as well as the "oppressed" qualities, of being a man.

The Reluctant Patriarchs:
A Review of *Men and Masculinity*

Carol Ehrlich

Men and Masculinity is a collection of articles written since 1971, largely by men involved in what its practitioners call "men's liberation." Although there are a variety of perspectives represented among the 31 authors, the basic theme is that men and women are equally incomplete, equally limited by an oppressive set of learned sex role behaviors. If only men could become gentle, expressive, interpersonally sensitive—if only women could become assertive, independent, strong—then our present society of crippled half-humans would have liberated themselves. And, by extension, they would have brought about the good society.

Most feminists, I think, believe that sexism will not be destroyed by the efforts of women alone. Although the majority of men undoubtedly will continue to resist any lessening of their power, there is a small (but hopefully increasing) number of men who are reluctant patriarchs—men who are searching for ways to reject the privileges automatically conferred upon them because they were born male. These are men who genuinely care about ending sexual oppression so that women and men can one day live in a truly egalitarian manner. They must, of course, be sifted from the hip characters who drool over the presumed opportunity to lay "liberated women"; the opportunists who want to cash in on the literary action; the movement males who see political women as useful "tools" for whatever brand of male-dominated actions they are pushing at the moment; those men—cynical? frightened? perhaps an unstable mixture of both?—who learn to recite the ritual disclaimers so that the heat will be off them; and the academic empire-builders who see a good new rip-off in "men's studies." (The Pleck-Sawyer bibliography indicates that MIT has "an extensive archival 'men's studies' collection." In its own way, this seems like the height of insensitive academic sexism: Women's Studies developed because all of academia already *was* "men's studies.")

My impression is that the editors of *Men and Masculinity* and many (if not all) of the men anthologized in this short (184-page) volume do genuinely care. For that reason they should be encouraged; and for that same reason I feel a certain ambivalence about criticizing *Men and Masculinity*. Negative comments may be interpreted as an act of purism by an embittered feminist. After all, a good book—in fact, any number of good books—on the subject of sexism, written by and for concerned men, is badly needed. The Pleck-Sawyer anthology is a well-intentioned start in that direction, but it is unbalanced and without scope.

Not only do most of the male writers assume something that cannot be assumed (i.e., that men and women are somehow equally oppressed—but more on that later), but the focus is almost exclusively on the personal aspects of the masculine role. Perhaps this is because both of the editors are psychologists; or perhaps it simply reflects what Barbara Katz, one of the three female writers included in the book, said about male liberationists—that they are "more introspective than political." Whatever the reason, few of those represented here look beyond the circumference of an individual man's individual navel.

Another cause of the overemphasis on the personal may be the class and race characteristics of most of these writers. As the editors state frankly, this is a book by and for "males who are white, middle-class, heterosexual, and live in the United States." It is, by and large, about relatively privileged men who have become aware of the personal costs of the "good life" open to them in a capitalist society. It is about men who know that the good life requires conformity to the masculine role, and who—to extend the capitalist motif—aren't buying it. These are men who have learned that a man who is successfully socialized into the twin role demands of "getting ahead" and "staying cool" loses touch with other valuable aspects of himself, such as gentleness and caring for others.

Inevitably, the reader becomes witness to the inner journeys of men who describe the relationships of *individual* men with other men, with women, with children. We learn of the traumas suffered by males who are good at sports/not good at sports; males who have erections when they don't want them, or—far worse in our culture—can't have them when they want them. We learn that the latter problem is called "sexual dysfunction." We read about men who cannot decide whether to relate sexually to men or to women. There are males who can't talk to each other, can't cry, can't love. We read approvingly of men who become involved in child care, but the emphasis in three of the four articles is on the *man* rather than the children, on men getting in touch with their buried inner selves. We read of men in relation to work, but with the exception of a provocative article by ex-sociology professor Michael Silverstein, the articles stress the personal problems involved in tying one's masculine self-image to financial or corporate achievement. Of the three articles in the section on "men and work," only Silverstein's questions whether men should want to be part of the capitalist political economy at all. Interestingly, the male author who most successfully describes the "fit" between masculinity and our political economy (I.F. Stone, "Machismo in Washington") is one of only two who does so from outside the perspective of self-absorbed "male liberation." There is a political lesson here: the personal is not self-evidently the political. People must make the connections between their individual problems and the inhumanity of our political and social institutions. As long as we live in a capitalist society, the stress on hierarchy and dominance will operate in some ways to the detriment of most women. And then, once they have made that crucial connection, they must decide what they are going to do to change the political economy as well as to end the crippling effects of sexism in their everyday lives.

Yet, most of these writers seem barely aware of the power of institutional sexism, and relatively little space is given to its discussion. As a result, any politically aware reader has to struggle with contradictory reactions of sympathy for the personal pain expressed by these men, and anger at their apolitical self-indulgence.

There is something else that is disturbingly present in many of the articles and editors' commentaries. It is a patronizing attitude toward women. There is an attempt, doubtless inadvertent, but nonetheless arrogant and ugly, to trivialize the women's movement (and, by extension, all other movements) by insisting that "all liberation movements are equally important; there is no hierarchy of oppression " *(Berkeley Men's Center Manifesto.)* Parallel to that, the very necessary search of aware men for another way of life is raised to the revolutionary status of a "liberation movement." Or, as co-editor Sawyer neatly puts it, "being a master has its burdens." Imagine the reaction if this solemn comment were translated into a situation of racial or economic dominance! Imagine white telling black, boss telling worker, slave-owner telling slave, "Being a master has its burdens."

As many feminists have pointed out—I think correctly—men are a privileged *caste*. An individual man may reject what he sees as undesirable elements of his role, but because he is male, he will still retain certain privileges of his caste, *even if he does not want them.* He will still be part of a group that by birthright has more power and is more valued than is the lower caste, women.

Another way of putting this is in terms of institutional versus personal sexism. A man may refuse to oppress the women he knows; he may share housework and childcare; he may reject every unsavory element of machismo. Yet, if he makes more money than his female co-worker, or is hired in preference to an equally qualified woman, or is promoted because he has a family to support, or qualifies for a job because of an irrelevant height requirement, or is listened to in a discussion because he is a man, or sees that men are featured in the mass media, or can pick up a textbook in his high school or college class and know that all human achievement is ascribed to him, or can routinely walk past strangers without being whistled at or propositioned or fearing rape, or doesn't have to cope with the horrors of trying to stretch welfare payments so he and his children can survive another day, or need never worry about the ill effects of contraceptives on his body—he is still part of a privileged group.

For all these reasons, Sawyer is only partly correct when he writes: "The battle of women to be free need not be a battle against men as oppressors. The choice about whether men are the enemy is up to men themselves." He is right when he says men can choose which side to be on. But that choice must entail something more than modifying inappropriate personal behavior. Sawyer will make no friends among the women he wants to join by trying to lay equal responsibility for their own oppression on them. Nor will women take at face value a man who announces that he "joins his feminist sisters in a common struggle" when that same man relates how he dropped his first girlfriend when he decided she was "simple-minded and boring" (after two years!), and criticizes another for becoming "too dependent and weak" (Jeff Keith, "My Own Men's Liberation"). Our only rational, self-protective response is to find out whether or not he has ever discovered what women's struggle is all about. Until we can be sure, women cannot be blamed if we find it hard to take "men's liberation" entirely seriously.

Those men who are reluctant patriarchs have an obligation to become revolutionaries. Now, then, how does a white, middle-class, heterosexual, American male become a revolutionary? For these men a revolutionary life style has often meant a rhetorical or gun-toting machismo—a radical-hip version of the "hairy chest syndrome" mentioned in Gloria Steinem's description of America's belligerent political and military elite ("The Myth of Masculine Mystique"). As political women know all too well, male-dominated Left organizations have tended to reproduce patterns of class and sexist dominance, and writers represented here rightly reject such a model. But what they present as an appropriate alternative model is not enough.

It is not enough because men must work simultaneously to change their individual relationships with women (and with other men) and to change our political-economic system that thrives on the power of a few privileged men over the masses of Americans, both men and women. Changing our political economy will be immensely difficult, and it will not come about through a few men rejecting the demands of masculinity. So, Sawyer, Pleck, and their male friends "give up power" over others. Then what? Outside their own immediate circles, where it will undoubtedly make a considerable difference, what differences can it make in the lives of everyone else? Will it end American manipulation of the economies of Third World countries? End our support of military dictatorships? Prevent another intervention such as the one against the socialist government of Chile? End the widening income disparities between white men and everyone else? Destroy institutional racism and sexism?

It will not change these and similar things because—to make an obvious point—most persons in privileged positions do not want to give up their power over others, even assuming that they are fully aware of the extent of that power. And if they do not want to give it up, it must be taken from them. Not from a few of them, but from all of them; and not by individuals, but by people acting together.

For this reason, when we look at what has to be done to create a genuinely non-hierarchical society, telling men that their major alternative is to join a consciousness raising group is grotesque. Consciousness-raising is one important means to an end—the end of personal and social change—but it is *not* the end itself. To act as though it is, is a cop-out. The Pleck-Sawyer reader has too many examples of hip academics and gentle drop-outs who are striving for quiet personal change. One wishes them well. But Pleck and Sawyer, at least, should know that this social system can easily accommodate a few renegades, especially if these renegades confine their activism to Getting Their Heads Together, alone or in concert with like-minded men. And today, tomorrow, in the foreseeable future, nothing else has to change very much.

From *Win,* February 1975. Reprinted by permission.

Warren the Success Object

Don Andersen

I've recently become aware of Warren Farrell, a man publicized by such mass media as the *Today Show,* the *Mike Douglas Show, Cosmopolitan,* and *People* magazines. The media say he's "the foremost spokesperson for Men's Liberation," and list his achievements: forming over a hundred consciousness-raising groups, the only man to be elected three times to the Board of Directors of NOW, and the forming of the NOW Task Force on the Masculine Mystique. Farrell also happens to be coming to Lewis and Clark College (Portland, Oregon), April 9 and 10, for a symposium on "human liberation." I recently heard him speak at the University of Portland and have just finished reading his book, *The Liberated Man: Beyond Masculinity.* He leaves me with serious misgivings.

Warren Farrell is a contradiction who, like all media stars, both reaches farther and compromises more than others struggling with the same issues. Unlike most feminists, and many men supportive of the women's movement, he is not responsible to a group or mass movement. He is a lone wolf, isolated by his media coverage. Farrell is bringing a message to the vast numbers of people who watch national television, read *Parade* magazine, and the *New York Times.* Living in this society inevitably involves compromises and contradictions, but the first thing that strikes me about Farrell is how isolation deepens his contradictions.

Between the typical dust jacket quotes proclaiming his "male values" credentials (PhD, professor teaching the sociology of sex roles, etc.), he delivers his personal doubts about those credentials and some clear statements about the women's movement's analysis of sex roles and our male dominated society. But as I read I began to feel that the compromises went beyond the external ones necessary to distribute the message as far as possible—and (not coincidentally) permeated the message itself. Throughout the book his arguments rely on stereotypes and implications which contradict the point he is making. He is also careful to pull back from a serious examination of the issues which really threaten male power: Women's Separatism, Homosexuality, the Nuclear Family, Economic Class, and Capitalism.

The tone of the book is safely within the privileged world of the heterosexual nuclear family-oriented businessman or middle-class student. Although he gives brief lip service to other realities (just to affirm their existence and return home), his major thesis is that Women's Liberation is *not* threatening to men, and indeed that its main effect is to relieve men of many of the pressures they now experience (e.g., freedom from nagging wives). The struggle to reach this freedom takes place completely internally and changes neither men's economic nor, ultimately, emotional security. After touching other men's hands for a while and doing half the housework, men will be free to consider "liberating" careers of their own choice.

When discussing the family, Farrell says he wants to examine sex roles in the setting with which most people presently identify. This seems to be the orientation he is trying to set up in the book: to appeal to, and explain women's liberation to, "the average man." The context of the book is overwhelmingly heterosexual, white, and bourgeois. While this may be where most of his readers are, he reinforces the supposed blameless normality of their position.

He always refers to homosexual men, third-world men, and working class men peripherally, so as to include everyone in his examples, and often to pretend their position is parallel to white, upper class men. In one such instance he demonstrates that his interest lies in obscuring the thrust of the women's movement rather than clarifying it: "The white middle-class American male likes to think that everything is always someone else's problem. He can see that blacks have a problem, that women have a problem, that Chicanos have a problem, but not that he has a problem . . ." But to say that men *have* a problem is obscuring the fact that men *are* the problem. This is more than an omission; it's a complete distortion. This allows Farrell to deny the oppression of women by men.

Farrell basically supports status quo power relationships. This accounts for the peculiar sections in *The Liberated Man* where he argues in favor of child-care on the basis of the capitalist consideration that it's good for business (taking child-care out of the hands of parents and into the hands of corporations). While reading the book, I sometimes got the feeling that businessmen are finally reacting to the threat of the women's movement, and that Farrell is here to take the bite out of it and to demonstrate how women can be compromised. His distortions, which seek to attain equality of the sexes within a male-created system, maintain male power by co-opting the threat of the women's movement. This is why the media is behind him; he does not threaten them. He is here to save their system by watering down its opponents and incorporating a few reforms. It's the same kind of back-flip that FDR pulled off when he incorporated socialist-like reforms, against the opposition of laissez-faire capitalists, to save their system for them.

In order to assure men that they have "nothing to fear from women's liberation," Farrell ignores the lessons of lesbian, faggot, third-world and working class struggles. He ignores the importance of separatism in developing strength and independence from the oppressor and attacks the position, both explicitly and implicitly throughout the book, but he never examines it as it's defined by women who support it. From the questionnaire and personal introduction, through accounts of a joint C-R group in the latter part of the book, he undermines the separatist idea in a number of ways. Although he is always talking about freeing men and women from limitations, he never discloses separation of the sexes as a positive option. All of the beneficial qualities men can attain are presented in the context of living with a woman. The questions distributed to men test their attitudes toward the female they live with. His personal introduction talks about the process of examining sex roles that he and Ursie (his "attaché") shared. The examples throughout the book reinforce heterosexual bias, by never commenting on it.

Farrell denies the reality of women around the country who are uniting with each other to create a new society. At one point he talks about the "sacrifice" that a segregated women's movement involves, the separation from the "intimate association that almost every woman has with a man . . ." This is an inexcusable denial of the culture women are developing with each other. He denies this reality again when he says: "For many women, ignoring the simultaneous resocialization of men means closet liberation. Or it can mean drastic conflict. It can be lonely living one's life on principle and waking up alone every morning. The radical approach that 'all women can change best without men' makes men the enemy of change. In creating this stereotype of women without men, Farrell shows himself to be an enemy of the changes that have already occurred in many women's lives.

I think he creates this image of separatist women in order to pave the way for men to continue ripping off women's energy. A blatant example of this power he claims for himself and other men is found in his *Open Letter to NOW Members* (1975), where he suggests

148

that members (mostly women) turn some of their attention from women's oppression to men's problems and the recruitment of men. He refuses to allow readers to see the positive energy women are directing toward each other without men. To do this he must lie: "few women change without at least a partially cooperative man."

Farrell seems to take a defensive attitude about his desire to maintain privilege and his fear of homosexuality. He gives personal accounts of his struggle with breaking out of sex roles throughout the book, but there is no indication of his attitude about homosexuality other than what can be gleaned from the way he presents it. Largely, he ignores it, thus affirming heterosexuality as a norm. For example, the questionnaire he administered to a random selection of men has questions which assume a heterosexual relationship. None assumes a homosexual relationship. This is true of all the references and examples in the book.

Homosexuality is mentioned peripherally several times, usually without comment. Generally the references ignore any possibility of heterosexual men learning from faggots. No reference is made to homosexuality as a possible path to liberation from masculine role-playing. The three longest passages dealing with homosexuality promote negative stereotypes. This is in a book which supposedly opens options for men to break out of socialized roles and develop such qualities as emotionality, humility, sensitivity, and sensuality. While most of the book challenges men to break out of their narrowly defined roles, it is Farrell himself who contradicts and undermines his challenge, and puts the shackles back on the reader's mind.

Most of my objections to the book are in the response to Farrell's pretense of advocating liberation while carefully keeping the discussion within his self-prescribed limits. The tragedy of Warren Farrell, and the necessity of understanding all this, lies in the fact that he is carrying the message that men should be nurturing, emotional, humble, in touch with children, open to other men, listening to women, non-competitive, non-domineering, and free from their de-humanizing socialization. And that while he is carrying this message to the vast numbers of people touched by the mass media, he does so with his elitist, white, hetero-sexual, sexist biases intact. This ultimately undercuts everything he says and oppresses all less privileged people, most of all, women.

From *A Forum for Changing Men,* April, May and June, 1975. Reprinted by permission.

Men

Kirsten Grimstad and Susan Rennie

While some men unquestionably regard the women's movement with feelings of benign curiosity, the overwhelming majority quite rightly see feminism as a threat to male privilege. The standard male response ranges from masked to overt hostility. Recently, however, we have witnessed the emergence of individuals and small groups of men who, calling themselves anti-sexists or "men's liberationists," appear to have exchanged the more conventional attitudes of fear and loathing for postures of sympathy and support for the women's movement. The beginning of the end? Not quite yet. A superficial reading should reassure even the most ardent masculinist that most of these men are not selling out their sex or going weak in the gonads. With few exceptions, which we detail below, "men's liberation" is exactly *that*. It has little to do with freeing women, but much to do with increasing the well-being and furthering the self-interest of men.

First, there are the out-and-out hucksters. Watch out for the men who peddle soothing messages assuring the males in their audiences that they have nothing to lose but everything to gain from the women's movement. These men have built careers—complete with lucrative lecture fees, book advances, foundation grants, magazine articles, media appearances—out of hawking the delights of moving "beyond masculinity."

Watch out also for the "brothers" whose "struggle" with sexism amounts to a program for increasing their own sensory awareness. Taking to heart what feminists are saying about the damage inflicted on human personality by artificially imposed sex roles, these clever fellows have seen the light, i.e., that they too suffer from the restrictions of role conditioning. "Look, guys, see what feminism can do for *us*!" they cry (and crying is lesson number one of "men's liberation"). "We have been robbed of our full humanity!" proclaims the "Manifesto" of the Berkeley Men's Center—a discovery which has prompted a vigorous program of enriching masculinity to get more out of life: learn to cry, love other men, masturbate without guilt ("getting in touch with your body"), develop nurturing and enjoyment of children, interact cooperatively as a relief from the anxieties of competitiveness. Most women soon find out that a little bit of crying does not root out that deeply embedded patriarch.

Watch out too for the men who prefer intelligent, independent feminists to Barbie Doll companions, but who are not about to confront the real sacrifices required to shed sexism, or seriously examine the issues which threaten male privilege: alternatives to the nuclear family, the separatism of the women's movement, lifestyle choices other than heterosexuality. Women are becoming hip to these types who use their "raised consciousness" as a weapon for sexual conquest.

And watch out most of all for the "liberationists" who try to move in on the women's movement itself. A letter published in *Ms.* makes commentary on this ilk almost unnecessary: "I . . . believe the Movement has reached a degree of autonomy that will allow the introduction of men into a larger role . . . The Women's Movement has become too important to male feminists, on a personal and political level, for them to be bulldozed out of at least ideological participation." Here it is, right out in the open, the quintessential cop-out of so many men who claim to be "feminists," or "liberationists," or "anti-sexists": they refuse to fight sexism where it exists—*not* in the women's movement, but on the front lines, where the *men* are.

What is to stop this man, or any other, from "participating" by putting time and energy into any number of crucial fronts—organizing and staffing child care facilities; fighting the economic exploitation of women; lobbying and pressuring to alleviate the physical abuse of women, such as rape and wife-battering—just to name a few. Note that this man is not volunteering to do the movement's KP. He wants "ideological participation" because the movement is "too important" to exclude men from that area. Is translation necessary? "The movement is too important to leave the definition of priorities, strategy, and tactics exclusively in the hands of women." The motives for this brand of male intrusion could hardly be more transparent.

By this time some readers might be wondering what efforts on the part of men do constitute authentic (that is, non-oppressive and supportive) struggle against sexism. For starters, we've drawn up an elementary check-list to help anti-sexist men examine and improve their feminism quotient.

1. Identify the extent of your male privilege and your participation in the sexist oppression of women through reading, rapping, consciousness-raising. (Most men can't even get through this beginning stage.)

2. Make the personal political—on the home front and in everyday relationships. If you think this means taking out the garbage, you haven't made it through phase one.

3. Carry your anti-sexist consciousness into public arenas, confronting *other* men with their sexism and trying to raise their consciousness.

4. Support the efforts of women, without getting in the way, expecting rewards, diverting our energies, or trying to take control. Any men wanting desperately to "participate" in the movement can get a few ideas from the efforts of those men in Portland and Tucson for example, who provide child care at feminist events and do typing for feminist publications.

But these suggestions only touch on the very basic levels of men's anti-sexism. A more profound examination of the issues can be found in *Changing Men,* the newsletter of the Portland Men's Center, and especially in *Double F, the Magazine of Effeminism.* The ideas expressed in these two publications alone affirm our belief that men are capable of radical breakthroughs in consciousness and in action. And while such breakthroughs can yield very great rewards, they can only be achieved at the cost of immense personal sacrifice and the total divestment of male privilege.

There are ample grounds for women to voice suspicion, if not cynicism, about the "men's movement." Movements are grounded in the problems commonly shared by a given group of people and their collective efforts to overcome these problems. The women's movement aims to free women from their ancient subordination to men. Men's liberationists ostensibly aim to free themselves from *being* oppressors. Women, however, see a very real danger in men grouping together because the focus of their bonding can so easily shift to dealing exclusively with the side-effects of being oppressors rather than with the disease itself. There is the very natural tendency for men to confuse their specific woes with oppression in general, blunting their sense of exactly who is being oppressed.

This is not to deny that men—even that most powerful and privileged group, white males—have real problems engendered by sexism. Take for example the question of "feeling." It must be very rough to be encased in a personality from which most emotional expressiveness has been cauterized. And it is understandable that much stress in the "men's movement" is placed on enlarging the capacity for intimacy, gentleness, sensitivity—especially where it has been most taboo, among and between men. But, however desirable the reduction

152

of machismo may be for the enrichment of the individual male personality, it has nothing to do with women's freedom *if it is divorced from the struggle to dismantle institutionalized patriarchal privilege.* Such male "liberation" can, in fact, co-exist with the most ferocious subjugation of women. We are only too well aware of the patriarchal cultures—Latin and Islamic, for example—that allow men unrestrained expressiveness, and even intimacy among themselves, while women are treated like shit.

As far as feminists are concerned, men are the problem—and that should be the central focus of any movement struggling to overcome the deformities caused by sexism. Look at it this way: no one would deny that institutionalized racism is destructive to the oppressors as well as to the oppressed. But show us the white male who would dare to respond to racism by centering his struggle on "the burdens of being white." We are not asking men to abase themselves in "the politics of guilt." We are simply insisting that the only kind of men's movement which we can take seriously is one which explicitly recognizes that the oppression of women is the lynchpin of sexual politics.

Nearly two hundred years ago there was a man who well understood this truth. Charles Fourier's statement should be the catechism of all serious men, repeated again and again: "Social progress is brought about by virtue of the progress of women towards liberty, and social retrogression occurs as a result of the diminution of the liberty of women.

Copyright (c) 1975 by Susan Rennie and Kirsten Grimstad. From 1975 *The New Woman's Survival Sourcebook,* 1975. Reprinted by permission of the authors.

Men's Movement Hype

Bob Lamm

We live in a world of men's movements. The United States Government is a men's movement. The Soviet Government is a men's movement. Exxon, I.T.T., and General Motors are all men's movements. The American Medical Association and the National Rifle Association are men's movements. Left politics is a series of men's movements.

Now, among all these many men's movements, there is one in particular that I wish to examine. It is the only men's movement which formally calls itself a men's movement. In fact, it calls itself *the* men's movement, or the men's liberation movement.

In thinking about the politics of this men's movement, I was reminded of an old question back from deep in my childhood. When Passover arrived, and the Seder began, we asked: "How is this night different from any other night?" In the same way, I've begun to wonder: "How is this men's movement different from any other men's movement?"

There are two principal ways of answering this question. One is to examine the *composition* of the men's movement. Here the results are striking. Virtually every member of the men's movement benefits from white skin privilege. The majority of these men benefit from class privilege. Most members benefit from heterosexual privilege. And, lest we somehow forget the obvious, *all* members of the men's movement benefit from male privilege.

When you add all this up, it turns out that most men in the men's movement enjoy white skin privilege, class privilege, heterosexual privilege, and male privilege. This makes the men's movement similar in composition to some other men's movements—such as the officers of the Chase Manhattan Bank, the agents of the Central Intelligence Agency, and the faculty of Yale University. Note also that the men's movement—while less exclusively heterosexual than some men's movements—is noticeably more privileged in terms of class and race than men's movements like the Chicago Police Department, the United States Army, the Oakland Athletics baseball team and the United Auto Workers.

So much for the composition of the men's movement. But what of its politics? People can change, goes the humanist credo. And it is a fact that, throughout history, small numbers of people from privileged groups joined the struggles of the oppressed. American whites harbored runaway black slaves; bourgeois intellectuals helped workers and peasants to make the Russian Revolution; and so forth. Thus, it at least seems *possible* that privileged men might choose to fight against a racist, capitalist, patriarchal system.

A small minority of men within the men's movement have made such commitments. There are men—both gay and straight—who have made serious efforts to combat male supremacy. Some work with child care groups or men's anti-rape groups; some fight repressive abortion laws or lobby for the E.R.A.; some participate in study groups focusing on feminist literature. There are also men who see the need to end racism, capitalism, imperialism, and heterosexism.

Yet all of these men do not represent the politics of the men's movement. The men's movement is *not* a movement of men fighting male supremacy, though some men in it may wish to. It is *not* a movement which consciously attacks heterosexual privilege, class privilege, and white skin privilege. The men's movement has no formal or unified commitment to any of these goals.

In fact, on a superficial level, it is tempting to state that the men's movement has no formal or unified commitment to *anything*. Some see the men's movement as a diverse, open movement, without a political line. If this were really the case, we could at least praise the men's movement for its spontaneous, decentralized, anarchistic spirit. But it is not true; it is a deception.

The men's movement has a line all right. Note the cover statement from the first "national newsletter" of Men's Awareness Network (M.A.N.—get it?) from Knoxville, Tennessee—"A newsletter dedicated to consciously creating awareness between, among, and about men and men's issues and concerns." Read the quote carefully, because *this* is the line of the men's movement. Not because the Knoxville men are a powerful vanguard, but because this has *always* been the line of the men's movement. The Knoxville collective has merely spelled it out.

What are the implications of this line? Does this line express or even imply any commitment to fight male privilege, heterosexual privilege, class privilege, or white skin privilege? Not that I can see. What it does do is reveal the essential *male bonding* of this men's movement, which is awfully similar to the male bonding of all other men's movements.

There is no mention of women in the quote. There is no mention of feminism. There is no mention of male supremacy. There is no mention of woman-hating. There is no mention of rape, abortion, child care, or forced sterilization. Just men "sharing men's issues and concerns with other men." How is *that* different from other men's movements? Women are as invisible and unimportant to this men's movement as they are in any other corner of our male supremacist society.

Reflect for a moment on the term itself: "men's movement." A *movement* of *men.* Now when men think of the men's movement, wonderful images often come to mind: awareness, sensitivity, warmth, "raised consciousness," a new level of trust among men. But how does this look to women—the 53% of the population that men oppress? How does the men's movement appear to women working in offices, to women in prison, to women on welfare, to rape victims, to lesbian mothers? How do these women—and all other women—feel about men focusing on "men's issues and concerns"?

When women see a movement of privileged men uniting to talk among themselves and build greater trust *among men,* how do they react? Do they feel hopeful; do they believe that "men's liberation" will lead to positive changes in women's lives? Or do they feel a little worried—having experienced all too well the politics and power of many other men's movements run by men of similar privilege?

I can't answer these questions, and it's not my business to try. But I do know that the more I've read feminist literature—and the more that I've listened to friends who are radical feminists, lesbian feminists, women-identified women—the more I've had to ask myself some difficult questions about this men's movement. About its politics, about its literature, about its "leaders," about its members, and about myself.

For almost four years, I believed in the men's movement and worked hard to help it grow. But, more recently, I've started to really study and learn about feminism. As a result, everything has come to look different. I wish I could communicate a thousand experiences, conversations, readings, arguments, etc., that have turned my head around.

For now, all I can say is that this men's movement strikes me as *very similar* to other men's movements. And I find that frightening. I've been in this men's movement and heard men feel absolutely free to call women "girls"; to say that radical feminism is "bullshit"; even to argue that they should organize to protect the jobs of men (meaning white men) from preferential hiring of women and Third World males. So much for "men's liberation."

I don't know where this leaves me. I do know that I'd like to live in a world without male supremacy and without men's movements. How that can happen is hard for me to imagine. But, increasingly, I have a feeling that either women will provide the answer—or there won't be any answer. Maybe men had better start listening.

Bibliography
Men who are sincerely anti-sexist should be reading every bit of feminist literature they can find. I'm including a brief list of materials that have been particularly meaningful in my own reading and learning.

Books

Ti-Grace Atkinson, *Amazon Odyssey* (Links).

Phyllis Birkby, et. al., editors, *Amazon Expedition* (Times Change Press).

Rita Mae Brown, *Rubyfruit Jungle* (Daughters, Inc.).

Susan Brownmiller, *Against Our Will: Men, Women, and Rape* (Simon and Schuster).

Charlotte Bunch and Nancy Myron, editors, *Class and Feminism* (Diana Press).

Barbara Ehrenreich and Deidre English, *Witches, Midwives, and Nurses: The Sexual Politics of Sickness* (The Feminist Press).

Noreen Connell and Cassandra Wilson, editors, *Rape: The First Sourcebook for Women by the New York Radical Feminists* (Plume).

Andrea Dworkin *Our Blood: Prophecies and Discourses on Sexual Politics* (Harper and Row).

Andrea Dworkin, *Woman Hating* (Dutton).

Barbara Ehrenreich and Deidre English, *Complaints and Disorders: The Sexual Politics of Sickness* (The Feminist Press).

Shulamith Firestone, *The Dialectic of Sex* (Bantam).

Eleanor Flexner, *Century of Struggle* (Atheneum).

Betty Friedan, *The Feminine Mystique* (Dell).

Doris Lessing, *The Golden Notebook* (Ballantine).

Kate Millett, *Sexual Politics* (Avon).

Robin Morgan, *Monster* (Vintage).

Nancy Myron and Charlotte Bunch, editors, *Lesbianism and the Women's Movement* (Diana Press).

Marge Piercy, *Small Changes* (Fawcett).

Sylvia Plath, *The Bell Jar* (Bantam).

Agnes Smedley, *Daughter of Earth* (The Feminist Press).

Mary Wollstonecraft, *A Vindication of the Rights of Woman* (Norton Critical Editions).

Publications

off our backs (1724 20th Street, N.W., Washington, D.C., 20009. $6/year).

Quest (1909 Que Street, N.W., Washington, D.C., 20009. $9/year).

Special Issue on Lesbian Culture, *Win,* June 26, 1975 (Box 547, Rifton, New York, 12471).

First published in *Morning Due,* November/December 1975. Also published in *A Forum for Changing Men,* December 1975, and in *Win* January 29, 1976. Reprinted by permission of the author.

A Critique of "Men's Lives"

Jon Snodgrass

"Men's Lives" is a forty-three minute color documentary. It is the story of, and a film made by, two male Antioch students who return to their hometowns with a movie camera to interview a variety of people about men and masculinity. They seek an understanding of the people and the process which brought them to manhood and they question the male role. The filmmakers were originally participants in the Oberlin College conference on masculinity, "Snakes 'n' Snails 'n' Puppy-Dogs' Tails," held in the Fall of 1972. Both the film and the conference are productions of the men's liberation movement.

The film is an accurate, and in parts, touching account of what it is like to grow up male in North America, particularly if one is also white, heterosexual and middle class. It shows small boys fighting on playgrounds and learning to hate girls. It shows adolescents saying they love football for the kill and hot cars for the sexual thrill. In general, it shows how men are trained to suppress, affect, and release aggression.

But the film's exclusive concentration on the limitations of the male role constitutes its greatest weakness, for it completely neglects the benefits. This sexist negation is epitomized in an interview in *Jump Cuts* (Summer, 1976) with one of the filmmakers who states, "Certain parts of the women's movement have mistakenly identified the source of their oppression as men." Here a man violates one of the cardinal principles of anti-sexism by speaking for women and attempting to define their oppressor.

Early in the film, a black child states that she would rather be a boy because "boys have more fun," but male privilege is not explored. Thus, the film is one-sided, emphasizing what is bad about being a man and not what is good. It assumes that straight men and women are equally oppressed. This position implicitly denies that sexism exists by denying the hierarchical structure in which men dominate women. If growing up male "is just as worrisome and wonderful as growing up female," which is the theme communicated to one reviewer and presumably to most viewers, then there would appear to be no reason for a women's movement. Thus, this male perspective is a negation of feminism.

Just as "Men's Lives" ignores the subordination of women, it excludes the oppression of male homosexuals. The film is only about heterosexual men's lives. Since exclusion reflects not only an absence of consciousness, but is an exercise in power, "Men's Lives" is anti-gay. It consistently assumes that all men are straight—that the only desirable relationships are male-female in character. In the few instances in which male homosexuality cannot be excluded by the biases of the filmmakers, it is forced to surface by the comments of those who are interviewed. For instance, a young man tells us he is stereotyped for being a dancer and gymnast; or a father implies that hugs and kisses won't affect his son's maleness. However, the subject of gayness in men is unacknowledged and unexplored.

One striking feature of "Men's Lives" is the number of Blacks in the film. While this is effective in demonstrating that Black men have experienced patriarchy and are therefore sexist, too, this stress on the sex role identification of both black and white men leaves out the political context in which Blacks have experienced racial oppression. Thus, it fails to take into account Black men's history of being treated like boys by whites. White men must comprehend that there is another dimension beyond "maleness" in *Black men's lives.*

In addition to lacking an awareness of women's, gay, and racial oppression, "Men's Lives" has no class consciousness. There are numerous scenes of working men, but work is seen as a requirement of masculinity rather than the function of the working class under capitalism. This perspective completely ignores women's work inside and outside the family as part of the female role. In seeing only male labor the film perpetuates women's oppression by assuming women's work is negligible.

"Men's Lives" and men's liberation literature are often politically naive, probably a result of their authors' more comfortable social origins. Consequently, what is class oppression is often mistaken for sex role oppression. Men are seen as oppressed by masculinity, not by a ruling class. By sex role, however, men are actually oppressors and the benefactors of sexism. Straight men are only alienated from their full human potential by sexism, not "oppressed" by it. If straight men are conceived as oppressors and oppressed, then the word, and the power relationship, and the feminist struggle, lose their meaning.

One of the connections between capitalism and masculinity is competition, so toward the end, "Men's Lives" alludes to a "competitive, aggressive, profit-oriented society" as the cause of it all. Several jump shots show us an executive boardroom, the masses, a computer, red tape, even Henry Kissinger, but the analysis in terms of capitalism, patriarchy or both is mystified and fleeting.

To conclude, "Men's Lives" is anti-woman, anti-gay, and anti-working class. It accurately portrays, however, the socialization and quality of life for one class and sex in society. And it reflects the kind of resistance men exert when threatened by the women's liberation movement. Men assert that they are oppressed equally by their masculine "conditioning." This makes them the victims, instead of the perpetrators, of a sexist system. This film demonstrates the need for men to recognize and give up their privilege rather than defending it. The anti-feminist qualities of "Men's Lives" needs to be recognized by anti-sexist men.

From *Los Angeles Women's Union Newsletter*, November/December 1975. Reprinted in *Brother*, Summer 1976, and *Changing Men*, September 1976.

Part Two:
Gay, Class & Racial Oppression
Introduction to Part II

The remaining three sections of the anthology are organized around the social divisions of class, race and sexual orientation, divisions which are also important to anti-sexist men. The relationship of these divisions to women's oppression, however, is problematical. Most of the articles are descriptive and do not develop theory about the various forms of oppression.

I would like to take up briefly the relationship between gay and women's oppression. Attempting to explain the relationship between these two forms of oppression raises questions about the nature of sexism itself. Sexism, patriarchy, is the assignment of people to dominant and subordinate orders according to gender. It is maintained by repressive sex role socialization which attempts to polarize individuals by making males masculine and females feminine. This polarization simultaneously forces sexuality toward heterosexual lines and is an essential element in male domination. Heterosexuality is the main pillar of patriarchy because the attempt to create separate masculine and feminine beings who are sexually attracted to one another results in the reproduction of children, the historical basis of women's oppression. Thus, patriarchy dictates heterosexuality in order to perpetuate itself. For this reason, the repudiation of and rebellion against heterosexuality by gay people has long been the advanced element in the historical struggle against patriarchy.

Because sexism is primarily a division between men and women, however, the meaning of homosexuality is different for lesbians than for gay men. Lesbians are oppressed because they are both women and gay. Gay men, however, are indoctrinated into patriarchal culture and trained as male supremacists to oppress women, including lesbians, and to identify their interests with male rule. Therefore, they have the contradictory position of being oppressive as men and oppressed as gays. Consequently, sexism is the oppression of women *in a total way* on account of their gender, an oppression which prohibits women's sexual preference for one another. Sexism is also the oppression of homosexuality in men. While on the whole, men benefit from sexism, gay men are *specifically* oppressed in terms of their sexuality by patriarchy. Therefore, both forms of oppression, women's and gay men's, are inter-related. As stated by Gayle Rubin, "The suppression of the homosexual component of human sexuality, and by corollary, the oppression of homosexuals, is therefore a product of the same system whose rules and relations oppress women." (*Toward an Anthropology of Women*, Rayna Reitor, editor, Monthly Review Press, 1975.)

Because women's and gay men's oppression is linked through sexism, the common source of their oppression, misogyny must also become an important issue to gay liberation. Gay male liberation lies with the women's movement. An independent gay male liberation movement is a struggle by men with men for patriarchal power and is supportive of male supremacy. Gay liberation arose out of the women's movement, as a result of the inter-dependence of both forms of oppression, and must return to support it. Gay men are oppressed because women are oppressed. To be free, gay men must challenge and participate in the revolution against male domination.

The material on gay men is a collection of articles arranged as an introduction to the subject and oriented toward educating the heterosexual reader. With the exception of the first essay, the articles describe the various ways in which gay men have experienced, and organized around, their sexual oppression.

In the first article, Claude Steiner takes responsibility for his anti-gayness by acknowledging first of all that it exists. As a psychiatrist and a member of the Radical Therapy Collective in Berkeley, he discusses the homophobic qualities of his previous books and practice. His acknowledgment was initiated by criticism from Anthony Eschbach, who authors "Gay Men's Work" in this anthology. By recognizing his heterosexual biases, Steiner attempts to end his contribution to gay oppression. I would like to have seen Steiner discuss in greater detail the process by which his anti-gay consciousness changed, and his ideas about how to support gay liberation in practice.

In the next article, "Homophobia and the Left," Tom Kennedy criticizes men in the left for not coming to terms with their fear of homosexuality and their oppressive treatment of gays. Homophobia among socialists both limits its members and retards the movement. Kennedy believes that straight left males must acknowledge their privilege and struggle against their own sexism in order to build "a more integrated socialist movement."

In the third article, "Gay Romance," Darca Nicholson interviews two gay men who are in love. Over three years ago, when they had known each other for only a few months, they "made a commitment to be together forever." The interview contradicts many of the false images about caring relationships among homosexual men and describes some of the problems they face in a heterosexually dominant society. Although the article has been criticized, fairly I think, for its reliance on a romantic conception of love and its liberalism about homosexuality, I feel that it is important because of the stereotypes it helps destroy.

In "The History of A Short, Unsuccessful Academic Career," Michael Silverstein describes the repression of his sexuality during his early life. He began to discover his gay identity in the early 1970's through the gay liberation movement while he was an assistant professor at a New York university. Because of his gay activism and radical politics he was fired from his job. In a "Postscript" written for this anthology, he up-dates the changes in his life, repudiates most of his previous article, and asserts his new political stand.

There are also articles about gay men in the final two sections of the book, "Working Class Men," and "Third World Men." Anthony Eschbach, in "Gay Men's Work," discusses the kind of employment traditionally available to gay men. In "Beyond the Binary: Race and Sex," Charley Shively acknowledges and explicitly reviews the racism in his sexuality. Shively's purpose is to use himself as a case study in a preliminary attempt to understand the interdependence of racism and sexism. The experience of being black and gay is contained in "Personal Reflections on Gay Liberation from the Third World," by Leonard Andrews, Jr. Andrews' article was originally written as a contribution to a special combined issue of *Fag-Rag* and *Gay Sunshine* in commemoration of the fifth anniversary of the Stonewall Rebellion in June, 1969, a date which historically marks the beginning of the gay (male) liberation movement. In this version, revised especially for the anthology, Andrews recounts his history of identification as a gay person and analyzes racism in the gay liberation movement.

The final two sections of the anthology are devoted to class and race. The articles describe the oppression of working class and third world men, but do not analyze the sources of oppression nor the theoretical relationships between sexism and class, and sexism and racism. The descriptive content of the articles in these two sections reflects the need for theoretical development in these areas. Perhaps the materials brought together here may serve as a starting point for that development.

GAY MEN

"Times Are a' Changing"

Claude Steiner

Anthony Eschback has pointed out to me that in my book *Games Alcoholics Play* especially, but also in *Scripts People Live,* it appears that I believe that homosexuality is a mental illness and that I have a strong bias against it.

I must agree with this criticism in regard to *Games Alcoholics Play*. I wrote that book between 1967 and 1969 and at that time my position about homosexuality was that it was an unfortunate choice of life styles. Unfortunate, I felt, because gay people were so mercilessly persecuted, and unfortunate also, because men in particular seemed at a great disadvantage in meeting male companions with whom to have intimate, long-lasting relationships. While I did not think of homosexuality as an illness or a perversion, I was willing to work with men and women who wanted to make a contract to "go straight." I was also capable of allowing into print the following sentence:

"The script is a consciously understood life plan decided upon before the age of fourteen, and psychopathologies such as alcoholism, depression, schizophrenia, homosexuality, etc., often represent a script . . ."

This sentence is a segment of a larger paper reprinted in its entirety in the book. The paper itself was written even earlier with a professional audience in mind; I did not really think of homosexuality as a psychopathology, but I called it that as a concession to, and in order to communicate with, those who I considered my colleagues and who I now see as our opposition. My true feelings at the time would have been more accurately expressed by putting psychopathologies between quotes.

My views on homosexuality, as are the views of so many psychotherapists, were liberal. This implies that my views were theoretically positive and emotionally negative. I believed that people had a right to choose their sexual preferences. I would never claim that homosexuality was wrong or immoral, and I felt that the laws against homosexuality were wrong. But I also did not believe that homosexuals had as good a chance to be as happy as heterosexuals. I believed that they were more prone to alcoholism, physical violence, loneliness, and severe emotional disturbance because I only knew homosexuals in therapy. Most importantly, I was afraid of gay men physically and found discussions of their sexual activities repugnant and therefore avoided them. I believed that a gay man who wanted to go straight was making a wise choice. I also quickly noticed that I had absolutely no success in helping gays change their sexual orientation. Above all, I felt, in some subtle way, that homosexuals were separate and different from me. I wished them well but had no feeling for their lives except that it was in some way tragic, not at all "gay."

It is also dismaying to recall that many of the people whom I worked with were referred to me by a gay psychiatrist who must have felt, though he never said so openly, that it would be harmful for him

164

to work with a homosexual. That is a commentary on how things were in those days and probably still are in most of the country even now. I was also publicly attacked for suggesting elsewhere in *Games* that alcoholism and homosexuality were not diseases.

Yes, the book does reflect heterosexist bias. I regret this because I realize that most readers do not check publication dates on books and I realize how gay men and women who read this book will react to some of my statements about homosexuality.

It may seem here that I am backpedalling, trying to defend what I did in terms of my background and the context in which I worked at the time. I guess that I am confused by the facts of the situation; on the one hand I was in the vanguard of tolerance working in a place which was considered friendly to the gay community (Center for Special Problems in San Francisco). And yet, well-meaning as I was, I contributed to the subtle but very real oppression of gays. It is a fact of life for me and I am sure for many other white men, that we don't really know what we can do about our membership in a class which has been so oppressive other than feel guilty or try to explain away our acts.

Scripts People Live reflects my current views more accurately, though I am sure it still reflects my inevtiable heterosexual bias. By the time I wrote *Scripts* I had been a member of the radical therapy movement for some years and I had come to see that the most important fact about gay people is that they are an extremely oppressed minority. Therapists must take responsibility for their biases and their subtle contribution to the oppression suffered by gays. I want to solicit, and I appreciate all, criticisms which point out these biases to me.

Professionally trained therapists are prone to have extremely distorted views about homosexuality because we have been taught that it lurks at the core of emotional disturbances such as schizophrenia and alcoholism. For instance, any time that a person exhibits paranoid symptoms, I was taught to look for "latent homosexual impulses" so that in my mind homosexuality became associated with the ominous, eerie, bizarre qualities of extreme paranoia. Because homosexuality is believed to be an important factor in psychiatric disturbance, most trained therapists feel compelled to comment on it regardless of how ignorant they may be on the subject, and that is something I did in *Games* and even, to a certain extent, in *Scripts*.

I want to say that I support gay liberation and that I support the development of a strong, aggressive gay liberation movement. I am opposed to all laws, employment policies or social trends which treat gay people differently from other people, or to procedures designed to change sexual orientation, even by contract. With respect to therapy, I also believe that the pervasive nature of heterosexist bias requires that a therapy group that has gays in it should have at least three gay members, and that if at all possible one of the therapists should be gay as well. I don't believe that most heterosexual therapists, including myself, can claim to be sufficiently free of heterosexist bias not to oppress or collude with the oppression of gays in their groups.

From *Issues in Radical Therapy*, Summer 1975. Reprinted by permission.

Homophobia in the Left

Tom Kennedy

Last June (1975) marked the sixth anniversary of the Stonewall Rebellion in New York, where several hundred gay women and men battled with police, and symbolically with straight society, in response to a police raid on the Stonewall Inn Bar. In an atmosphere of social change, gay liberation emerged to vocalize centuries of rage, anger, and oppression. This article is dedicated to those gay people who have perished physically and psychologically throughout the centuries in our struggle to survive in a heterosexist society. This article is also dedicated to those feminists whose strength and courage paved the way for the emergence of a gay liberation movement.

At a recent program on feminist therapy sponsored by Bay Area NAM (New American Movement), one of the key points and criticisms was that men have yet to begin to combat sexism by themselves without the support, the encouragement, or the prompting of women. With the exception of gay men, the speakers pointed out, men have yet to see sexism as an issue that relates to them personally. A common attitude among those men who are attempting to support the struggles around sexism is that it is basically for the benefit of women or gays— always for some other rather than something that relates to them directly. This attitude of straight men, that the struggle around sexism is primarily for the benefit of an outside oppressed group, coupled with the fear of homosexual/gay feelings (homophobia), is not only a serious handicap for the non-gay men themselves, but a handicap that is certainly holding back certain aspects of the socialist movement.

For far too long, the contributions and analyses that gay men have to offer the (male) left have been ignored and/or dismissed. As men victimized by a male heterosexist society we have considerable insight into the crippling effect of male dominance. Many of us have been married or at least have had to fake heterosexual roles and have insights into the negative aspects of the nuclear family, monogamous relationships, and heterosexual relationships.

Yet the (male) left has rejected, trivialized and dismissed us for so long and so consistently that it has not allowed gay (male) theory to be presented and digested. Gay socialists spend most of their time trying to reconcile the contradiction between their gayness and a predominantly anti-gay socialist movement. However, within NAM and among a very few other socialist groups, gay people are beginning to be acknowledged as people who have much to contribute to socialist revolution and, in fact, whose absence is a serious loss to any organization that sees itself as working to build a socialist party and movement.

As a gay man who has been working within the left for several years, I am always amazed at the ability of straight men to dismiss me and my political beliefs because I am gay. When I first noticed this happening, I assumed it was my own projected paranoia. But as time went on and I compared notes with other gay brothers I could see that there was a definite pattern developing. There are many reasons for this attitude, such as actually believing stereotypes and shallow analyses that state we are products of bourgeois decadence.

Yet one of the major reasons for our dismissal is the fact that we are feared because straight men fear the gay aspects of themselves. For the most part straight men still see something wrong with the possibility of involving themselves in any sexual/emotional contact with other men. Granted, fear is fear and it is not something that can just be dismissed, but the source of these fears must be identified for what it is—bourgeois morality. At the very least, I feel the eradication of homophobia is a very positive political/personal act that definitely liberates an individual.

Unlike some early radical lesbians who stated that a woman wasn't a "real" feminist unless she had sexual/emotional relations with other women, I don't feel that every man committed against sexism must have gay as well as straight experiences. Yet I am certain that almost all gay socialists would agree that a gay experience would

167

have a positive radicalizing effect on any straight man. The fear of homosexuality is a fear that has been drilled into the minds of men and women since they were children. It is a fear that patriarchal capitalism has had to perpetuate in order to sustain itself. A society where men take pride in gentleness, emotional tenderness and its application through gay sex is incongruent with patriarchal capitalism. Capitalism needs competition between workers, not cooperation, and it is male competition that helps sustain divisions among workers. Likewise, capitalism cannot allow a society where women are strong, assertive, and independent of men, as characterized by lesbianism. The fear of the positive, revolutionary aspects of gayness within oneself is a perpetuation of the system of patriarchal capitalism.

One of the most unfortunate dynamics existing between gays and non-gays is the fact that we get penalized for the fears of non-gay people. Straight men often hold back their emotional support for us for fear that it will be misinterpreted as a "come on." They are afriad to touch us or have any kind of physical contact for the same reason. These types of actions leave us feeling ignored and alienated.

In the realm of politics, dealing with issues of gayness and/or sexuality is often much more anxiety-filled than with any other issue because one must deal with real sexual and emotional feelings. Gay people are, fortunately and unfortunately, a very real "threat" to those who are insecure and attached to their sexual identities. This is one of the major reasons that gay people are not welcomed into the left—we bring a part of the revolution right along with us. We take the theoretical and by our very existence make it personal.

Again I will say here that the fear of gayness and gayness are two different but related things. I am not stating that everyone must become gay. But I and many other gay people will testify to the fact that smashing the fear of gayness is an incredibly liberating and joyful experience. It is an experience that the homophobic ruling class will excourage you in every way not to have. If we are to expand the concept of revolution past a limited economic revolution to one that includes a sexual/emotional revolution as well, we must begin to acknowledge in ourselves the potential to develop male-male and female-female relationships as well as female-male relationships. Likewise, we must free the oppressor within us.

For men in particular, there must be an end to hiding in our intellects and the beginning of developing relationships that may or may not involve gay sex but that *will* involve loving, sharing, and the pride and acknowledgment that same gender relationships are just as valid as a mixed gender relationship. Men loving men is a major aspect of gay liberation. In a society based in male aggression and competition, it is a revolutionary act.

Clinging to heterosexuality is clinging to privilege. If men are sincere in their struggle against sexism, they must begin by not only respecting their gay brothers and sisters but by struggling on a personal level by allowing emotional and/or sexual feelings toward other men to surface. Likewise, gay people must end any attachments they have regarding their gay identities. I am avoiding stating that we must evolve toward a bisexual society because until the privilege of heterosexuality is ended, bisexual is not the neutral term it is implied to be.

Hopefully together we can create a society where labels are meaningless and people can function freely as they so choose. But until that day arrives, straight men dedicated to socialist revolution should acknowledge the privilege they have as heterosexual men over women, gays, and children. Likewise, that privilege and power must be shared. The mistrust for straight men shared by lesbians and gay men, as well as by some feminists, must partially be resolved by the men themselves dealing with their sexism on a personal level. Hopefully, this process will lead to a more integrated socialist movement with a broader representation than currently exists within the left.

From the *New American Movement Newspaper,* Summer 1975. Reprinted by permission.

Gay Romance

Darca Nicolson, Richard L. Stein and Thomas F. Merrifield

Darca: I would like to know how and when you met, and how your relationship developed.

Dick: We met during homecoming 1971 at the University of Iowa. We both went with the same group of people to watch the homecoming parade.

Darca: Tell me something of your life at the time.

Tom: I was finishing graduate school, getting my Ph.D. I was living in a house with some friends and at that time I wasn't really deeply involved with anybody. I was gay and I was out and this was widely known at that time. I was seeing a couple of men and a couple of women, but mainly I was enjoying being single.

Dick: For me, I was sleeping with two men and two women, although I didn't consider myself gay or even bisexual. I thought of myself as straight. I had known these people quite a while, all four of them. When I met Tom I could see right away that the relationship had more potential in it than the others—it was going to be a lot better. We had a lot more in common. After spending time with him I saw that the other relationships weren't that good and so I just dropped them. Just a few days before meeting Tom, I had written in my journal that I really needed someone I could love fully. I wanted a truly intimate relationship, not the kind I was already involved in.

Tom: For me, our meeting was pretty romantic. I remember the first time that I saw Dick. I was watching him that evening, and thinking how nice he looked. Shortly thereafter we ran into each other in a bar and got into a long discussion and ended up going out for breakfast and talking until dawn. We talked very openly about ourselves, our lives, our hopes, dreams, and fears. I think that's when I fell for Dick. I told him that if he ever wanted to do anything, to give me a call, and he called the next afternoon. That was pretty much it; within six weeks we were living together and we have been together ever since, a little over three years now. Within a few months we had made a commitment to be together forever. We told each other we loved each other on New Year's Eve, only two and a half months after we had met.

Darca: What were some of the problems you had? Either between you or imposed from the outside?

Dick: I can remember one night when we were driving around and Tom made some reference to me as a gay man. We had known each other three or four weeks at the time, and I was really surprised to hear that term used to refer to me because I didn't consider myself gay. The big thing that I had to deal with was my being gay and what it meant and how I thought and felt about it. I realized that I did know Tom and that I had more fun and better times with him than I ever had with anyone else and I wanted to keep spending time with him. So I decided it was all right to be gay.

Tom: Right away I saw that Dick did not consider himself gay and that really scared me. Prior to that, my most tragic romance was with a man who never faced up to being gay, and that was an awful experience for me. I knew that I couldn't go through another bad experience like that, that if we were to stay together he *had* to face up

170

to it, but it was something that couldn't be rushed. The night that he said I shocked him, I knew exactly what I was saying and I knew that he would be shocked and I knew that the subject had to be approached, but I gave him space to think about it and accept it. A major problem from my side was that I came from a basically unhappy family, a very unstable family. I never expected really to love the person I ended up with. There were a lot of bad marriages and people stayed together for the children and I had never had any positive models for straight couples, let alone gay couples. Everything that I had ever heard said— that gay people don't stay together, that they can't stay together because they are unstable—I think is totally untrue. But it was difficult for me to trust in a relationship, and trust that Dick loved me and that he could stay with me. It was hard for me not to get upset and worry, which is what I had done in previous relationships. When we came to problems, when there were things that upset us, or that we couldn't handle without quarreling, what we would do typically would be, first we would get close physically. We would lie down and hold each other and say, well, this is a problem that we can work out eventually, but we can't work out everything all at once. So we would just put it off for the future. We needed to know the difference between problems we could handle now and problems we could handle in the future. If we'd tackled all problems at once we'd have never made it together, but we were committed to working things out at a proper pace, and it worked for us. Now we have few problems between us. Our problems tend to be external, such as job pressures.

Dick: After about six weeks I left my apartment and moved in with Tom, who was living in a house with two women and another man. Tom had an enormous, comfortable room and it became my room also. One thing that helped me feel OK about my gayness was the friends that we had, and the people who just totally accepted it and gave us a lot of positive reinforcement. There were other couples in the house and we were looked on as another couple, not any different from anybody else. That was a good foundation.

Tom: Yeah, I think that was really important. I did have a lot of good friends, old-time friends, and I felt totally accepted by them as a person. Although I identify very heavily with the gay civil rights movement I've never really considered myself as gay in one sense, because I never thought of myself as different. A lot of people think of gay as being very different and I just think of myself as a very average person. I think that most people who get to know me have that opinion. A lot of people, when they first find out that I'm gay, say,

171

"Well, gee, I don't care; I don't understand it but I don't care." From my point of view there isn't anything to understand. A lot of straight people imagine that being gay is something really different—that I have different feelings than they do or different perceptions—and I don't think that that's true at all. I think that I love Dick just the way that anybody loves a spouse. There's no qualitative difference in the love that we experience.

One other thing that made it easier for us to develop a good relationship is Dick himself. He comes from a very healthy family where his parents love each other and where his parents both really love and respect him. He's warm and giving and kind and wants me to be happy. Dick naturally does all the right things. For me it's harder. Sometimes I have to think about what's the right thing to do. I think, "a good lover would do this," or "if I do this then this will happen so I shouldn't do it." With Dick it just flows. He always knows what I need and does his best to give it to me.

A lot of people have the idea that gay couples follow stereotyped sex roles like a lot of straight couples do. We've never done that and other gay couples we know don't do that either. I think that one of the fallacies about gayness is that there is a connection between being a male homosexual and femininity or female homosexuality and masculinity. I don't think that's true at all. Dick and I are very typical men and there's nothing that would distinguish us from straight men. One of the advantages to being gay is being free to set up a relationship more like we want than how we should. We both definitely knew that we didn't want to act in a parody of straight couples.

Dick: I grew up in a very middle class family, an all-American family, two boys, two girls, etc. I always thought that I would grow up, get married, have kids, take out the garbage, and live happily ever after. So I think that until I met Tom and decided that I was gay and started living in that lifestyle, I did have some real preconceived notions about how I would act when I got married. I don't know how that would have turned out, since I didn't do it.

Tom: Dick still gets stuck with taking out the garbage.

Darca: How do you feel about marriage? Do you want to marry?

Dick: We feel married, but neither of us wants to get married. It would feel like a parody of straight relationships, a desire to be "valid" in the eyes of the world.

Tom: In my mind, marriage should be a celebration of an already existing relationship. We have the relationship and don't need a license from some county clerk. That's certainly not a celebration. We have talked about and plan on some kind of legal contract that will guarantee our rights as a legitimate couple if one of us dies.

Darca: Could you talk a little about how the women's movement has affected your lives?

Tom: I knew I was gay when I was five years old, and in my family being gay meant being feminine, that there was something feminine about me. I was interested in art and I read a lot and men in my family were supposed to work on cars all the time and do things like that. It was considered feminine to be bright and to be interested in books. It upset my father a lot that I didn't want to help him work on cars. I was quiet and liked to be by myself reading or with my pets. My sister wanted to work on cars. The way my father treated me caused a lot of conflict and pain for me because I had the idea that because I didn't fit my father's ideal masculine image I was less of a person. The women's movement gave me an understanding of sex roles and the way in which the white, heterosexual male structure puts down women and keeps them powerless. This let me see that all of my bad feelings about myself were coming from the same place; that the things women were fighting against, and are still fighting right now, were the same things that were hurting me. I realized I couldn't accept the white heterosexual male premises, that basically I just really couldn't give a shit about what those people thought. I simply had to live my life the way I thought best. One good thing about the people that I was living with when Dick and I met was that they had a feminist consciousness. That was one reason they could accept me. It wasn't just accepting or tolerating your friend even though he's strange; they could accept me as a person and see me clearly for what I was without a lot of societal prejudices standing in the way.

Dick: I think what the women's movement did was give people of both sexes permission to do what they wanted, regardless of their sex. I can embroider a shirt and one of my best friends who is a woman can go play basketball with me in a real competitive place with a lot of other men. It just gave people permission to break their sex roles and fulfill their potential.

Darca: I'd like to hear about how you handle being gay at work.

Tom: Well, I work at a big university here in the Bay Area and I just came out at work. I'd become increasingly vocal at work in support of gay causes and had told many people individually, and I had given a lot of thought to whether I should make a public statement or just continue the way I'd been doing. Then the other day, in a staff meeting, there was an appropriate place and I just announced that I was a gay man. My bosses were wonderful and totally supportive. I feel their support is genuine. It's no "liberal" guilt trip. Many of my co-workers congratulated me and I feel confident there will be no repercussions. It made some people feel much closer to me, because it meant I trusted them. But it also means I trusted myself.

By no means do I believe that everybody really accepts me, but I believe that it's necessary to come out. I think that the whole homosexual issue has to be centered around our demanding our civil rights. We don't need to wait around until people accept us; that's their problem, not ours. We need to make a political statement of who we are and what we want; basically my political statement is I'm a person and I want my rights as a person and that's it! And I want my rights completely and fully—I don't want to suffer any pain or discrimination being a gay person. Therefore I feel that I have no choice about coming out. We all have to come out! People need to see that we're just ordinary people, their brother, sister, son, daughter, mother, father, neighbors, and co-workers. As long as we stay in the closet straight people are going to have horrible fantasies about what's behind that door. But I also believe that it can be very hard to come out in this society and I don't believe in putting pressure on other gay people to come out.

Dick: I feel the same way Tom does. I feel I should be accorded the same civil rights as a straight person and not be discriminated against because of my sexual preference. My job is teaching retarded adults, and I'm not really sure what would happen there if I were to openly let it be known that I was gay. There would probably be repercussions from the parents who might think that I would make their son or daughter a homosexual. At my previous job I told all of my co-workers privately and within the course of a year everybody knew and most approved. I think that there were a few who didn't approve, but felt it would be uncouth for them to say so. Even my boss knew that I was gay. I don't know what he thought about it but the fact that I hadn't announced it publicly made it so there was really nothing they could do to make a scandal out of it. At my current job I'm telling people individually. I would like to be able to say flatly, yes, I'm gay, that's the lifestyle I choose. But the parents' consciousness is not at a place I would hope it would be. So my coming out might really jeopardize my job.

Darca: How do your families react to your being gay?

Tom: Within my family my coming out caused some trouble. My parents have been absolutely wonderful. They're lower-middle class working people who had really no preparation for my coming out, but they have totally accepted Dick as a son-in-law. They treat him exactly the way they treat their other son-in-law. I'm very proud of them for that. I have a lot of aunts and uncles also who treat us like any other couple. We're accorded full status. The difficulty I've had has been with one of my sisters who became very upset about it. She was fearful that this meant that it's something catching, or hereditary and that her children might come up with it, that they might be homosexual. She went to see some minister who was also a shrink. He told her I was unnatural, would never go to heaven, and that it was environmental. He said my mother made me a homosexual. Now she's afraid to have me or my mother around her children, and that's where the stress has come in the family. She's been horrible to my mother. The rest of our family is very angry at my sister, but they see it as her emotional problem. Although most of them don't know the word, they can see that Carol's homophobia hurts other people but that my homosexuality hurts no one and makes me happy.

There was a period of shock for my family and some ugly scenes, but they love me and that passed quickly. My coming out totally changed my relationship with Dad. Now we're very close. I can feel that he loves me and is proud of me. He's the most vocal gay rights supporter I have in the family; his views are very close to mine.

Dick: I think that part of my family suspects that I'm gay but I haven't discussed it openly with any of them. I've discussed homosexuality and prior to being gay I had some gay friends and I had talked to part of my family about them. My feeling is that it would be pretty much OK with most of them, and I wouldn't expect any insolvable problems. I would have to talk to them and re-educate them about what a gay person is and is not; it would involve a lot of time and effort on my part and this is pretty much why I haven't done it. There's a 2000-mile physical separation between us. I'm pretty much just waiting for a really convenient time to tell them in person. All my family has met Tom. They like him a lot, and I think he'll fit right in as a part of the family.

Tom: I know that Dick's parents like me better than any of their sons- or daughters-in-law, and while my family doesn't know Dick as well as I know Dick's family, my family has had to face up to the fact that Dick's and my relationship is more stable and healthy than the marriages of my straight brother and sister. Both of them have been divorced and have had and continue to have lots of trouble in their relationships.

Darca: I would like to hear how you envision the future of your relationship.

Dick: I don't know when we decided that we wanted to spend the rest of our lives together. We decided it a long time ago. We both see this as permanent.

Tom: We know that we have a good thing, and we want to grow old together—we think about that and we fantasize about that. Our biggest commitment in life is to each other. Nothing else in my life is that important. My career is important in the sense that I enjoy my career, I get a lot of satisfaction out of it, and I worked very hard to be where I am, but it's very secondary. I have a lot of friends who are very close and very important to me, but none of them is close in the way that Dick is close. I like that. I like that specialness. I like to feel that he's my man and that we're going to be old and rickety together. We won't be old and rickety alone—I know that there are friends who will be our friends when we're old together. We have plans to travel a lot and to enjoy ourselves and to take big blocks of time off and really indulge ourselves in having a good time.

Dick: I think I've known for a long time, in my head and in my guts, that Tom is the absolutely best person I could ever get to live with and to love. In fact, the further we go, the more this sticks out in my mind. Thinking of being without Tom sends a chill through my body. I couldn't imagine not living with Tom and he feels the same about me.

Darca: I was thinking about how much I enjoy coming over here to be with you—I enjoy my relationship with each of you individually and I don't feel as if you are doing a heavy couple trip at all. I also really enjoy a lot seeing you two love each other . . . Is there anything else you two would like to add?

Tom: Last night we were talking with our friend Alice about what it means to be gay, and I said that homosexuality and heterosexuality, to me, is not, who do I have sex with, but who do I fall in love with. I fell in love with a man. I use the term gay because it has fewer sexual connotations than homosexual. Recently, a bill was introduced into the House of Representatives that would guarantee civil rights to individuals without regard to "affectional or sexual preference." I think that's an important distinction and that adding the term affectional gives a more balanced view of gay people. If sex were all we had, we'd never have lasted three and a half years. What's most important is I love Dick and Dick loves me.

From *Issues in Radical Therapy,* Winter 1975. Reprinted by permission.

The History of a Short, Unsuccessful Academic Career

Michael Silverstein

PART I

The usefulness of a history is to show the operation of process. In this case, the process is the development of an identity. By using my experiences as an example, I hope to show the experiential reality of the one-dimensionality of this society in determining an individual's identity. This is done through the key institution of sex roles. What I must grow up to be, what it must mean to be a male human being, was presented to me as inevitable and unquestionable. Masculinity was defined for me by the social world I was part of as a set of personal characteristics that must become a part of my identity. I, like all male children, was taught that my value as a person depended on my power over others. I was taught that I must compete for personal power, and that to be successful I must conceal feelings of weakness, tenderness, and dependence, and present myself to other men as self-sufficient and insensitive.

In spite of the all-pervasiveness of this lesson, I finally found myself in full rebellion against manhood. The source of this rebellion was something that seemed entirely external to the reality of the world I was taught about—the fact of my Gayness. To those of us who identify with the Gay Liberation movement, Gayness has come to mean far more than the original fact of our homosexuality. The description of how I came to reject the definition of myself as a man is also a description of how I came to understand the concept of Gayness, by coming to an understanding of the political reality of the psychological characteristics of manliness.

Our lives are lived in the context of social institutions. In my case, these processes worked themselves out in the context of Academia. This was not accidental. I found myself in Academia because it had been presented to me as a less masculine milieu than most social institutions. Yet it turned out that success in this sphere is as much dependent on those personality traits defined as male as it is in any other part of the society. Thus in describing my academic career, I can show how the social needs men are taught to act upon are essential to the functioning of even the less masculine-appearing social institutions.

Ultimately, this assertion leads to the generalization that the masculine personality, man's learned drive for interpersonal dominance, is the psychic engine required for capitalist society to function. Those with real power, ruling class white males, in order to perpetuate the existing social structure and thus ensure their continued control, use their control of the educational, communications, entertainment, and religious institutions to create men who seek a positive self-image in their power over others. Thus they have at their disposal middle class men motivated to operate the organizational machinery of capitalism by a desire to achieve power, and working class men who can be reconciled to their real powerlessness by personal power over their women and the possibility of successful competition for personal power with rivals of their own class. In addition, white working class men are given at least a vicarious power over third-world peoples. Similarly, those in power also require women to learn to evaluate their self-worth by their success in emotionally and materially supporting a man in his struggle for power, rather than acting as competitors themselves. The present paper illustrates how the masculine drive for power is the essential motivating force in the functioning of academic institutions.

But these abstractions can only define the argument; they can never advance it. My experiences aren't abstractions for me; my life depends on them. Manhood now appears to me not as a sociological concept, but as a Procrustean bed the society would force me into; my struggle against it is a struggle to keep from being mutilated out of all human shape. My academic career was a life-and-death struggle I just barely survived. It is the reality of this struggle I want to communicate. It was well under way by the time I was ten years old.

PART II

By the time I was ten, the central fact of my life was the demand that I become a man. By then the most important relationships by which I was taught to define myself were those I had with other boys. I already knew that I must see every encounter with another boy as a contest in which I must win or at least hold my own. School was the major arena of this contest, especially the playground and P.E. The same lesson continued everywhere, after school, even in Sunday School. My parents, relatives, teachers, the books I read, movies I saw, all taught me that my self-worth depended on my manliness, my willingness to stand up to the other boys. This usually didn't mean a physical fight, though the willingness to stand up and "fight like a man" always remained a final test. But the relationship between us usually had the character of an armed truce. Girls weren't part of this social world at all yet, just because they weren't part of this contest. They didn't have to be bluffed, no credit was gained by cowing them, so they were more or less ignored. Sometimes when there were no grownups around we would let each other know we liked each other, but most of the time we did as we were taught.

So I knew what I had to do to be a man. One could only succeed at establishing his manliness or be a failure, a sissy, someone who couldn't stand up and fight. One didn't choose to be a sissy, a loser— one lost. Since manliness was, of course, what everyone would want, the unmanly must be those who were too weak to make it as a man.

By the time I was in junior high, I defined myself and was defined by the other boys as a loser, as the class sissy. Largely this meant that I saw myself as a failed man. Yet (I now realize) the beginning of my Gayness was the beginning of my attempt to choose to be what I was. I began to redefine myself positively, to redefine what it meant *not* to be a successful man. In so doing I was moving outside the social reality I had been born to.

My first attempt at self-affirmation was to insist to myself that I didn't really want to be a man anyway. Much of this was sour grapes, of course, and I knew it. But there really was a part of me that, in opposition to everything I had been taught, really didn't want to be a man. I didn't know anything about homosexuality then; I didn't even know about sex. But from the time I was five years old I had wanted to touch and hold the bodies of other boys, and when I had done so I had felt warm and comfortable, and affectionate toward them. By the time I was eight or nine I had learned how bad and dirty, how unmanly, this was, and I was so scared of being caught at it that I stopped. But the desire remained, a gigantic thing always there. It was totally outside the reality of what it was to be a man. Yet it was so real, so undeniably a part of me, that it forced me to see myself as outside the world of all the other boys I knew. It was not just that I couldn't be a man, it was also that I knew about this part of me that could never be satisfied by manhood, because it wanted something that no man would ever want. For the reward of success as a man is power over other men— and I understood that this need I had could never be satisfied by power. I wasn't exactly sure what I wanted, what I actually wanted to do with another boy. But I knew that whatever it was, it required that we both want it, that it was only itself if given freely. All sorts of fantasies were going on in my head, completely dominating my consciousness. They were all rather vague, but they all involved relating to other boys in very unmanly ways, ways that had nothing to do with power.

So although I tried to be a man, I could never entirely put my heart into the contest when the reward for success seemed incompatible with what I really wanted. This may seem rather abstract for a 13-year-old, but I believe I understood the reality of the world far better at 13 than I did for a long time thereafter. It was at this time that I set out to find an alternative to manhood, something else that I could grow up to be. (Ultimately, this would lead to the goal of Gayness, the rejection of the whole dimension of masculinity-femininity as a scale on which people find their proper status, and the attempt to create a new concept of peoplehood. But that came later.)

I didn't feel ready yet to take on the world in junior high, so I started looking around in the world as it had been presented to me to find a place for myself. One choice I could have made was to decide that since I wouldn't be a man I would be like a woman instead. Many young Gay males make that choice. I thought I saw another alternative, something else I could be, which was a recognized part of the world I knew, yet wasn't a man. In fact, this alternative turned out to be a twenty-year-long detour into a blind alley, the blind alley of an academic career. But at the time I thought I saw an escape route: I would grow up to be a Brain.

Intellectual abilities and attainments had always been presented to me as essentially unmasculine, something a real man wouldn't take seriously because they weren't practical (that is, they didn't lead to power). Thus they were an escape from masculinity into asceticism and the source of the only positive self-image I could imagine. I had hoped that by graduate school, with the Big Men On Campus off to the professional and graduate business schools, I might find myself among other people like myself, and that as unmanly intellectuals we might find some new way to relate to one another.

Instead, now that all the Big Men were gone, it seemed that all the other Brains wanted to play at being men. Only now they'd play their way. But their way was my way. My sanctuary from manly competitiveness had become another one of its arenas. And the weapons being used, words, were something I was accomplished in the use of. For the first time in my life I could be a Big Man, a winner. Moreover, I started doing this without even knowing it. I just went on as I always had. Suddenly I started finding myself being proclaimed a winner in a contest I never knew I had entered.

The graduate Sociology Department at UCLA was as masculine as any locker room. The female graduate students were self-effacing, weren't taken seriously in the competition, and didn't seem to take themselves seriously. (Of the three exceptions I can remember, two are now radical feminists, and the third killed herself.) But I didn't recognize the games being played, because the main way I had recognized them in the past was from the perspective of a loser. Suddenly finding myself in the middle of the game as a winner, I didn't know where I was for quite a while. But I knew that I was one of the bright young men of the department. I was awarded a Special Research Training Fellowship of the National Institute of General Medical Sciences. I talked more than anybody else in all the seminars and could keep the other men from getting in a word edgewise. And I found myself enjoying the hell out of doing it.

For the first time in my life I had some taste of power over others. While I still appeared to my teachers as rather naive and erratic, nonetheless I was finally treated like a man. Even my family decided that college professors did pretty well after all. For the first (and last) time in my life, my family regarded me as a success. I just about forgot about being the sissy of my junior high, and I started believing that I was just a late bloomer, that now I was coming into my manhood at last.

At least I tried to believe this. But to do so I would have had to totally repress what I knew to be the truth about myself, that I was a homosexual. I could never succeed in doing this, so I could never believe in the reality of my masculine power. I could use it only as a defensive facade. Although I had access to masculine power for the first time, I still didn't want what this power must be used to purchase if it is to be actualized in this society. And I was sure that as soon as this became apparent, people would realize that I wasn't a man after all.

Thus the power I started to attain in the academic world never meant the same thing to me as it would have to a heterosexual man. I believe this power was typical of that wielded by "successful" homosexuals, in that I experienced it as essentially defensive. It was not a weapon to win for myself that masculine prize I still didn't want, but a shield to hide my failure from public view. No matter how powerful I might appear to others, the most I could ever hope from this power was security, safety—never gratification. If this is true of apparently powerful homosexual men, then no matter how much they appear a part of and committed to the society, their attachment is based on fear and defensiveness; their only hope of gratification lies in abandoning their power and abandoning their commitment to the society in which it is the greatest possible gratification.

None of this is to deny the objective reality of the power actually wielded by middle-class, white, male, educated homosexuals, such as myself. From the perspective of the students I would teach, of third world people, of women, I had the power to act as their oppressor. I would have this power by virtue of my academic position, my credentials, and the "expert" skills I had been taught. All of these are rooted in class and male privilege. I am only saying that the benefits I got from such power were not meaningful to me. This does not mean my exercise of power would be any less real or oppressive to my subordinates, and implies no obligation on their part of accepting the legitimacy of my power. The tendency of powerful men to ask oppressed people to feel sympathy for their feelings of inauthenticity and powerlessness seems essentially hypocritical to me. What I expect from those I have power over is nothing but the demand that I relinquish such power. Similarly, when more powerful men tell me that their power is of no benefit to them, my only response is to point out that this should make them more willing to relinquish it. This brings me back to my point. I believe that homosexual men such as myself can give up class and sex privileges more easily than straight men, because the benefits we gain from them are not so real. Only then can we assert any solidarity with other oppressed peoples.

At this time in my life I wasn't willing to give up my privileges, because I saw no alternative way I could live. So I set out to be a success after all. Academia might just be another masculine cage, but at least it was one where I found myself on one of the higher perches. Just to be confident I could pass for a man, especially with my family, was something to be grateful for. I had even picked out a specialty: I hoped to make it as the Big Man in alienation theory.

But now, just when I was ready to play at being a man and strive for success, the game changed again. As I reached the end of graduate school and started looking for a job, the most important arena of competition moved from the polemics of the classroom to the use of entrepreneurial and managerial skills within the bureaucracies of academic departments. Success was now determined by the sale of products and future products: writing and research projects. These were to be sold to academic departments, publishers, and agencies that funded research grants. While the polemical skills that let me argue successfully for the correctness of my analysis of things were relevant to this kind of competition, other skills were more important, such as the ability to write long, formal, highly structured, and bureaucratically sound research proposals. I first ran into this new set of required skills in applying for fellowships. Then came applying for a job. I was already getting scared by the prospect that a successful career would require a concentration on these things. I could do them if I had to, but they didn't bring even the spurious gratification of power in the classroom. They didn't seem to be any fun—only drudgery, alienated labor. They were the means to a successful career, but the end never seemed worth it.

Again the world seemed to have changed around me. Without any self-conscious change on my part, the gratification I could draw from my environment began to lessen. By this time I had gone to my first sociology convention, and any hope I had left that I might find some other non-men around was smashed by the sight of all the bustling young executive-types, drinks in hand, buttonholing one another to sound out prospects. Seeing this, I realized why my family had decided that it would be all right for me to be a college professor.

PART III

Nevertheless I got a job at City College of New York. Arriving in the fall of 1967, I had a whole personality ready for presentation, down to a bushy beard. By now I knew that as long as I kept things on an abstract and intellectual level—and we men kept them there—I could be articulate to the point of glibness, and self-confident to the point of of smugness. I was distantly friendly and impersonally cheerful to everyone. I was pretty sure I could pass as a man now.

But I still knew that passing as a man wouldn't help. And thus the dirty, ugly, angry city of New York pounded into me every day I spent in it—I was too lonely to give a damn about making it, too lonely to take seriously anything as meaningless as a successful academic career. I'm still grateful to New York for this. When I got there and felt what it was like, I needed people so badly I wanted to die most of the time. This forced me to get down to the real business of living and start finding out how to get in touch with other people, and with myself.

So, once in New York, my most urgent need was other people. Looking around me, I saw two groups of them: my colleagues and the students. Since my colleagues were the group from which I was supposed to draw my friends, I turned to them first. What I found should not have been surprising: they were not so different from me as I had thought. Many looked as if they had been pretty lousy at sports as kids, and had had a hard time hustling up a date. They had ended up in the academy for reasons similar to mine, but they were still very different from me, most importantly because as adults they had finally found that they could make it as men, if they worked at it, and they certainly were working at it. The rewards of manliness were real goals for them.

My colleagues could not meet my needs for friendship. So I turned to the students. My first encounter with them had been the first morning of the semester. At 8:00 a.m. I found the first of three groups of 80 persons staring at me. As a promising graduate student, I had been continually groomed to do research, and to define myself as a researcher. Teaching was a minor chore I'd pick up on the side. Consequently, I had never been in front of a class before in my life, and I was very scared. I stammered through the first day, but made it somehow. By the end of the week it was much easier, though there were occasional flashes of panic. By the second week I was starting to get into it, and by the end of a month, I was home. The endless, effortless flow of words that had made me the terror of the graduate seminar would still turn the trick. In a class of 30 graduate students, I had kept the other men from getting a word in edgewise; with undergraduates, inexperienced and already accepting my right to speak as much as I wanted, it was all my show. This was just opposite to the pattern of most of my colleagues. Since they tended to shy away from verbal encounter and argument, from masculine competition on that level, they were generally intimidated by any direct contest with students. Their ability to compete was exerted at a distance, by paper proxies; their victories were in endurance contests in the production of paperwork evaluated by weight. They were particularly afraid of young people, who represented an enigmatic and possibly hostile force to them. They knew young people so little that they feared they were on the edge of revolution. In the social sciences, there is an additional reason for defensiveness: The faculty suspected the students regarded both the ideas of the social sciences and the methods by which they are arrived at as trivial and irrelevant to an understanding of the real world around them, thus calling into question the faculty member's authority as expert. Most students regard the kind of concepts and analysis found in social science texts as obtuse and pretentious, and they are right.

Consequently, most of the faculty needed to use their power as teachers to force students to acknowledge the legitimacy of their authority as experts (and thus the truth of the conceptual system within which their expertise lies). This is how our system of higher education works. All the requirements—texts, tests, papers—are designed so that the student's success or failure depends on her/his ability to understand, interpret, and work within the teacher's definition of reality.

Thus, the connection that men make between self-esteem and power works as the psychological underpinning in the operation of such institutions as the educational system. Even the most independent student can only be on the defensive, since she/he has to work within the teacher's conceptual world, and the teacher has not the slightest obligation to understand the student's perspective at all. The most independent response most students can make is a sullen resentment, and an anti-intellectual skepticism denying the relevance of any abstract analysis, while meeting requirements as superficially as possible. This well describes the attitude of most of the students I've known.

As a teacher, I didn't have to resort to any of this. I didn't need to use my formal authority to have power over my students. First of all, I didn't find them particularly intimidating. As a vicarious hippie, a vicarious radical for years, I understood the youth culture as only an envious outsider could. (Neither hippies nor radicals have much use for queers.) Most importantly, I didn't see students as an outside threat to an establishment of which I was a part—I saw myself as far more outside it than they were. I was defending neither a system of analysis in which I believed—I'd considered the practice of American sociology garbage for quite some time—nor my authority as an expert in the understanding and teaching of these concepts.

In fact, my real power over students lay in just my ability to give up formal authority. By abdicating my sole right to define the situation I seduced the students into speaking up, presenting their own ideas, disagreeing with me. Then I'd smash them. I put on quite a show. But I was intimidated by students, too (male students at least—I was just starting to see women as people); I was intimidated by them as men, usually men who were bigger, stronger, better looking than I was. But in class they were on my home ground. I was more than eager to give up all external power, professional authority, and fight on a man-to-man basis. I was finally getting back at the kind of man who had always beat the shit out of me. This was far better than just making him study hard for tests.

And on top of all of this I was loved. For I could afford to be generous. I didn't actually humiliate students..I just wanted a general acknowledgment that I was smarter than they were. The atmosphere was one of easy informality, with an undertone of benevolent paternalism, typical of the classroom of the "radical" teacher. Since this is about the freest atmosphere any student is likely to find in a classroom, I was appreciated. Within a few months I had a reputation as one of the grooviest of the hip, young, radical teachers. By the second year, I could depend on all the Big Radical Men of the school being in my class, considering me an ally, or even something of a guru.

Soon, most of my close friends were students, former students, and other people I met through them. They were generally younger than I was, poorer than I was, and didn't have their lines down nearly as well as I did. I was guru, father-figure and host. My apartment was a meeting place for young, hip radicals. Usually a few of them were crashing there. In my office or the cafeteria, I usually had an entourage of half a dozen students or so.

(Some of this was real. Sometimes I did manage to establish real human contact. There are people—students and colleagues—whom I love, and who love me, whom I met while I was teaching. I'm still in contact with some of them. We've talked about the past, and have gone on to more authentic relationships. To dismiss the four years of experience I've just come from is not only unfair to myself, but to many other good people. In spite of everything, there was some real contact, some authentic friendship, some little love.)

But with so much game playing, so many power trips, I came close to being a man after all. Finally, though, with all the gratification, victory, power, and recognition, it still wasn't real; I still couldn't believe in it. For what I got from people still depended on the power I had over them—that was all society would ever offer to me as a professional success, and it wasn't enough. I could make it as a teacher, guru, advisor, but I never believed I was any of these things; they were never real enough to satisfy me. Outside these roles, my friends who were straight men would never give me what I really wanted from them. Sex was part of it, of course. In fact, at the time I believe I experienced it as the major part, since I lived in a seemingly eternal state of sexual tension and frustration. The whole atmosphere of the milieu I'd built up for myself reeked of sublimated sexuality. But looking back on it (from the perspective of having had a lot of sex, and finding out that didn't help much either), the real reason I couldn't settle for the kind of life and relationships I had was less direct. My friends were the most important part of my life. But for them, no matter how much they liked me, their relationships with me were of secondary importance. Their most important relationships were with women—wives or girl friends. Our time together was when they didn't have dates, or when their wives had something else to do. Or I was a guest of the family, or was dragged along on a date.

This wasn't due to any personal failure either on my part or theirs. They were part of a society in which a man's real intimacy and commitment can be expressed only toward a woman. That is, he can reveal himself and make himself emotionally dependent only on someone who is not a potential rival, but who, on the contrary, has been trained to be emotionally supportive of men and to expect a position of dependency. Before another man, a rival, a display of emotional commitment is an indication of weakness. Masculine solidarity is a real phenomenon in this society among straight men. It is a coalition of equals against inferiors for the maintenance of power. The personal relationships within such coalitions are a grown-up version of the armed truce that has existed among men since boyhood. Such relationships are satisfying to straight men who are interested in maintaining power and can turn to subservient women for emotional support, but they were not satisfying to me at all. And these were the only kinds of relationships with other men that my straight male friends were really comfortable with. I needed close emotional relationships with other men; my straight friends did not. Such relationships are threatening to the masculine facade of self-sufficiency; this threat is behind much of the straight man's revulsion for Gayness. Even the best-intentioned, most liberal straight male friend is not going to place the same value on a friendship with a Gay man that the Gay man places on it.

Everything I had been taught about Gay men had made it totally unthinkable for me to accept myself openly as one of them. Ever since their existence had been admitted to me, I had been taught increasingly sophisticated reasons why they were not to be taken seriously as people. For years the only knowledge I had of the category of people in which I was included came through dirty jokes. Later I learned that Gay people were to be pitied as cases of arrested development. The message that came across was that they were pitiful, crippled, tormented creatures, always good for a laugh. But in any case, Gay people could not be taken seriously. Since it was tremendously important for me that I take myself seriously, I was completely unwilling to see myself as part of a group depicted as vain, frivolous, childlike, foolish—or as a tormented, mutilated metaphor for human loneliness.

My fear of this image was so great that it prevented me from having any real contact with Gay people, which might have shattered the image. The only way I saw open to me to avoid self-hate was telling myself I must be different from the rest of those fairies. Thus the image of the homosexual presented in this society not only teaches all men to be afraid of, to hide their own Gayness; it teaches those of us who cannot hide our Gayness from ourselves to avoid and be contemptuous of other Gay people. Even when our sexual needs bring us together, there is often a mutual distrust and contempt based on our early internalization of the society's stereotypes, and this works against any real solidarity among us. Then the isolation of Gay people from one another can be pointed to by the society that creates it as evidence of the neurotic inability of homosexuals to relate to one another.

This describes my life up to my twenty-eighth year. But I was desperate enough now so that very little was necessary to break me out of the pattern I was in. Gay Liberation did it. The Gay Liberation movement is a very complicated thing; it requires extensive analysis. But for me, in 1969, there was nothing complicated about it at all. I went to the November Peace March in Washington, and I saw five Gay men with a Gay Liberation banner. I don't think I can ever communicate how important a thing that was for me. Nothing would ever be the same again. I saw five people with a Gay Liberation banner. People. They didn't look ridiculous, silly, or grotesque. They were talking to one another like friends; they didn't seem tormented, lonely, miserable. They were people, like me, at a peace march, and proud of being Gay. They looked like people I could talk to about serious things, about my life.

As before, the change seemed not so much in myself as in the world around me. This time a new part of the world seemed to open up to me, a new space, the space to be Gay without conforming to the stereotypes that I had rejected. The motivation to move into such a space was provided by the desperation that had been inside of me for a long time.

Nothing happened right away. But all sorts of things were going on in me. For a while I was extremely depressed. Some time around the middle of December I reached the decision that I wanted to be Gay. In the middle of January, I went to my first meeting of the Gay Liberation Front. I started becoming a different person, and the world started appearing to me as a different kind of place. Before, my homosexuality had made me an outsider, alienated from society. But the social reality I had been taught still gave me the terms in which I defined myself. I had seen myself from the perspective of the dominant society as a tiny isolated satellite revolving around an immense social universe. Now I had contacted other people out there, and suddenly it appeared that what I had been taught about such people wasn't true. There were people like me, and I didn't have to be isolated. I didn't understand at first why I had been lied to. But now that I could talk to others like myself, it gradually dawned on us that the lie was essential for the ruling class to keep America running. Men, if they are to be driven to function by a need to prove their masculine power, have to believe that anyone who chooses not to be a man is a failure or a fool. As we understand this, all the self-hate of our isolation started to turn outward in a growing torrent of rage. I had never really hated anything before—except part of myself. Now I began to hate this society, and I began wanting to destroy all of it. It was this wave of rage that finally broke through the conditioning of a lifetime, and what had seemed true and unalterable before now appeared as something monstrously evil that must be destroyed. I hated what this society had done to me, then what it had done to us.

And that led me to really see what it had done to still others. I had always been against racism from the usual liberal perspective of paternalistic altruism. Now I could connect it to my own experience in having been taught that I was less than human. This didn't make me sympathetic toward black people; it made me look to them and the rest of the third world as people who might be willing to join with me in the destruction of America. I was able to listen to women now and understand something of what they are saying. All oppressed peoples, all the people whom the ruling class has defined as incapable of determining their own lives, share the same need to destroy the present reality of this society, if they are to assert their right to determine how they will choose to live. This is getting ahead of myself, because all of this happened gradually—in fact, it has just begun. But the Gay Liberation Movement set this process in motion for me. For me, all of it became inevtiable when I saw five Gay men carrying a banner in a Peace March.

Meanwhile, my academic career was quietly dying of neglect. My emotional life was the focus of all my energies. Teaching was very much a part of it; the rest of the package wasn't. I applied for no grants, set up no research projects, and served on no committees in more than a perfunctory way. The only thing that still meant anything to me aside from teaching was writing. But as my conception of sociology became more subjective and problem-oriented, it became harder and harder to write about something that didn't touch on my personal experience as an extremely alienated closet Gay, and I wasn't ready for that yet.

More and more, I felt detached from the motivational system that was supposed to keep me functioning in the academic context. An academic career had never seemed to me to be more than a *faute de mieux* excuse for a life. With the possibilities that Gay Liberation offered, I didn't feel any need for settling for academic life any more.

Now I was up for tenure, and the alternative to tenure was dismissal. The sociology department faculty committee, much to my surprise, recommended me for tenure. Perhaps it was because they wanted one "experimental teacher" around, who had rapport with students. Also I believe they liked me, since I was the least manly of the radical teachers. I didn't try to bully them personally, and I wasn't trying to take over power in the department. I was seen as radical, but not as personally threatening. They, like the radicals, perhaps sensed they didn't have to take me seriously as a man. However, the real Big Man of the department voted against me, higher authority supported him, and I was fired. The reasons, as tradition dictates, were kept as obscure as possible, but one official suggested to the student newspaper that my behavior was "unprofessional." Quite a number of radical faculty were fired that year, eight in the sociology department alone. I got to be one of the Sociology 8, and a building was taken in our honor and held for several hours. In any case, I was out.

PART IV

My academic career was now drawing to a close. I had finally stopped being a Brain and had become a Gay person working at being a teacher. I was out of the closet and working actively in the Gay Liberation Front. The whole academic world was becoming increasingly peripheral to my social reality, as I struggled to redefine myself within a new Gay community we were and are struggling to create.

But being a "good teacher" still seemed meaningful, and was still an important source of gratification for me. And I still felt too isolated, too cut off from the support of a community, to live without a job. So I looked around for another place to teach. Several senior colleagues who liked me helped me. I wanted to stay in New York, to continue working with the Gay Liberation Front, but I could not work it out.

So in the fall of 1970, I found myself starting the second and last job of my academic career, at California State College, Hayward. It was essentially an epilogue. Teaching there was never the central part of my life that teaching at C.C.N.Y. had been. My life was in adjacent Berkeley, and in the Gay community there. A whole new set of struggles had begun for me, including my first real attempts to define and explore my sexuality. But that is another story, outside my academic career.

In any case my experience at Hayward was brief, a smaller-scale replay of events at C.C.N.Y. I found it more than ever impossible to associate with my colleagues without getting quite depressed. There was an almost metaphysical air to the unreality with which they viewed the world. They were equally out of touch with the social and historical events proceeding around them, and with their own emotions, desires, and weaknesses as human beings. To be in the same space with them was to be sealed in a crystalline little world, out of time, out of space, where all the world, for all eternity, was precisely determined by clearly specified guidelines, set down by the appropriately designated authorities. They drew about them a world without creativity, without passion, without morality.

In such an atmosphere, far more bureaucratic and technocratic, far less intellectual than C.C.N.Y., I nonetheless felt more free to teach and act as I felt I should, since I now had so much less commitment to survival in such a world. Consequently, this time I was fired at the end of one year. The suggested reason was that I had failed to develop a professional self-image and tended to identify with students. That was the end of my academic career.

PART V

Well, where does that leave me now? Coming out of the blind alley of Academia I had been led into by my failure to see that Brains turn into men after all, trying to get back to where I was when I was ten. Back then I had decided I didn't want to be a man. I never entirely gave up that decision. Defensiveness, a desire for security, and the surprising fact of my masculine competence in an academic setting—all of this led me into being a male impersonator for far too long, and I got so used to it that it was very hard to stop. But I am not now, nor have I ever been a man.

When I was ten, what I really wanted to be when I grew up hadn't been invented yet. It does not—cannot—exist within the capitalistic social system. Those of us who are now trying to create it call it Gayness. Being Gay means relating to other people without a need for power over them, or a fear of revealing yourself to them. It is the ability to love equals, like other men or women, defining themselves as equals, without being humiliated by the exhibition of unmasculine interdependence. Gayness is revolutionary because it requires the end of capitalist society and the creation of a society in which Gay people can live.

The concept of Gayness has come a long way from homosexuality but it grew out of the efforts of the people defined by this society as homosexual to redefine and recreate themselves. What Gay people will really be like none of us knows yet. We have had to survive in America and that has made it impossible to be really Gay. We cannot even entirely renounce power yet. We must be able to defend ourselves against a society that will increasingly attack us as it comes to perceive the danger we are to it. Thus we talk about Gay Power. But this must not be power for its own sake. We must not define ourselves in terms of power. The first step we can take toward Gayness, the first concrete thing Gay people can do now, is to relate to one another without a reliance on power.

That's the theory. It becomes reality only as it becomes a real part of one's life. Right now my life is learning what it means to be Gay. At the moment, I'm living in a big old house in Oakland, California, with five other Gay men. We've been living together for a year now, supporting ourselves with savings and various odd jobs, and trying to learn to relate to one another. We are breaking up soon. We didn't make it. We are still too frozen in the old patterns, still too much men. But we learned something in the process. Two of us are working at setting up a new collective, and we'll try again. There's no turning back; there's only a void behind us. And what's ahead of us only begins to exist as we create it.

I also have to decide what to do with all the knowledge and skills I've learned in my life in the straight world—with the resources and power these give me access to. Now that I don't define myself as an intellectual, I have come to terms with intellectualism. When I was a Brain, things of the mind were the source of my sense of self-worth and a consolation for loneliness. Now I have other, less alienated sources of self-worth, but it will be a long time (if ever) before I can live without such consolation. As an academician, I learned to use ideas as weapons to establish my power over others. Now I reject a self-concept based on power. Yet I am involved more than ever in a struggle against all the power of this society; in this struggle, it is only through the use of ideas that I can feel I am fighting back against my oppressors. Thus this paper.

Finally, I have no answers. I don't know where I am going, only the direction in which I must proceed. I often feel alone and isolated in this journey, but that is changing. Slowly, with many false starts, we are coming together. We are frightened because we are leaving all of the world we knew behind us, with whatever security it provided. It is still very hard to trust one another with our lives. But there is no going back, and we are building the future as we go. We must create a new world, if we are to be able to go on living. We are determined to live, so the future is ours.

Postscript

It's been more than five years since I wrote the "History of a Short, Unsuccessful Academic Career." Re-reading it now leaves me with all sorts of feelings—strong and hard to define. My life has moved on since then, so much so that the person who wrote that article now seems as far away from me as the Michael Silverstein who wanted so badly to be a college professor.

My life has changed very concretely in terms of how I live and earn my living, and along with these changes have gone changes in how I see the world. These changes aren't unique to me. I've changed because I am part of a changing gay and left movement. Through struggling together, many of us have come to understand the limitation of the Gay Liberation ideology of five years ago. By learning to link up with other people who have similar political perspectives, we've all been able to change.

Before I started this postscript I noticed how I had been described in the journal that originally published "History": "Michael Silverstein is a part of the Gay Men's Collective of the Berkeley Free Clinic. He lives in a gay men's house in Oakland, California." I wrote that identification myself to let people know that "gayness" was at the center of my identity. At the time, I believed it was the fact of gayness that set me apart from other white, middle class men and led me to radical politics; for me, this was true. The strength of my own feelings led me to believe that the same must be true for most other gay men. If they could only be shown how society oppressed them for being queers they would understand that they must take their stand on the side of all oppressed people against our common oppressors.

The greatest single disillusionment of the last few years is being forced to admit that the revolutionary potential of gay men just isn't true. Not all of them even feel the kind of pain I felt. Fewer connect that pain to masculine roles or see the need to change these roles. And fewer yet see roles as part of capitalist society that can only be changed through a struggle for socialism. Many gay men, maybe most, want their piece of the pie, and if they're already doing pretty well in terms of class and race, gayness by itself doesn't seem that big a barrier. This isn't to say I no longer experience the reality of gay oppression, but I see it as one part of a person's identity that might be offset by other characteristics, especially by class privilege.

My overriding commitment now is with those people whose understanding of their oppression leads them to become part of the overall struggle against all oppression. I feel a special closeness with gays, but I no longer think of myself as united with "Gay People." Gayness, no longer capitalized, is no longer the center of my identity. More positively, the emergence of third world and working class oriented gay groups has helped me to understand their oppression on a more fundamental level. Consequently, I feel far more connected to a general left movement now.

When I wrote my "History" I was aware of racism and the class system, but they were not as real to me then as now, because I identified with my privileges.

One of my major reactions to the article is the language—the way it sounds. I originally worked hard on it, writing and rewriting. It was far and away the classiest thing I ever wrote. Perhaps I wanted to tell academicians to go to hell, that I didn't want to be a success at their game, but at the same time I wanted to show that I could be an intellectual, that I was still a better analyst than most of them. It was necessary for me to act like I was renouncing the role of professor on my own. I wasn't entirely able to accept what was happening to me. I was being booted out of my niche as an upper-middle class intellectual. I had failed to produce and had been found unreliable. I was being declassed. The content of the article is my acceptance of this, but the style is a denial of it. Now when I re-read it, it seems self-defeating in that the people I claim to care about, people who haven't gone to graduate school, wouldn't have understood what I was writing.

This brings me to the life I'm leading now which has been the source of my change in consciousness. If I were to write another "identification," it would probably read: "Michael Silverstein is a member of the June 28th Union, a socialist pro-feminist organization of gay men struggling against racism and imperialism as well as gay oppression." I still live and work largely among gay men, no longer because I see them as my ultimate community, but partly because of my history and partly because I feel that for now it is the best place to do good political work. I have a job that at the time of writing the article would have seemed ideal. As a Program Specialist of The Gay Community of Concern, I'm paid to work with mental health and counseling agencies, lecturing on what they don't know about gay people. I also work with the Gay People's Union of Stanford (where our office is) organizing activities such as peer counseling. I feel pretty lucky to have this kind of job.

First, in the last few years I've learned that jobs are generally something to be grateful for (the year before, I ghost-wrote term papers). Also, I am getting paid for what I used to do for free. Sometimes it's fun, I'm pretty good at it, and it is of some value in helping gay people. However, I don't see this work as a particularly important part of making the revolution or as necessarily leading to any far-reaching social change. The limitations have been made clear to me by the people with whom I work. Both the mental health professionals of the agencies and the gay men of the men's collective of G.P.U. (I don't work very much with the women's collective, which is in fact more political), are united in their conviction that gay people, especially Stanford-type gay men, can fit into the American way of life with a minimum of change. The "gay community" can be just one other "specialty community"—peculiar but harmless—for which room can be made. Gay people are seen by both groups as variations on the norm. Other individuals in the G.P.U. have a somewhat broader conception of the gay movement, especially around the idea of creating a community, but given the class background of the Palo Alto gay community, that's about as far as anyone goes.

The gay movement may be a progressive force in the long run, but it is not that central to my life at this point. One of the things I like about my job is that it's half-time. The rest of my time and most of my energy goes into political work in San Francisco, where I now live. This is work I see as socialist organizing within the gay community. We work in a disciplined, collective way with other gay socialists, directing ourselves more toward gay workers and unemployed people, than toward an elite of intellectuals andsstudents. I still feel the importance of outreach to gay people because the American left, sharing a history of heterosexism with the rest of American society, has ignored the gay segment of the working class. As a result of heterosexism, gay workers have been considerably isolated from working class movements. I share a view with many gay socialists to work within the overall left while our primary task is to build a socialist, worker-led gay movement. Our long-range goal is a political force that includes the rights of gay people as an essential part of a socialist-feminist society.

The other major change I've gone through is the struggle against individualism. I now try to see my life in a collective, political and materialist perspective. Through collective struggle, I have come to understand how individualism has impaired me. More and more the self-awareness and depth of insight that the article conveys seems to be the more attractive side of the sense of aloneness, isolation and alienation that I gloried in and suffered from. My pain was unique to me, I felt. It made me unusually valuable in the depth and richness it gave to my character, and would be resolved individually on the basis of my own powers of self-examination and self-determination. As with the language of the paper, the content emphasized collective process and mutual support, while the tone celebrated the process of exceptional self-awareness. I am critical of the tone's claim to superiority over ordinary people who hadn't experienced the pain which sharpened my sensibilities. I do not imply that pain and gay oppression aren't real or sources of insight. But pain and oppression aren't unique to me or to gay people. My interpretation of them as something uncommon and unsharable was elitism. Individualism is the core of the elitism that has always divided the intellectual left from the masses of the people in this country. Middle class intellectuals must come to understand that they have much to learn from the "insensitive" masses of people who are forced into lives of poverty and drudgery; perhaps more to learn than to teach.

In my life I'm less concerned with things like "self-actualization" and "getting in touch with my feelings," and more concerned lately with "struggle," "solidarity," and "criticism/self-criticism." There is a contradiction in the middle class "growth movement" including the men's movement, which I see largely in this context: the emphasis on sensitivity and awareness rests on economic privilege. I feel that to be concerned with such things is only possible for people whose income and life-style leave them with the time and energy to devote to personal development, and that few people who work forty hours a week or more are likely to spend their spare time "raising their consciousness." The people who identify with "the human growth movement" seldom are willing to face the reality of their privileges. The opportunity to spend time and money on personal growth is paid for in the long run

196

by the oppression of workers and the unemployed in this country and throughout the world. I don't believe this is "just" a guilt trip. I believe it is an objective social fact that the "growth movement" is based on this underlying contradiction.

The real political meaning of the "growth movement," and the men's movement, will be determined by how they deal with this contradiction. Will the movement as a whole, or individuals within it, be led by their sensitivity to actively work to eliminate the system of privileges from which they benefit? Will they come to see that a sensitivity to one's own feelings that is rooted in a deadness to the suffering of others is ultimately self-deceiving? If so, then the "growth movement" can be a vehicle by which those members of the middle class with a genuine moral sensitivity will betray their class origins and join the struggles of the oppressed. But if one's "finer feelings" are an *excuse* for one's privilege, then consciousness-raising will increasingly become a game played by aristocrats.

Where does all this leave me? Coming to understand the above contradiction has been a real growth experience for me. The most important personal aspect seems so obvious—I'm not nearly so alone anymore.

This article, without the "Postscript," is from *The Insurgent Sociologist,* Fall 1972. Reprinted by permission.

WORKING CLASS MEN

Labor Pains

Andy Weissman

I want to communicate two major concepts—the first being how my background and politics led me to become a more or less blue-collar person, and the other, how it looks from my perspective to see other people—primarily men—work together.

I come from a family in which work has played a big part. My father was a carpet layer and my mother a short-order cook and bookkeeper. My father hated working. He would drag himself off to work in the morning. Sometimes I could hear him through the early morning, moaning and crying to my mother in despair. My father had worked most of his life. He came from a poor family and in the Depression dropped out of school and helped in the supporting of the family. He's 54 now and has been working for 41 years. Work took a toll on him. He would come in in the evening and be all tied up in self-hatred and hatred towards us, whom he saw as the reason he had to go through all this shit. He wouldn't talk—just go off to his room. Sometimes he would spend just enough time to shout "get away, leave me alone." He would go off to his room and cry. After a while he got into taking pills and then running around and getting loaded. Then he disappeared for a while.

While he was gone, my mother had to take care of the family. She didn't have any marketable skills. She learned to be a bookkeeper and got a job doing that, which didn't pay very much. It was left to my sister, who was the eldest, to watch after the house. My sister resented this. She and my mother would fight all the time. My mother would feel terribly guilty. It was hard for her to see what she needed for herself. She would blame herself for my father's leaving, crying out, sometimes, what had she done wrong—she had loved him. My mother had been trained early to believe it was her place to give to other people. Often she would come home and just fall onto the couch and cry. I would hold her and she would cry to me and fall asleep, asking me to forgive her for the way things had turned out. We got by on what my mother made, and in the course of time my father (after spending a year in a state mental hospital for being manic-depressive) returned to the family.

It seems that most of the pain in my family is that they never lived up to their fantasies of what they wanted out of life. I watched my father torment himself with stories of the great athlete he could have been, if he had only had the time. I watched my mother put three hundred pounds onto her 5'2" frame through self-hatred. I know now, after talks with them, that a lot of the anxiety in their lives was that they were afraid of not surviving, and that they held little or no respect for what they had to do with their time in order to survive. (I remember when people asked me what my parents did, I would lower my voice and hope they couldn't hear me. My father stressed that he wanted me to become something better than himself.)

I'm the only person in my immediate family to have graduated from high school. Also, I am a first-born male. For years there had been pressure on me to achieve. I don't know whether this kind of pressure is typical for lower-income people to place on their first male child, but I believe it is. I was made very aware that some day I would have to support myself, and hopefully a family also.

Relatives would play guessing games with what the future would hold—always they would imagine a lawyer or doctor or some such professional. It appears that their training to believe in their own unworthiness got projected upon their children so as to prime us for the old achievement game. I remember all the stories of how this cousin or that had gotten through school and become a success. Apparently when my relatives felt unsuccessful in their own lives they needed to use their children to grant them meaning.

After I graduated from high school the pressure really came in. I wasn't much of a student, but to my parents the fact that I had graduated from school made me superior, and in some ways superior to them. The maps for my future started to be printed. I was to be famous. This was heavy for my father to deal with. He was proud that a son of his had made it to this new intellectual world, but he couldn't handle feeling inferior.

For a summer we worked together at his job. The competition between us was remarkable. He would always berate my capabilities as a worker, and he would push himself very hard to be the one to produce the most. It was really painful to work with my father and see him push himself and play these self-hate games with the people he worked with. Also, for the men he worked with, sexual capabilities really became a status symbol. He would tell them what a great lover I was, and would prod me to come to work with hickies and display them to the other men. It's weird, but I guess this was the first time I became aware of how important it was for men to use feelings about women to prove to each other that they were OK.

I continued to work while I was going to college. My parents were very proud of this and would always bring it up with their friends. But having to work so much had quite an effect on me. Teachers wouldn't understand why I was so tired, and would be irritated. Or else they would be paternal and say "How nice it is to work yourself through school." I resented this a lot.

Also, there was the war in Southeast Asia. Some of my friends who didn't have 2S deferments or had never wanted to go to college were getting drafted after graduating from high school (1965). One friend especially sticks out in my mind. We talked all through the night about whether he should go or not. I had believed all the war movies and shit I was told and I argued he should go to war. He wanted to go to Canada and become a fisher. In the end he decided to go to war. In 1967 he was killed—he stepped on a land mine. I went through a lot of guilt and pain about his death.

I started to think more and more about the wars and who fought them. I joined SDS and talked and read and began to realize why students didn't have to fight wars—the bosses had plans for students, so they wanted them not to have to go. I got lucky, if you want to call it that—I have high blood pressure and that's one of the things the army rejects you for. I guess that's the best I ever felt about a rejection. I continued to work in the antiwar movement, becoming more and more enraged at all the complicated manipulations used to keep us at one another's throats. By 1970 I had been arrested a couple of times and had learned the meaning of justice. And when, in one of my trials, paid informers and university officials took the stand and told supportive lies about each other, I knew my place was not to fit in on their privilege ladder. I dropped out of school and became a full-time movement professional, doing some paralegal work and being interested in becoming a movement lawyer. I had swallowed the meal of success and real importance, and was going to become a great lawyer for all the poor. (Here I chide myself for needing to be important and helping the "little people." But I also believe some really committed and honest people are lawyers for the oppressed, and I don't want to trash them.)

I went into this until I took some time in the mountains and realized how far I had gotten from myself and my roots. I wanted to get back in touch. I discovered that I wanted a skill and to work with people, not for them (the idealist that I was). Also, I feel it's important for revolutionaries to have skills to share and build with, to utilize machines for the benefit of those who produce them.

I made a transition from being an intellectual to being an intellectual who also works with blue-collar stuff not because I was going to organize the people I was working with (though I will admit to some fantasies about that), but because I felt I had to work. I wanted to be closer to my roots and to feel that I could be creative with my hands. My situation separates me from the people I work with, and often from myself. It separates me because I can leave. I'm not married, or totally identified with my work. In fact, I hate having to work for a boss under huge pressures to produce. I can't joke about blacks or women or my own pain, and sometimes that leaves me just shuffling my feet. And too often the other people can sense the separateness in me and I feel a bit impotent to bridge the gap. It's hard to do when I know I could leave now because I've saved some money, and because the intellectual or aesthetic in me needs to see more of life.

I remember the day I called my mother to tell her of my decision to be a mechanic. I remember the disappointment in her voice. It was really hard for me to get into being a mechanic. All through the years, my father had told me that I was clumsy and that I should work with my head and not be a schmuck like him. I was lucky though—I met some people who helped me learn to work on cars. I worked collectively for a while, which gave me a lot of space to be wrong and to admit it and to also ask other people for help. In the two years that I worked in the collective I started to overcome my feelings of manual inadequacy.

I'm a blue collar worker now, and in the class and prestige system of blue collar workers I am a skilled worker, but that does not feel good enough for me because I still am hounded by a need to prove myself superior or special. Many of the people (men) that I work with are constantly needing to compare themselves to people they consider more important. For instance, they say a mechanic has as much skill as a doctor. Or, "There are a lot of flakey mechanics around—you really have to be on the ball to be a good one." Many of the people I work with are small-time landlords or big-time story tellers. The amount of bluffing that goes on is amazing. At work they have production sheets, and every morning one of the men I work with goes and reads the sheet to check out how he did compared to the rest of us. He knows exactly how much each of us has produced. He really freaks out if someone produces as much as himself. He is older than I am—perhaps 20 years—and if I produce more than him, he will remind me that my work or the cars I work on are gravy jobs. Or he will recall some of the mistakes I have made.

The men I work with sometimes get very angry and start calling me the worst thing they can imagine, and that is a cunt. That is very much like the way the men my father worked with responded to each other—always competing and grading themselves and using women to grade each other. The lowest grade is to be like a woman. Even though I am 27 years old, it's important for the other men to treat me like a very young boy. They affectionately call me lad, and almost go about patting me on the head. I guess that is their way of rationalizing me in their existence—to get along with me they either have to be my fathers so as not to take me as a threat because of my youthfulness, or else they excuse my reality by making me an inferior youth.

That setup is so hard to get past. Sometimes I talk to the other men about how my back hurts, and how the work is taking its toll. They get into talking about their own injuries, and we share a knowledge of some common feelings. It's hard to talk directly when we are so divided. Sam will joke when Bob makes a mistake. I will mutter to myself when I need to scream. Jim berates everyone as flakes. We battle and accuse each other of being the problem, and work till our bodies are diseased and tired, forgotten hulks. My father's body broke down a couple of years ago. He can't work any more—two years shy of retirement benefits, and cast off by society. That was the last time he freaked out. Sam talks despondently now and then that he will have to find some other way of making a living, but what can he do? We each kiss up to the boss, and drive ourselves and hurt each other till we disappear with time and age. It's frightening.

I don't think that the way people work happens by accident. There is a whole procession of events which adds up to make people work readily at jobs they hate. What I wanted to communicate here was how these little events in our lives slowly guide us along the paths of alienated labor, and how these things divide people at work. My mother cried when I became a mechanic and not a lawyer—but I believe it was because she felt this primed me to be an unhappy person, as unhappy as she had been, unhappy because the way we work takes from our lives and does not add.

I want to point out ways we hurt each other, and fall into the game plans for people who want to use our lives and abilities for their own gain. I think of the ways that the men I work with separate themselves from their jobs and each other and the people they care about. That is where I want to put my eyes—seeing how to break down those barriers.

From *Issues in Radical Therapy,* Spring 1975. Reprinted by permission.

Gay Men's Work

Anthony Eschbach

When I was called "sissy" at age ten, people (father, older brother and other boys) were not talking about my sexual behavior (who I was fucking) but about other "characteristics" I showed. These were the result of permission I received in early childhood to be in touch with my feelings (cry if hurt, yell if angry, etc.); I preferred being with people who were also into their feelings (women) and who were nurturing (again women). I had a lot of permission to ask for nurturing, both physically and emotionally, and similar permission to express it. I preferred cooperative and familiar situations to competitive ones and I and my friends (girls and boys) usually spent our time in group and non-competitive or slightly competitive activities (i.e., roller skating, exploring the neighborhood parks, jumping rope, climbing trees, ring-a-lee-vio, hide-and-seek, etc.). The threat of being called sissy or feeling bad about myself was not present. We played for the fun of it and that fun was not contingent on whether we won or lost. Our games went along with our energy cycles and spontaneity and were not set in rigid game rules and time durations. In short, I was not being scripted with the competitive, alienated, heterosexist, rigid components necessary for the survival of capitalism. In fact, the only times I felt "not OK" were when some macho schmuck, threatened by my humanness (read gayness), would take my power away either by beating me up or ridiculing me in front of others too threatened to side with and support me. I feel I was probably given a lot of permission for the above because I was the younger of two male children and didn't get a lot of pressure to achieve, "succeed," and prove myself as my brother was scripted to do.

I don't want to go into the development of my sexuality and why my preference is for men. I feel to do so would collude with the "pig" idea that men attracted to or able to love other men are a problem (at best) and therefore must have a common cause or causes. What I want to show here is that I was relegated to a position of non-man (powerless), not because of my sexuality, but because I retained characteristics not compatible with capitalism. I would not be "successful" in competing with other men if I valued cooperation (equality). I would not be able to work one-third of my life in some alienating job if I were spontaneously in touch with my work/rest/play cycles. Since I enjoyed the company of women, I would find a male-dominated work/social world a pretty limiting place. The only career I thought of was to become a priest (at that time priest equalled gentleness, nurturing, defender of "goodness", living communally, etc.). Success for me was not couched in terms of acquiring money or power, or feeling my own worth through oppressing others. Now it is the "pigs" I've had laid on me because of the above qualities that have oppressed me and made me feel "not OK," . . . not the qualities themselves. The pigs are, *"You're weak," "You'll never amount to much," "You don't have what it takes," "You're weird, crazy, queer," "You can't take care of yourself," "You're too emotional."* With these "pigs" are injunctions such as *"Don't assert your needs," "Don't try to do anything," "Don't think," "Don't be powerful," "Don't feel your feelings," "Don't ask for what you want."*

Between the ages of fourteen and twenty-two, I learned two very important things. First I learned how to pass (more or less successfully) for straight. I learned that if I oppressed the right people (mainly women and "weaker" men) I would have power. With power I would then be in league with other "real" men. The second thing I learned was that certain sexual behavior was OK among men (circle jerks and sometimes cock-sucking); the real taboo was the display of direct affection—i.e., hugging, kissing (making out . . . necking), or saying "I love you" to another man. I mean, come on, sweetheart, you can't love someone when tomorrow you may have to cut his balls off for a job!

At fourteen I also entered the work force. I usually quit or was fired pretty quickly from my jobs. I just couldn't get jived behind my first one where I made sixty-five cents an hour and spent all my after-school hours and Saturdays as a delivery and stock boy. I would try to liven things up by masturbating in the stock room but the roaches, rats, and water bugs were more than I could handle. For the next four years it was one boring, exploitive job after another. I don't mean those jobs came consecutively, I only got a job when the pressure became unbearable at home, and I would quit or be fired as soon as possible. After high school I joined the Navy. I'm sure I would never have stayed in it for four years had it not been for my father's farewell words, "You'll never make it, you don't have what it takes." (As you can see, my "pigs" were delivered with a certain lack of subtlety.) This was the

204

last test; I would really be a "man" if I got through the USN . . . whoopee!!

With my "Honorable" discharge in hand, I kissed the Navy, New York, and my family and all the shuck and jive goodby, moved to San Diego, CAME OUT and got the best job of my life. I became a hairdresser. While still having alienating aspects, i.e., competition, working with certain chemicals and furthering some sexist models of "women's beauty," this job still afforded me a place to be creative and nurturing, permission to schedule my own time, work with women and other gay men whom I could identify with and not have to play straight games with. Even as oppressed and oppressive as the Gay scene was in the mid-60's, I felt like I was reborn. I reveled in the knowledge that there were other choices to be made besides the dreary, boring, frightened life I was leaving behind.

I want to talk now about the kinds of work that Gay men traditionally do in this society, and the oppression that is associated with each kind of work.

For Gay men who are "out" or visible, there are basically four categories of work available. First are those of us that service, attend to and nurture women. We are the hairdressers, fashion designers, interior decorators, etc. Note the different connotation between us and men such as barbers, tailors and landscapers, who service other men. This first group resembles the eunuchs of old whose job was to "gild the lily" of sexism for the benefit of male supremists. The work we do is devalued, has little or no status, and usually implies other negative attributes (frivolousness, superficiality, immaturity). While some of us may become famous and part of the upper middle class, we lack power and prestige.

The second group is represented by those of us who are used to service the state's artistic pretentions. In this group are dancers, writers, painters and others in the Fine and Performing Arts, whose sexuality is ignored or tolerated because of our talents. The assumption is that you have to be a "bit odd" anyway to be an artist. While the work some do is valued, the vast majority go unrecognized, have little or no job and economic security, and are dependent on "sponsors" (elite) for survival. While some of us may socialize within circles of power and wealth, we ourselves have little. Another point of oppression for us is that while our sexuality may be known and tolerated, the "art world" is controlled by straight society and demands products which will support and glorify it. Gay writings by such men as Walt Whitman, W.H. Auden, Waugh and others have gone unnoticed and ignored until very recently and even now are mainly available in the Gay community and in gay publications.

In group three are "pseudo-female workers" who work in jobs traditionally held by women such as nurses (hospitals, mental asylums, convalescent homes, homes for the aged, etc.) and secretaries. Here we suffer in two ways. On the one hand we experience the oppression that women in the same jobs encounter . . . doing the shit work with little or no recognition, overworked and underpaid. Along with this we are also viewed as "failures." *Instead of being a doctor or the "boss," we "settled" for second place and a woman's job!* We've crossed sex-role programming and whether we become "head nurse" in a hospital or a "private legal secretary," it makes little difference. *("A nurse is a nurse, and a secretary is a secretary and they're both women. Women are second class citizens and for a man to do their work is demeaning.")* There is little status (except through hospital, boss or doctor) and not much chance of rising above a certain low economic level.

Group four is represented by those of us who "sell our time and use our bodies." Those in this group are models, houseboys, waiters in "gay" bars, baths, and restaurants, and escorts. Here again, we suffer some oppression that women in similar jobs (models, stewardesses, bunnies) experience. This work is available only to the "young and pretty." There is no job security (high turnover), little change to organize, low wages, and oftentimes the work is self-demeaning. These jobs are dependent on a sexist view of beauty and "typing." They lack status and prestige, are considered non-productive, unimportant, and not constituting "real" (men's) work. Selling oneself as a "sex-object" is considered within the sphere of woman's work. "Real" men do not consider themselves as sex objects, but rather as the possessors of sexual objects. To become a "sex object" is giving up one's power. These jobs are dependent on sexist and ageist values and on a society of lonely, alienated people.

There is another group of Gay men in the "job force"—our brothers in the closets. While many of us may achieve well-paying jobs with varying degrees of status and prestige, we maintain our positions in them by hiding our sexuality. To COME OUT would in most cases mean a loss of security and possible radical changes in life styles. This is often a frightening alternative and a choice we should not have to make to be visible.

Heterosexism, like racism and sexism, is another tool of paternalistic capitalism to keep workers from uniting and directing their power towards their true oppressors. It is one more way of eliminating people from competition for the inadequate number of good jobs. It is also one more pig that is used to make people feel powerless and "not OK" and like all pigs must be struggled against and offed.

From *Issues in Radical Therapy*, Spring 1975. Reprinted by permission.

Sexuality as Consumption

John Lippert

I work at a Fisher Body plant over in Elyria, Ohio. And so I spend about sixty hours each week stacking bucket seats onto carts. I used to spend all my time here in Oberlin as a student. But I had to give up that life of comfort as it became financially impossible and as it became psychologically and politically a less and less satisfactory alternative. I still try to remain rigorous about my intellectual growth, though, and so I still take a few courses here at the College. Such a schizophrenic role is at times hard to bear psychologically, and the work load is often staggering. But such a dual lifestyle also gives me something of a unique perspective on both Oberlin and Fisher Body. I feel this perspective is a useful contribution to this conference on men's sexuality.

One of the things that really surprised me when I went to work for Fisher Body is that it really is hard to go to work every day. I don't know why that surprised me. At first I thought that everyone around me was pretty well adjusted and that I was still an irresponsible hippie at heart. But then I found that just about everyone I know at the plant has to literally struggle to go back to work every day. Again I was surprised, but this time also encouraged, because I made the very casual assumption that I could look to the people around me for help in facing the strain of that factory. But I soon found that there is nothing "casual" about this kind of support: it is incredibly difficult to find. I have lots of friends now, from all over Northern Ohio and from all different kinds of cultural backgrounds. But most of these relationships seem based on a certain distance, on an assumption that we really do face that factory alone. At first I had to look to see if it was my fault, to see if there was something in me that made it hard to have nurturing relationships with the people I work with. I soon found out that it is my fault, but that it is part of more general phenomena. I began to explore these "phenomena" as completely as I could: this exploration became an essential part of my struggle to go to work every day.

In trying to look at these barriers between me and the people around me, I was struck immediately with the kind of role sexuality plays in mediating the relationships of people in the factory. I spend much time working with men in almost complete isolation from women. I soon found that instead of getting or giving nurture to these men that I was under intense pressure to compete with them. We don't seem to have any specific goal in this competition (such as promotions or status, etc.). Each member of the group seems concerned mainly with exhibiting sexual experience and competency through the competition. Past sexual history is described and compared in some detail: as a newcomer, I was asked to defend my sexual "know-how" within a week of joining the group. Also, we try to degrade each other's sexual competency verbally, through comments like, "Well, why don't you introduce your wife to a *real* man," or "Well, I was at your house last night and taught your wife a few things she didn't know." But it is important to note that none of what happens between men in the plant is considered "sexuality." That remains as what we do with (or to) our women when we get home. And so even though homosexuality is generally considered to be some kind of disease, most men are free to engage in what seems to be a pretty basic need for physical intimacy or reassurance. This can be expressed very simply, through putting arms around shoulders or squeezing knees, but it can also become much more intense and explicit, through stabbing between ass cheeks or pulling at nipples. But all of this physical interaction occurs within this atmosphere of competition. It takes the form of banter, horseplay, thrust and parry seemingly intended to make the need for such physical interaction seem as absurd as possible. But even through this competition, it is easy to see that many, many men enjoy this physical interaction and that they receive a kind of physical satisfaction from it that they just don't get when they go home.

My relationships with women seem somehow equally distorted. Entry of women into the factory is still a relatively recent event, at least recent enough so that contact between men and women is still unique and very noticeable. Much occurs before words are even spoken. Like every other man there, I discuss and evaluate the physical

208

appearance of the women around men. This analysis is at times lengthy and involved, as in "She's pretty nice but her legs are too long in proportion to the rest of her body." Of course this evaluation goes on in places other than the factory, but here it seems particularly universal and intense. Perhaps a reason for this intensity is that the factory is an ugly place to spend eight or ten hours a day, and attractive people are much nicer to look at.

I guess I really do get some sort of satisfaction from engaging in this analysis. But there is an incredible gap between the kind of pleasure I get when I sleep with someone and the kind of pleasure I get when I see someone attractive in the shop. And yet I behave as if there is some connection. Many men are completely unabashed about letting the women know they are being watched and discussed, and some men are quite open about the results of their analysis. Really attractive women have to put up with incredible harassment, from constant propositions to mindless and obscene grunts as they walk by. Men who call out these obscenities can't actually be trying to sleep with the women they are yelling at; they are simply making the women suffer for their beauty.

In this attack they are joined by some older men who just don't like the thought of working with women. Many women have been told they ought to leave the factory and get a husband, and then they are told in some detail what they have to do to get a husband! It is really difficult for women to work in that factory. In many cases women have merely added eight hours a day of boredom and frustration in the factory to eight or more hours a day of housework and childcare at home. And they have to contend with this harassment on top of all that.

But women are getting more secure in the factory. More and more now, men who are particularly offensive in this harassment are responded to in kind, with a flippant, "Up your ass, buddy!" In any case, by the time I get close enough to a woman to actually talk to her, I feel like a real entrepreneur. By that time I've already completed my analysis of the woman's physical appearance, and in the beginning of the conversation we are both trying to find out the results of the analysis. And to reinforce this feeling of entrepreneurship, when I get back to the men I'm working with, I get all kinds of comments like "Did you tap it?" or "Are you going to?"

But one thing that really amazes me about my sexuality at the factory is that it has a large effect on my sexuality at home. I first began to notice this when, in the first week, I began to feel an incredible

209

amount of amorphous and ill-defined sexual energy at the moment I left the plant. This energy makes the drive home pretty exciting and it influences my behavior the rest of the day. I often think something like, "Well, I have two hours before I go back to work, and it would really be nice if I could get my rocks off before then." I found that dissipating this sexual energy really does make it easier to go back. Also, I began to notice that my sexuality was becoming less physically oriented (as in just being close to someone for a while) and more genitally oriented (as in making love and going to sleep). Also, as household chores were becoming more formidable while working, I began to ask people who came into my house—and for some reason, especially my sexual partners—to take more responsibility in keeping the place fixed up.

In trying to understand how my sexuality was being influenced by the factory, this relationship between sexuality at home and at work became an important clue. Working is much more than an eight-hour-a-day diversion; it influences everything I do. If I'm not actually working I'm either recuperating or getting ready to go back. Because I confront this fact every day, it's not hard for me to imagine the changes in my sexuality as essentially in response to the fact that I have to go to work every day.

Now there is an important contradiction in this "I go to work." When I'm at work, I'm not really "me" any more, at least in some very large ways. I don't work *when* I want to; I don't work *because* I want to; I don't work *at* something I'd like to be doing. I don't enjoy my job; I feel no sense of commitment to it; and I feel no satisfaction when it's completed. I'm a producer; my only significant role is that I make money for Fisher Body. Now Fisher Body values me highly for this, and at the end of each week they reward me with a paycheck which is mine to consume as I like. But notice: I have to spend a large part of that check and much of my time off in preparation for my return to my role as producer. To a large extent, I don't consume so that I can feel some satisfaction or something like that. Now I consume so that I can go back to work and produce. And that part of my consumption which I actually do enjoy is influenced by my work in that what I enjoy has to be as completely removed from my work as possible. I build elaborate and often expensive systems (such as families, stereos, or hot rods) into which I can escape from my work each day. And this is as true of my sexuality as it is true of the music I consume for escape each day, the car I consume to get back and forth, or the soap I consume to wash the factory's dirt off me when I get home.

There is an important adjunct to this: the specifically asexual or even anti-sexual nature of the work I do. For the last three months my role as producer has consisted of stacking bucket seats on carts. That's it; nothing more and nothing less. Many parts of me are stifled by this type of work; we've all read about the monotony and so on. What is relevant here is that whatever dynamic and creative sexual energy I have is ignored for eight hours each day and at the end, is lost.

I hope that by now a picture is beginning to emerge which explains much of what is happening to me sexually as a function of this split between my role as producer and my role as consumer. What is the nature of this picture? The essential conflict is that in my role as producer, much of what is organic and natural about my sexuality is ignored for eight hours each day and at the end lost. I have to spend much of the rest of the day looking for it.

But notice: already I have lost much of what seems such a basic part of me. My sexuality is something which is no longer mine simply because I am alive. It is something which I have to look for and, tragically, something which someone else must give to me. And because my need to be sexually revitalized each day is so great, it becomes the first and most basic part of a contract I need to make in order to ensure it. The goal of this contract is stability, and it includes whatever I need to consume: sex, food, clothes, a house, perhaps children. My partner in this contract is in most cases a woman; by now she is as much a slave to my need to consume as I am a slave to Fisher Body's need to consume me. What does she produce? Again: sex, food, clothes, a house, babies. What does she consume for all this effort?—all the material wealth I can offer plus a life outside of a brutal and uncompromising labor market. Within this picture, it's easy to see why many women get bored with sex. They get bored for the same reason I get bored with stacking bucket seats on carts.

But where did this production/consumption split originate and how does it exert such a powerful influence over our lives? The essential conflict is that we really do have to go to work and we really do have to let our employers tell us what to do. There's nothing mysterious about this. People who will not or can not make a bargain similar to the one that I have made with Fisher Body are left to starve. If we are unable to convince ourselves of this by looking around this room or this College, we need only expand our observation slightly. Furthermore, Fisher Body and other employers have spent decades accumulating bureaucracies and technologies which are marvelous at producing wealth but which leave us with some awfully absurd jobs to perform.

We have no say in deciding the nature of these jobs; they are designed only from the point of view of profit maximization.

But to question the economic power of Fisher Body is to question most of what is to our lives essential and leads us to an intellectual tradition which most of us find repugnant. But if we are to have an adequate look at our sexuality we must begin with these observations: that our society is largely influenced by two relationships which are universal in our society: *that as producers we are forced into roles which we cannot design and which ignore our sexuality precisely because it is an unprofitable consideration, and that as consumers our sexuality becomes a pawn in our need to escape from the work we do and our need to return to work each day refreshed and ready to begin anew.*

Now what is the power of the conclusion we have just made? It is a conclusion which was reached through the exploration of day-to-day experience, but at this point it is an intellectual abstraction which leaves much out. For instance, it doesn't consider important influences of family and school on sexuality. At this point, the conclusion is general enough to apply equally well to blue and white collar workers (the main conflict is that we really do have to go to work). The conclusion doesn't attempt to explain every detail of the life of every worker. It does, however, attempt to describe a certain dynamic to which those lives respond and certain boundaries within which those lives occur. This conclusion is necessary for us in this conference if only from the point of view of intellectual clarity; we can hardly proceed unless we are aware that we as men and the College as an institution play a particular kind of economic role in society. Enough self-awareness to include the discussion of sexuality is a form of consumption that is simply not available to the mass of the people in our society. And it is to their time spent as producers that we owe our own extravagant consumption.

But what is the political significance of the conclusions we have reached? That is, can our discussion of sexuality affect the evolution of Fisher Body's power over us? For today, the answer seems no, that for today Fisher Body is incredibly strong because, like myself, the majority of people who work for it are basically committed to their jobs. But we need only consider individual survival for a moment to see that it can only be sought in the long run in a collective consciousness which is capable of challenging the power Fisher Body has over our lives. And this is why we need to confront our sexuality; because our sexuality is based on competition among men and at best distorted communication between men and women, it will make building that collective consciousness an incredibly difficult task.

In a short time we in the United States will feel the need for that collective consciousness much more sorely than we feel it today. The Third World is in revolt and the U.S. economy is in the midst of an economic collapse which rivals the collapse of the Thirties in proportions. As a result, we face massive unemployment in this country and the awesome prospect of battles between different groups of people fighting for the "privilege" of working for Fisher Body. If people see that it is only Fisher Body that can gain from such a battle, they may decide not to fight it. And if people see that a victory for Fisher Body means inevitably a return to a lifetime of alienation and oppression inside offices and factories, they may decide to fight instead for the right to control their own lives.

From *Brother: A Forum for Men Against Sexism,* Summer 1976. Reprinted by permission. This article by itself should not be considered representative of the politics of the staff of *Brother.* Each issue was meant to be seen as a whole.

THIRD WORLD MEN

Beyond the Binary: Race and Sex

Charley Shively

Sex between white men and Third World men must necessarily be shaped by the social circumstances in which we live. Out of these come the fantasies, opportunities, projections, prohibitions, taboos and chains in which we find love. Being "white," I want to talk about my own fantasies. As something I'm familiar with, my life is my place to look for social theory. It would be arrogant for me to pretend that I understand how every or any Third World man approaches this topic. Nor do I pretend to represent every white faggot. Ultimately I speak only for myself.

In part, this is a pathological study of the "white problem;" I present

213

myself as a specimen. I don't pretend to have transcended my skin color or my racism; they are a part of my past and will always be with me. But I hope to expose myself to scrutiny, question and study; wounds exposed sometimes heal faster than those buried in bandages.

I grew up in rural Ohio. Clermont County had only a sprinkling of Black people segregated in the county seat (Batavia). I don't recall ever seeing a Black person even in Batavia, although I remember people saying that Batavia always won the county basketball championship because they had Black players. (I never attended any games: lack of interest, lack of money, lack of a way to the games.) I went to the Williamsburg Township School which had no Black students.

The first Black people I ever remember seeing were two students who tried to enter Williamsburg School. (I don't exactly recall their sex—although I think they were female.) Their family had evidently moved into the township, but I'm not sure of the details. I was only in the second grade in October, 1943. I remember the Brown twins (whom I had played around with sexually) were sort of gang leaders in our class. They led the playground in taunting and stoning the two Black children (who were not in my class). It wasn't physically brutal (small sticks and stones). I don't remember what I did exactly: did I shove? yell? (if so, what did I say?) did I throw something? Only the feeling of wrong lingers. I can remember precisely the school door, the corner of the building where it happened, the undergarments of the Brown twins. Certainly, I did not say, "Stop! No! Don't!" I feared the ostracism of the twins. (Later I associated their conformity with all heterosexuality.) The two Black students withdrew from Williamsburg and went elsewhere (Batavia I would guess).

My next vivid memory more definitely associates Blackness with sexuality. I was then around thirteen and had begun a semi-affair with another boy, who worked with me setting up pins in the bowling alley. He was the toughest boy in our neighborhood (Gobbler's Knob): arrested several times, he was eventually given a stiff sentence for armed robbery. Earl was a little (but not much) older than I; still, at thirteen one or two years means a lot. He was certainly more experienced than me—the shy, quiet, studious, good-boy type. We had our first sex in a pig pen and he fucked me—rather gracefully. Earl told me things about the world—like Cincinnati. He confided in somewhat hushed and warning tones about Black men on Central Avenue in Cincinnati. They had such big cocks they would run a hole right through me. I guess he was projecting what he wanted (but because of

214

his butchness couldn't even entertain) onto me. My feeling was one of intrigue and desire. I suppose my relations with any Black man will always be touched by the things Earl said.

Of course, coming to Harvard in 1955 from rural Ohio changed a lot of things. On the racial side, I discovered who and what Jews were. In my high school we had not learned about the concentration camps or Hitler's anti-Semitism. I knew nothing about Judaism as a religion, although Cincinnati is one of the country's centers of Jewish theology. And although my roommate for two years was Jewish and I generally socialized with all the non-WASP's in my dormitory, I remained very much a country bumpkin as far as grasping the Eastern subtleties of ethnicity. Even with a Korean and a Chinese-American friend, I maintained a rather fraudulent idea of equality—that everyone was the same (i.e., potentially "American"), homogeneous. My college friends were all studious, hard working, poor and very much out of the social elite of Harvard. We all despised the "Clubbies." As far as sex goes, I don't think anyone did much of anything but masturbate. Certainly, if they were like me—busy in the tea rooms and bushes—they kept it totally closeted.

At the end of my sophomore year, in the summer of 1957, I met a man who fell passionately in love with me. He said he was a direct descendant of Sitting Bull—although I'm never too sure of such genealogies (my Father always said he was part Indian). We made out in the little town library and exchanged phone numbers. I still have the passionate letters he sent me (after our first meeting) saying "I love you with all my heart, and no one will ever take your place." After our second meeting, he said "I would be forever content just to wait for you." We rendezvoused a few times and I felt very uncomfortable not being able to return his passion. I think I was a bit snobbish about his taste in music (Frank Sinatra), his religion (Pentecostal) or literature (he gave me a Norman Mailer book, which was then considered "vulgar"). I felt very relieved when he moved to Indiana and I never heard from him again.

I did not know any Black students at Harvard (there were few if any in those days). Since I generally scored in the undergraduate library (Lamont) tearoom, I didn't meet many Black partners. My sophomore year was one of the busiest in my life, making it with something like three men a day every day of the semester, I was intrigued with the varieties of bodies, penises, personalities (whenever I could get into that) and generally going to bed with any man that was willing.

215

One night, going home from the library (it closed at ten then), I caught a Black man's eye by a camera store on Massachusetts Avenue, the main drag. He went down a side street and stepped into an unlighted doorway. Fearing assault or robbery, I nonetheless followed. We kissed and groped each other. And he invited me back to his place, which as we walked seemed miles into East Cambridge. He lived with his elderly mother and we made it together, alone on the living room couch. He was tall and thin, built like a dancer, short hair, mocha skin; his family was from the French West Indies. Those were the fifties and I was very much into playing a passive role: getting fucked or doing some stud. After he had fucked me wildly, Norman asked if I had ever fucked anyone and I said (quite honestly) no, I never had. He said, OK, I've always said that if I ever met a virgin like you, I'd want him to fuck me since I've never been fucked myself. So I did it, very easy and gentle; nonetheless he found it a little hard (I remember his back stretching and straining—sweating a bit down the spine). Whether his being a "virgin" was a line or not, he deeply impressed me. After I had breakfast in the morning with him and his mother, we exchanged addresses.

The next time we met, he gave me a pink shirt. (Pink was then considered very wild as a color—somehow associated unfavorably in my mind with Elvis Presley, whom I considered hopelessly vulgar.) I was totally floored by the idea of a gift: no sexual partner had ever treated me so nice in all my life. I was also worried. At the time I remained a totally dedicated, industrious student. I had never had a love affair and—sad to recall—I looked on such things as a great waste of time. My relation never developed further with Norman. I suppose I saw it as the career girl torn between love and promotion, and in my mind there was no question of not going for the sweepstakes. I later saw Norman from time to time, in fact moved into a house just around the corner from his. In the meantime he's moved on to New York; I once met him and his new lover, a Columbia professor. In retrospect now it all seems like an episode out of Langston Hughes' The Ways of White Folks. I was even then against the middle class, against the empire, war and the state, but I was more against the body, against my animal self, and dedicated to what I thought was pure thought.

In pursuit of "pure" history, I went to Madison, Wisconsin, for a year (1959-60). There I came upon the twentieth century beat poetry radicalism and other now familiar things. I remember only one Black man in Madison. He was a law student from Alabama—paid by the state to study in the North if he would stay there. William B. Hesseltine, a professor in the history department, said whites were beginning to make pets or teddy bears out of the few Blacks they ran into. Pete may have suffered from such saccharine attention as a member of the Blue Lantern Cooperative, where we ate together. The Lantern was then the small center of student radicals in Madison. We managed to get a good-sized crowd out to demonstrate against the local Woolworth's (whose lunch counters were the center of protests against segregation) and in April we had a large march from the university to the State Capitol Building. I wore a red and black lumber jacket and felt very righteous when I saw myself on TV that evening.

In Madison my sexual life remained very underground: library tea room by day, the Capitol grounds at night, or occasionally the one gay bar. I don't think I even saw a Black man in any of the cruising areas. I did meet a Mexican-American from the Southwest; he was a graduate student in Spanish literature. I had done him nine or ten times in the tea room (a marble altar he called it as he went down on his knees under the stall partition and I went down on his penis). Finally he invited me home to his room and we went to bed together. I liked him a lot, but he was deeply afraid of any emotional attachment; he was married and had two children at home. He showed me pictures of his family and told me how difficult it was being gay at home.

Back in Harvard in the fall of 1960, I passed notes in the Lamont tea room with a Black man, making arrangements to meet outside. Lester was tall, thin, still in his teens; he lived in Cambridge with his mother. He was slightly wild and outrageous to my sober, scholarly outlook but also immensely talented, charming and spectacular. Through Lester I met Edmund, who was much quieter, winsome, sweet, and affectionate. The three of us formed an almost inseparable circle for a couple of years; we didn't have much sex with each other, but we were "sisters" in the night.

Harvard graduate students are totally isolated; they lack the charm and attraction of the undergraduates (who include jocks, poets and thespians) to either the school or each other. They are supposed to dedicated entirely to cultivating their minds, reading everything and committing themselves to nothing. Edmund and Lester kept me alive through those dry years of torturous study; in a way they were wives to me: absorbing the psychic shocks I was suffering, strengthening me to survive in the straight world, keeping me going with friendship. Whatever else, they were my family; the only people I talked to; the only people I loved.

Ours was not, of course, a traditional family by any reckoning.

They each lived at home with their parents and I lived in a furnished room, later in a small apartment. Above all else we shared our love sexual adventure. New Year's Eve 1961 we picked up a pack of soldiers home on leave (Fort Dix basic training). Three, four, maybe more of them were hanging around the Hayes Bickford all-night restaurant in Harvard Square. They wore neat khaki uniforms. We all went to my room and turned off the lights; arrangements were a bit awkward. One of the boys was shy and couldn't do anything with the others around: so I took him into the closet and even there he was absolutely trembling, could barely get it up and was happy to get away. He returned later and robbed some of Lester's records and got to enjoy homosexuality more. One of the soldiers—"Johnny" was his name (and we used to sing, "When Johnny comes marching home again" in memory of the night)—wanted a woman and decided to check out the landlady (who was between sixty and seventy years old). The soldiers were all white and she was Black; either age, race or her motherly demeanor turned Johnny away.

We all three tricked regularly in Lamont. I remember a husky Santa Barbara freshman cruised me in the library and gave me what he said was his name and address to call for a later rendezvous. I then gave the note to Lester; he called the number and went over and made it with the other party, who it turned out had also cruised the freshman and had been given my number. (I eventually made it with that mischievous trickster.) Another time, Edmund brought a married friend along—partly I think just to shock him with our wicked talk. Then secretly the friend would come around to see me for a blow job; in fact he almost became a nuisance.

Not all my contacts were black and white. I remember seeing *Hiroshima mon amour* and on my way home meeting a Japanese man who looked like the star in the movie. He was a Harvard student and a swimmer with a perfect samuri body. I couldn't believe it: almost an instant fantasy fulfillment. Physically he gave himself totally to me, emotionally it was as though I did not exist. The experience was strangely unnerving: all those years not sleeping with a Japanese man; then suddenly there he was almost a total fantasy fulfillment. Was I the creature of random media stimulation—a sexual consumer always in the market for novelty?

Certainly Lester, Edmund and myself pursued novelty and variety in our sexuality. I wonder now that we got away with all we did. One evening Lester came by with a carload of Irish teenagers in a remade Mercury that was painted with the mouth of a dragon on the front and shooting flames all over the car. This was sort of a *Rebel Without A Cause* fantasy.

We decided to go to the country to give the boys blow jobs. When we got out to Waltham, they saw some young woman walking along the street and started to follow her. Then a gang of Watertown/ Waltham boys challenged and started chasing our car. Perhaps they were outraged that one of us was Black or maybe just pissed that we were operating in their territory. We began a high-speed drive to get a-way. Hoping to lose them, we managed to hide in a suburban driveway (the car was hard to hide) but the people living there yelled for us to get away and the pursuers found us. They had pikes and chains; the Cambridge boys told Lester and me that we would have to help fight or else. Luckily we got the car started and away (a few chunks of filling were knocked off the headlight).

As we streamed down the main drag in Waltham going fifty or sixty miles an hour pursued by the other car, we attracted a lot of attention. Two police cars began chasing. We approached a red light but shot around the other waiting cars, crossed the island and went through the intersection. The cop car pulled alongside and then in front of us; the pursuing car made a safe getaway.

On the way to the police station I coached everyone on a story that we had come to study the architecture of Brandeis and were chased by these hoods. Whether the police bought that story or not, we all stuck to it and they let us go with a speeding ticket for the driver. I was all for continuing on our way to the country for the blow jobs, but the teenagers would have none of that.

I think Lester, Edmund and myself had become enough of a family that we began to find lovers a bit like each other (though we didn't have sex much between us). That must certainly have something to do with my first full-time lover (that is, we got a place for living together). I met Lou in 1961 late one night in back of the Club 47; Joan Baez still sang there along with other jazz and folk musicians. I had never been inside because I didn't have the money; I was passing by that night on my way to cruise the Charles River bank. Lou was very spaced out, pissing, cursing, holding a broken beer bottle in his hand, crying. I asked him if he needed anything and he put his arm around me and we walked to his place. We took off our clothes and he fucked me with enormous passion and enthusiasm; he was very large but at the time I was totally loose, relaxed and happy to have him inside me. He went asleep and I left a note and went on home.

I actually didn't expect to hear from him at all, but in a couple of weeks he called and wanted to see me. We met and he said he remembered nothing of the night and wondered who I was and what the note meant. I explained that I was a faggot and we had fucked together. He said that was the first time for him and I said, well, I was always pretty much available. Lou was at the time a cult figure around the Club 47 crowd; he was an extraordinary piano player and had a whole act of being a wasted jazz star. He also dealt and used a lot of drugs, of which there was also a cult at the time. Lou had been officially deported for narcotics violations from Canada.

We made an unusual couple. While I may have been a faggot, I was still very academic, serious, disdainful of most pleasures—drugs, drink, music, smoke. Hardly a likely companion for a sophisticated jazz pianist; yet something clicked between us. My poetry perhaps: I wrote poems for him and he would play for me alone at night wearing only jockey shorts. I wrote a friend of my love for Lou: "the experience is a real one. It brings out my being and carries me to the limits of human experience—something I've never had before."

We got two baby kittens together from the Animal Rescue League. We would go to Cape Anne for sunrise on the rocks. We took pictures of each other by the sea. We walked along the Charles River, Easter morning sunrise. Lou was vomiting sweet-and-sour chicken, thanking me for being there. And when I had to take a Spanish test, he made love to me and gave me some speed to keep me awake (the two most helpful things he could have done); I was deeply touched that he knew what I needed.

Our relationship came to a rather dramatic end in Ohio. Lou, a drummer in his group, and I were going to Mexico on some dope business in this rich suburban woman's car. We got to Cincinnati and were stalled at my family's house (mainly because we were quite out of money). We went into Cincinnati to audition for a job in a downtown club. On the way home, Lou drove even though he could scarcely stand up. In Cincinnati, he ran a red light and just missed hitting a Cadillac by a microsecond. Nonetheless, the drummer and I went on with him driving; outside of town he ran the car out of control.

I was sitting next to him in the front seat and could see us moving off the road through the air. We hit a utility pole just six inches in front of me; I saw it coming like a rerun on a football movie. I was thrown out of the car and landed in the mud relatively unhurt. Lou and the drummer were also unscratched but still a little drunk. I was nearly sober and vomited quickly so as to have no alcohol on my breath and said I was driving when the police arrived. Not only drunk, Lou didn't have a driver's license. The woman whose car was totalled flew out and took him back (they were later married). I think Lou resented my keeping him out of jail or at least trouble. As he said, it was as though I had something on him. The drummer and I returned by Greyhound.

Back in Massachusetts, I could cry on Lester's and Eddie's shoulders, but they were relieved to see that adventure ended. Lester wandered on into Cambridge nightlife as he grew older and I saw less of him. Edmund and I grew closer. I shared the tribulations of an Irish lover with him; we went cruising a lot together and kept up an endless stream of gossip, tricks and cups of coffee. In 1965 I met my present lover who was very jealous of my friends and after that I didn't see a lot of Edmund. Later he moved out of town and we only get in touch with each other like old family cousins. I've since wondered if I shouldn't have stuck with my friends and forgot about lovers.

One of the common charges against those engaging in interracial sex/love/marriage/life is that the experience is self-destructive, pathological. The case of my liason with Lou certainly contains elements of that. I could see that Lou was a homosexual—physically attracted to Black men, while he had all his sex with white women and me. That among other things led to his destruction. He married the wealthy suburban lady for her car and money; she went insane; he went to Florida and (as informed sources report) shot himself.

For myself, I think I was not destroying myself but trying to destroy what Harvard-Conformity-Western Civilization would make of me. There was always in the middle class intellectual life enormous lures: the quiet harmony, soft chairs, fine offices, sociability and order. Whenever I left home in Ohio, I breathed easier in the relaxed atmosphere of school where nobody seemed to be scrounging for grocery money or rent. Where there was no weekly crisis of injury, unemployment, conviction, car wreck, breakdown, pregnancy, fights or disease. Harvard (and the middle class values it preserves) is a quiet, total self-destruction. What is really pathological is trying to hang on to that security while trying to escape it: the conflict and tension tear people apart. You must cut the umbilical cord in your heart to Western Civilization.

I think the issue is not the self-destructiveness of miscegenation, nor by extension the self-destructiveness of homosexuality, masturbation or sexuality in general. The issue is rather the destruction of capitalism, middle class culture and Western Civilization. Bakunin said, "Let us have confidence in the eternal spirit which destroys and

221

annihilates only because it is the unfathomable and eternally creative source of life. The urge of destruction is at the same time a creative urge." Do not cry/Let Western Civilization die.

The issue of Western Civilization and interracial sexuality are intimately linked: these were the two questions Malcolm X found white people most often asking about. The two issues are intrinsically tied together because Western Civilization is in itself a system of sexism and racism. The "Western Tradition" begins by dividing everything into two parts: Adam/Eve, Male/Female, Good/Evil, God/Devil, Sex/Love, Mind/Body, and by extension White/Black. These dichotomies do not correspond with any reality but they do have a devastating effect on believers in the system.

Race or skin color, for instance, cannot be divided into *only* two parts. The Supreme Court can only deal with Black/white segregation; when they face multiple groups as in Corpus Christi (Chicano, Black and white), their language cannot function. In Boston, Spanish-speaking students must by law be designated either Black or white by the individual teacher; under this system one identical twin was categorized white, the other Black. In writing this article, I have tried to think multiply—not only of my sexual contact with Black men but with all Third World men (American Indian, Japanese or Mexican-American). The effort is obviously somewhat strained: the mind focuses almost automatically Black/white.

The conceiving of race grows out of the conceiving of sexuality. Racism or fascism or imperialism needs to be perceived "in the light of patriarchal history, sexuality, pornography, and power, in which the first people turned into things are always women, and female (negative) qualities are attributed to every dominated group as the excuse for domination" (Adrienne Rich). Obviously white faggots carry a fantasy of Black men being more at home in their body (more animal, more thing). Good in music, dancing, basketball and bed. This grows out of a denigration not only of color but also of sexuality and humanity. Christians have long had a tradition of the "slavery of passion." That is, to submit to pleasure, desire, love, lust, the body—is to become a slave of something lower, inferior, less celestial—suicidal and self-destructive. To become *master* of the self is to stop giving in to sex. (Any number of religions share this sick philosophy.)

I would say that interracial sex only highlights a wider contempt and fear for sex, the body, flesh, lust, animal or whatever you will call it. Cocksucking as an act of revolution would go against this system, would celebrate the values of sex, desire, love, and animal in us all. If we fight the love, strength, humanity that is inside us we are self-destructive—we are suicidal. If we attempt to break down the tyranny of the binary system which would celebrate mind, mastery, power, authority, hierarchy and order—we can become truly creative, human, alive, beautiful.

From *Fag Rag,* Spring 1975. Reprinted by permission.

Personal Reflections on Gay Liberation from The Third World

Leonard   Andrews,   Jr.

Several distinct events in my life have guided the details and the subject matter of this article. When brought together they begin to tell a story about the peculiar experience of Third World people who are gay. My experience is obviously limited, and I do not mean to convey by my   words here that my personal history is anything like typical. I mean only to share some of it with the reader, along with some of my observations, so that a voice can at least be heard. It is my experience that Third World people who are gay do not really have a voice. We are in many ways voiceless, which of course also means powerless. And because of the psychological barriers in this country, most of us remain invisible.

Let me be more specific. All of the activity that has constituted the gay movement in the last six or seven years has been notable for its its absence of black, brown, red or yellow voices. While the Third World women's movement has acknowledged and supported the existence and the needs of lesbian women, the same phenomenon is not happening among men. There is unfortunately no organized men's movement at the present time, Third World or otherwise, but there is an active and viable gay movement, and few black, brown, red or yellow men have felt willing or able to participate in it. There are a lot of reasons for this. But what it boils down to is the fact that we live in a racist culture, and very few of us are allowed the psychological freedom to rid ourselves of taboos and restrictions that have so long been inter-woven within the framework of this society. It's ironic that the very people who helped to shape the political premises of the women's movement and the gay movement are not allowed to participate in them to any significant degree.

The black movement in this country demonstrated that oppression does not always take the form of geographical restrictions. It demonstrated a degree of discrimination, more subtle than separate drinking fountains or sitting in the back of a bus, that operates on a psychological level and deprives the individual of self-worth. In the end it demonstrated the extent to which the dominant culture had taken a race of people and had taught them, in the words of James Baldwin, "to despise themselves." With this discovery came the realization that the most devastating kind of oppression operates on a subconscious level, and that no significant measure of freedom could be achieved until psychological barriers were eliminated. In other words, until you rid yourself of the assumptions of the dominant culture, you are still trapped in a psychological prison more severe and more permanent than physical walls. This is where the phrase "come out" originated: the implication is to "come out" of the psychological prison dictating that you are not as worthy or as capable a human being because you are homosexual, or because you are a woman, or because you are not white.

Gays and women acknowledge their indebtedness to the black movement, usually through irritating and questionable comparisons. (And, incidentally, much of the hostility that homosexuals complain about coming from the black community is not so much intolerance as it is irritation at having the black struggle used as a band-wagon for white people. It's annoying to hear white gay activists speaking in public, compare being gay with being black, as if they had some kind of first-hand knowledge of what "being black" is like.) Though the black movement in various ways set the precedent for the emergence of the women's and gay movement, black people and other Third World sisters and brothers are noticeably absent from participation. As I indicated earlier, this is particularly true of the brothers. I suspect the reason for this goes beyond the conventional wisdom which insists we "just don't have the time." I remember walking into classes on behalf of gay liberation, and a group of maybe five or six of us would sit in front of a class and rap about our experiences as gay people. I got a lot of satisfaction out of those class "raps," but invariably mine would be the only dark face in the group. And what I remember most is the stares that came from the maybe five or six black students sitting in the back of the class together. The questions in their eyes asked: "What are *you* doing up there?" And sometimes a hand would go up and ask me that very question. And the hostility and disappointment that I saw in their eyes was the look of betrayal, as if I were being accused of betraying some unspoken agreement. It wasn't so much being gay that was the problem, it was being *publicly* gay. The betrayal was not in the fact that I had slept with men; it was in the fact that I had talked about it in front of "strangers."

Part of the ambivalence many black sisters and brothers feel toward the gay movement involves a silent consensus that black people can less afford to make sex a political issue, to "rap" about it in front of "strangers." Part of it has to do with the "visitor" status that black people in this country inherit from historical circumstances. This visitor status is why so many of us feel like "guests" in this country. It's reflected in our unwillingness to participate in anything as "brazen" as gay liberation. We haven't been made to feel quite that "at home" yet. And it keeps many black, brown, red and yellow brothers who are gay in closets of a different nature, with multiple doors to open. It makes the act of "coming out" more complicated than opening a single door.

My identification as a gay person began back in 1965. I was very young at the time, very impressionable, and very much in need of a hero. My hero eventually came in the form of one of my sister's friends, named Joe, who was five or six years older than I. At the age of fourteen, five or six years made a lot of difference. Joe had all the qualifications necessary to fill my hero-fantasies: he was tall, he was handsome, he was independent. He seemed always to be moving, I remember, always on the go, always being missed and pondered over by high school girls who fell in love with him, and by this fourteen year old boy who was searching for a hero. I never understood why he stayed away from his friends so much, or why he remained so elusive. As I got older it dawned on me that he acted the way he did because he was gay and was trying to manage two separate identities at the same time.

Joe was different from anyone I'd ever known. Because he came around so rarely, his very presence used to be something of an occasion in our household. I used to know whenever he was in the house because the smell of his cologne was rare and intoxicating. And if I was in my room reading or drawing, that smell would follow me upstairs, at which point I would sneak down, and find him seated on our couch, smiling. Joe's cologne would bring him into my mind whenever I passed someone on the street who had it on. It was roughly the smell of all the colognes together when you passed that counter in the department store. But whenever you tried to put your finger on it by sniffing all those bottles it would be impossible to find. You had to stand back, away from the counter, and sniff in the combined odor. The scent was elusive, like Joe.

Another thing odd about Joe was his hair. It was black like mine, only it was also covered by strands of silvery-white. I guess I was arrested by this feature of his. It seemed very unusual, and it made him attractive somehow. I was always puzzled by those strands of white hair. I wondered how he got them. They seemed to tell a story about Joe; about his struggles and his battles. To me they seemed to symbolize the after-effects of some long, forgotten war. In my fantasy world of fourteen or fifteen, they made Joe seem just a little heroic. And I guess they were also why he always seemed older than he was.

One day Joe began talking to me about his life and the shadowy gay world of Detroit. Because I was so young, and because he was really one of my sister's friends, I could never understand why he chose to confide in me. I suppose he sensed I would need someone to help me in my own eventual coming out. At the time, I was in the process of discovering a preference of my own for a certain boy in my neighborhood. But Joe never knew that. He confided in me out of some deep part of himself that was lonely and unsatisfied. And in a way, we both needed each other. Joe helped to put my vague sexual feelings into a context, and relate them to a concealed social life around Detroit. This life was so concealed that they had to invent a pseudonym to describe it. I was later to discover that this pseudonym had been in use all over the country as a code word for homosexual. And the word was "gay." And I first heard that word from Joe, back in 1965.

There were days before "gay" became proud and loud, when it had to be very quiet and very secretive, and somewhere in the underbelly of Detroit there formed a fraternal-like network uniting a diverse group of young brothers who were gay. It was possible to be an integral part of the black community and be unaware of this world. But it was always there, ever present, for whoever wanted to find it. And for me it held a fascination precisely because of its mystery. It was a mystery that I always connected in my mind with Joe. For it was through his words that I was able to construct an image; a picture of the gay world in Detroit. Joe's words were my only link to that world, and I relied on him to relate to me his story, as he relied on me to listen. Since that time I've learned that other gay brothers along the way had developed similar relationships with older friends who had helped make the transition we call "coming out" a little less difficult. It occurs to me only in retrospect that Joe's friendship accomplished that for me. In a way that has never been sexual, Joe brought me out during that autumn of 1965.

Five years later I found myself a part of a Third World Caucus that was formed out of the Detroit Gay Liberation Front. A small but courageous group of Third World men and women had taken it upon themselves to address the peculiar needs of non-white gay people. The result was a caucus that met every Sunday in someone's apartment. Most of us were black, but also among us were Native Americans and one Asian American. Most of us were male. I had stumbled across the Caucus by accident when a friend asked me to come over and help make posters for a gay parade. Gay people had organized a parade, marching down Woodward Avenue, the main thoroughfare in Detroit. I didn't have it together enough to participate in the actual march, which after all was in the center of my home town. But sitting in that apartment along with eight other brothers making signs that read, "Young, Gifted, and Gay!" was the beginning for me of a long continuing process called coming out. I had known I was homosexual, but I had never before been able to integrate that knowledge into a positive affirmation.

When I finished college in 1973 I moved away from Detroit and settled down in what was the only viable community left, if you're gay in Michigan—Ann Arbor. It's difficult to describe the gay community in Ann Arbor. It's diverse, and it makes an effort, at least, at being politically responsible. Coming out in Ann Arbor went smoother for me because I was away from home, and I was older, and I was in the midst of a community that was supportive in a way I had never experienced in Detroit. Ann Arbor is of course smaller and more manageable than Detroit, so Gay Liberation came easier. It wasn't the terrific effort it seemed to be in Detroit. To borrow a plant metaphor, Ann Arbor had more fertile soil in which a viable gay community could grow. And more importantly, it provided an alternative. It has already been suggested that the gay liberation phenomenon is in many ways an intellectual one, and it's no accident that in the midst of this thriving gay community stood the University of Michigan. But the gay community in Ann Arbor was more than a student community. It was made up of men and women who had no connection with the University, who simply lived in the town. And not a few of those townspeople were refugees from Detroit like myself.

It was in Ann Arbor that it was brought home to me the extent to which gay liberation is carried on primarily for the benefit of whites. Those few of us who were non-white and gay were very much like

227

"guests" in this little community. But the gay community that developed in Ann Arbor was a supportive one, and later on, after the integrated consciousness-raising groups started to wane, a few of us began to come out of the shadows and meet together among ourselves. It was, appropriately, at a Solidarity Conference back in 1974 that I first gained some insight into the predicament of Third World gays. In February of that year, Third World people from various parts of the country came together in Ann Arbor to hold a conference. There were a number of speakers and a number of workshops, and for the first time blacks, Puerto Ricans, Chicanos, Asians, and Native Americans came together under the assumption of a shared oppression. Those of us who participated learned how much non-white people in this country have in common, and how little we know about each other. We had reached the knowledge of our oppression slowly and separately, and it is just recently that we are beginning to pool our collective strengths and energies.

As I was listening to the speakers and participating in the workshops, and enjoying the camaraderie that was being developed among all of us, I was struck by the number of gay men and women who were hidden among us. I was struck by how utterly voiceless and powerless we were, and by how much we could contribute if given the chance to be open about our lives. I was struck because I realized I was one of them. After rapping about gay liberation in front of classes, picketing gay bars, yelling at psychiatrists at an APA Convention in Detroit, picketing a Catholic Church during noon Mass, and helping to effectively halt the proceedings of a session of the Ann Arbor City Council for their refusal to enforce the Human Rights section of their city charter, I was sitting here among hundreds of sisters and brothers unable to raise my voice, rendered effectively invisible.

The presentation staged by the Chicano group turned out to be blatantly sexist, and when the leader of the American Indian Movement made a reference to George Washington as being a "fag with a ponytail," I knew we had a long way to go. For the lesbians, it was a slightly different story. The women's movement had gained grudging acceptance, and the questions the Third World women presented to the conference at least hinted at the development of a world consciousness that could incorporate alternative lifestyles. The next time I attended a Third World women's coalition in New Haven, the lesbian issue was treated with the same determination as childcare, rape, and other concerns of Third World women.

The New Haven conference presented me with an unusual

opportunity to meet together with a group of Third World men, ironically because the women who planned the conference created a workshop specifically for men. Not only was this workshop created *for* men, it was also the only workshop open *to* men, but instead of using the time creatively, the majority of men spent the time feeling left out and voicing their outrage at being on the fringe of an entire conference held by and for Third World women. It was amazing to me. Slowly I began to feel like I was surrounded by insecure heterosexuals instead of by Third World brothers. It became very clear that the source of their outrage was based on assumptions about their relationship to "their" women that "their" women did not share. Men who had always called the shots when it came to Third World priorities couldn't deal with the fact that women were now calling the shots.

Third World men who are gay must contend with dishonest relationships with straight brothers who usually come equipped with various macho hang-ups, feel threatened by women's liberation, and share an open disgust toward men who are homosexual. Our predicament is that few of us feel strong enough to challenge the values of our straight brothers. During the Sixties Black Muslims used to tell us that homosexuality was part of the decadence that developed when the white man began taking over the world. We didn't argue. Today, black nationalists interested in furthering the race tell us that homosexuality represents a "death wish." We still don't argue. Third World gay radicals are a rare breed. Most of us pride ourselves on how successful we are in concealing our gay identities. We stay invisible. And those of us who do get involved with gay liberation must contend with "visitor status" in an organization that is predominantly white and has made only superficial provisions for the needs of gays who are not. This could be described as the "double jeopardy" confronting many Third World gay men. Most of us don't feel it because most of us are too busy attending to the business of plain survival: "getting over" and "making it" against formidable odds. We go to the discos and dance to the music and share a social camaraderie that is usually too dependent on an exploitive gay bar system to be sustaining.

There are hundreds of Third World brothers in Detroit, Ann Arbor and even here in New York City, whom I'll never talk to except against the background of disco music and a strobe light. Maybe we don't need to talk to each other. Maybe it's enough to just dance to the music and "have a good time," as Paul Simon implores in his song. But I suspect we need to find some common ground other than a gay bar on which to level with each other and to pool our collective energies, our resources, and our support. I suspect we need some alternatives; a place to sit and rap as Joe and   I used to do. It occurs to me that I've gotten a long ways away from my friend Joe since those days he used to come over and talk to me. We've both gone off in very different directions, and I miss him very much. I miss him mainly because I suspect he still has a lot to tell me, and maybe there are even a few things I can now tell him.

From *Fag Rag/Gay Sunshine Stonewall Fifth Anniversary Issue,* Summer 1974. Reprinted by permission.

Black Manliness: Some Fatal Aspects

Sedeka Wadinasi

Research into Black self-revelation has shown that Black men typically reveal less personal information about themselves to other Blacks than Black women do. Since Black men have as much "self" or "I-Am-Ism," i.e., inner experience, as Black women, then it follows that Black men have more "secrets" from the interpersonal world than Black women. Black men, seeming to fear being known by Black others, must be continually more tense (in a neuro-muscular sense) than Black women. It is as if being "manly"—particularly in Black terms—implies the necessity to wear "a gaudy mask," the character mask which Countee Cullen wrote about with such lucidity in his poem "We Wear the Mask." (And on an even higher level, there is Ralph Ellison's "Invisible Man.") Furthermore, if a Black man has something to hide, it must follow that other people (particularly his Black Brothers and Sisters) will represent a threat to him; they might seek to pry into his supposedly well-hidden secrets, or he may, in an accessible moment, reveal his true Black self in its nakedness, thereby exposing his areas of weakness and vulnerability. Naturally, when a person is in hostile territory, he must be continually alert, imperceptive, hypertensive, and desultory. All this suggests that attempting to appear manly is a kind of "work," and work imposes stress and consumes energy. Black manliness, then, tends to carry with it an inveterate encumbrance of stress and energy-expenditure which would be a factor related to the Black man's relatively shorter life-span.

If Black self-revelation is an empirical index of "openness," or "real Black self-being," and if openness and real Black self-being are factors in health and wellness (i.e., from a Black perspective), then the research into Black self-revelation tends to point to one of the potentially fatal aspects of the Black male role. Black men keep their selves to themselves, and impose thereby an added encumbrance of stress beyond that imposed by the exigencies of everyday life. (Hypertension is a prime example of this contention.) Psychotherapy is the art of promoting self-revelation and authentic being in patients who withhold their real selves from expression, and clinical experience shows that when psychotherapy has been effective with psychosomatic patients, the latter change their role-definitions, their self-structures, and their behavior in the direction of greater spontaneity and openness, with curative effects on their body.

There is another implication of the fact that Black men reveal less about themselves than Black women, an implication that relates to self-insight. Black men, trained by their upbringing to assume the "instrumental role," tend more to relate to other people on an I-IT basis than Black women. They are more proficient than Black women at relating impersonally to others, seeing them as the embodiment of their roles rather than as persons enacting roles. Black women (often to the chagrin of business-like Black men) seem to find it difficult to keep their interpersonal relationships impersonal; they sense and respond to the feelings of the *other* person even in a supposedly official transaction and they respond to their *own* feelings toward the other person, seeming to forget the original purpose of the impersonal transaction.

Now, one outcome that is known to follow from the persistence of the Black female (that the Black male reveal more) is that the Black male becomes increasingly sensitized to the variations of his own feelings (and those of his partner) as they ebb and flow in the relationship. Thus the Black male becomes more proficient at labeling his feelings, diagnosing his own needs, and understanding his own reactions. Concomitant with this increase in insight is an increase in empathy with others, an increase in his ability to "imagine the real." Studies of leadership show that the leaders of the most effective groups maintain an optimum "distance" from their followers, avoiding the distraction thereby of overly intimate personal knowledge of the followers' immediate feelings and needs. But not all of a Black man's everyday life entails the instrumental leadership role. For example, a Black man may "lead" his family, but he is not a father twenty-four hours a day. Personal life calls both for insight and for empathy. If practice at spontaneous Black self-revelation promotes insight and empathy, then perhaps we have here one of the mechanisms by which Black women become more proficient at these aspects of their so-called "expressive role." Black women, trained toward motherhood and a comforting function, both engage in and receive more Black self-revelation than Black men.

If Black men are trained, as it were, to ignore their own feelings, in order to more adequately pursue the instrumental aspects of Black manliness, it follows that they will be less sensitive to what one might call "all is not well signals," as these arise in themselves. It is probably a fact that in every case of outright physical or mental illness, earlier signs occurred which, if noted and acted upon, would have averted the eventual breakdown. Vague discomfort, boredom, anxiety, depression—thus hypertension—arose as consequences of the afflicted person's way of life, but because these signals were "faint," or else deliberately or automatically ignored, the illness-condusive way of life persisted until breakdown finally forced a respite, a withdrawal from the illness-producing role.

Loving, including love of self, entails knowledge of the unique needs and characteristics of the loved person. To know another person calls for empathy, the capacity to "imagine the real," and the ability to "let be," that is, to permit and promote the revelation of being. Black men's concepts of the subjective side of other people—of other Black men as well as of Black women and Black children—are often naive, crude, or downright inaccurate. Black men are often alleged, in fiction, to be mystified by the motives for the behavior of others, motives which a Black woman observer can understand instantly, and apparently intuitively. If this conjecture is true, it should follow that Black men, in spite of good intentions to promote the happiness and growth of Black others by loving actions, will often "miss the target." That is, they will want to make the other Black person happy, but their guesses about the actions requisite to the promotion of this goal will be inappropriate and their actions will appear awkward or crude.

The obverse of this situation is likewise true. If a Black man is reluctant to make himself known to another Black person, even to his spouse—because it is not manly to be psychologically naked—then it follows that Black men will be difficult to love. That is, it will be difficult for a Black woman or another Black man to know the immediate present state of the Black man's self, and his needs will thereby go unmet. Some Black men are so skilled at dissembling, at "seeming," that even their wives will not know when they are lonely, bored, anxious, in pain, thwarted, hungering for affection, and the like. And Black men, blocked by pride, dare not reveal their despair or need.

The situation extends to the realm of love of Black self. If true love of Black self implies behavior which will truly meet one's own Black growth, the Black men who lack profound insight or clear contact with their real Black selves will be failures at self-loving. Since they do not know what they feel, want and need (through long practice at repression), Black men's "essence" will show the results of self-neglect or harsh treatment of the self by the self.

It is a fact that suicide, mental illness, and death occur sooner and more often among "Black men whom nobody knows" (that is, among unmarried Black men, among lone wolves) than among Black men who are loved as individual, known persons. In addition to obvious economic differences, perhaps loving and being loved enables a man's life to take on value to himself and to his loved ones. Moreover, if a Black man is open to his loved one, it permits two Black folk to examine and evaluate their inner experiences and present conditions. Black men who are inadequately loved often fall ill or even die without warning, which shocks everyone who hears about it. If one had direct access to the Black person's real self, one would have had many earlier signals that the present way of life was generating illness.

The hypothesis may be proposed that Black women, more sensitized to their inner experience, will notice their "all is not well signals" sooner and more often than Black men, and change their style of living to one more conducive to health—e.g., consult a doctor sooner, or seek bed rest more often. Black men, by contrast, fail to notice these "all is not well signals" and do not stop work or take to their beds until the destructive consequences of their manly way of life have progressed to the point of a stroke or a total collapse. It is as if Black women "amplify" such inner distress signals even when they are dim, while Black men, as it were, tune them out until they become so strong that they can no longer be ignored.

It seems clear that the Black male role provides many opportunities for fatalities to arise. The best example is provided by the data on aging. It is a well-documented observation that Black men in American society, following retirement, will frequently disintegrate and die not long after they assume their new life of leisure. It would appear that masculine identity and self-esteem are predicated on a narrow base. If Black men can see life as worthwhile only so long as they are engaged in gainful employ, or are sexually active, or have enviable social status, then clearly these are tenuous bases upon which to ground one's existence. It would seem that Black women can continue to find meaning and reasons for living long after Black men feel useless and unneeded. Thus, a Black man's sense of masculine identity has numerous fatal components.

From *Osagyefo*, Winter 1976. Reprinted by permission.

Sources and Selected Bibliographies

Names and addresses of publications that first printed the the material in this anthology.

Brother: A Forum for Men Against Sexism. 10 Issues/$3.00. Box 4387, Berkeley, CA 94704.
Double F: A Magazine of Effeminism, 3 Issues/$5.00. Box 98, FDR Station, New York, NY 10002.
Fag Rag. 12 Issues/$7.00. Box 331, Kenmore Station, Boston, MA 02215.
A Forum for Changing Men. 12 Issues/$5.00. Men's Resource Center, 3534 S.E. Main Street, Portland, OR 97214.
Gay Sunshine. 12 Issues/$8.00. Box 40397, San Francisco, CA 94140.
The Insurgent Sociologist. 4 Issues/$6.00. Department of Sociology, University of Oregon, Eugene, OR 97403.
Issues in Radical Therapy. 4 Issues/$4.00. Box 23544, Oakland, CA 94623.
Liberation. 10 Issues/$7.00. 339 Lafayette Street, New York, NY 10012.
Male Bag. Project Redirection—Detroit. 15770 Heyden, Detroit, MI 48223.
Men's Issues. 12 Issues/$3.00. East Bay Men's Center, 2700 Bancroft Way, Berkeley, CA 94704.
Morning Due: A Journal of Men Against Sexism. 4 Issues/$4.00. Box 22228, Seattle, WA 98122.
New American Movement Newspaper. 12 Issues/$4.00. 16 Union Square, Somerville, MA 02143.
Osagyefo. 4 Issues/$6.00. Department of Pan-African Studies. California State University, Los Angeles, Los Angeles, CA 90036.
Win. 44 Issues/$11.00. 503 Atlantic Avenue, Fifth Floor, Brooklyn, NY 11217.

Selected Bibliography on Feminism

BOOKS

Abbott, Sidney and Barbara Love. *Sappho Was A Right On Woman.* New York: Stein and Day, 1972.

Angelou, Maya. *Gather Together in My Name.* New York: Bantam Books, 1974.

Asian Woman (editors). *Asian Women.* San Francisco, CA: China Books and Periodicals, Inc., 1971.

Atkinson, Ti-Grace. *Amazon Odyssey.* New York: Links Books, 1974.

Beal, Frances M. "Slave of a Slave No More: Black Women in Struggle," *The Black Scholar* VI (March 1975), 2-10.

Beard, Mary R. *Women as a Force in History.* New York: Collier Books, 1946.

Beauvoir, Simone de. *The Second Sex.* New York: Vintage Books, 1974.

Bengis, Ingrid. *Combat in the Erogenous Zone.* New York: Bantam Books, 1972.

Boston Women's Health Collective. *Our Bodies, Our Selves: A Book By and For Women.* New York: Simon and Schuster, 1971.

Brown, Rita Mae. *Rubyfruit Jungle.* Plainfield, Vermont: Daughters, Inc., 1973.

Brownmiller, Susan. *Against Our Will: Men, Women and Rape.* New York: Simon and Schuster, 1975.

Bunch, Charlotte and Nancy Myron (editors). *Class and Feminism: A Collection of Essays from "The Furies."* Baltimore, Maryland: Diana Press, 1974.

Cade, Toni (editor). *The Black Woman: An Anthology.* New York: New American Library, 1970.

Connell, Noreen and Casandra Wilson. *Rape: The First Source Book for Women.* New York: New American Library, 1974.

Covina, Gina and Laurel Galana (editors). *The Lesbian Reader.* Oakland, California: Amazon Press, 1975.

Cott, Nancy F. (editor). *Root of Bitterness: Documents of the Social History of American Women.* New York: E.P. Dutton & Company, Inc., 1972.

Chesler, Phyllis. *Women and Madness.* New York: Avon Books, 1972.

Dalla Costa, Mariarosa. *The Power of Women and the Subversion of the Community.* Bristol, England: Falling Wall Press, 1972.

Davies, Margaret Llewelyn (editor). *Life as We Have Known It: Co-Operative Working Women.* New York: W.W. Norton & Company, Inc., 1975.

Dworkin, Andrea. *Our Blood: Prophecies and Discourses on Sexual Politics.* New York: Harper and Row Publishers, 1976.

Dworkin, Andrea. *Woman Hating.* New York: E.P. Dutton, Inc., 1974.

Davis, Angela. *Angela Davis: An Autobiography.* New York: Random House, 1974.

Dreifus, Claudia. *Women's Fate: Raps From A Feminist Consciousness-Raising Group.* New York: Bantam Books, 1973.

Firestone, Shulamith. *The Dialectics of Sex.* New York: Bantam Books, 1970.

Flexner, Eleanor. *Century of Struggle: The Woman's Rights Movement in the U.S.* New York: Atheneum, 1974.

Gilman, Charlotte Perkins. *The Yellow Wallpaper.* Old Westbury, New York: Feminist Press, 1973.

Gornick, Vivian and Barbara K. Moran (editors). *Woman in Sexist Society: Studies in Power and Powerlessness.* New York: Basic Books, 1971.

Guffy, Ossie. *Ossie: The Autobiography of a Black Woman.* New York: Bantam Books, 1971.

Hartman, Mary S., and Lois Banner (editors). *Clio's Consciousness Raised: New Perspectives on the History of Women.* New York: Harper and Row, Publishers, 1974.

Hole, Judith and Ellen Levine. *Rebirth of Feminism.* New York: Quadrangle Books, 1971.

Horos, Carol V. *Rape.* New Canaan, Connecticut: Tobey Publishing Co., 1974.

Jay, Karla and Allen Young. *Out of the Closets: Voices of Gay Liberation.* New York: Pyramid Books, 1972.

Kahn, Kathy. *Hillbilly Women.* New York: Avon Books, 1972.

Klaich, Dolores. *Woman + Woman: Attitudes Toward Lesbianism.* New York: William Morrow & Company, Inc., 1974.

Koedt, Anne, Ellen Levine and Anita Rapone (editors). *Radical Feminism.* New York: Quadrangle Books, 1973.

Kraditor, Aileen S. *The Ideas of the Woman Suffrage Movement: 1890-1920.* New York: Anchor Books, 1971.

Kraditor, Aileen (editor). *Up From the Pedestal.* New York: Quadrangle Books, 1968.

Lerner, Gerda (editor). *Black Women in White America: A Documentary History.* New York: Vintage Books, 1972.

Lynn, Naomi, Ann Matasar and Marie Rosenberg. *Research Guide in Women's Studies.* Morristown, New Jersey: General Learning Press, 1974.

Medea, Andra and Kathleen Thompson. *Against Rape .* New York: Farrar, Straus and Giroux, 1974.

Mellen, Joan. *Women and Their Sexuality in the New Film.* New York: Dell Publishing Company, 1973.

Millet, Kate. *Flying.* New York: Ballantine Books, 1974.

Millet, Kate. *The Prostitution Papers.* New York: Avon Books, 1971.

Millet, Kate. *Sexual Politics.* New York: Avon Books, 1970.

Mitchell, Juliet. *Psychoanalysis and Feminism.* New York: Random House, 1974.

Mitchell, Juliet. "On Freud and the Distinction Between the Sexes," *Women and Analysis,* ed. Jean Strouse. New York: Grossman, 1974.

Mitchell, Juliet. *Woman's Estate.* New York: Vintage Books, 1971.

Morgan, Robin. *Sisterhood is Powerful.* New York: Vintage Books, 1970.

Morgan, Robin. *"Goodbye to All That."* Philadelphia: Know Inc., 1970.

Myron, Nancy and Charlotte Bunch (editors). *Women Remembered: A Collection of Biographies From "The Furies."* Baltimore, Maryland: Diana Press, 1974.

Piercy, Marge. *Small Changes.* Greenwich, Connecticut: Fawcett Publications Inc., 1972.

Pomeroy, Sarah B. *Goddesses, Whores, Wives and Slaves: Women in Classical Antiquity.* New York: Schocken Books, 1975.

Postan, M.M. *Medieval Women.* Cambridge, England: Cambridge University Press, 1975.

Redstockings. *Feminist Revolution.* New Paltz, New York: Redstockings, Inc., 1975.

Relter, Rayna R. *Toward An Anthropology of Women.* New York: Monthly Review Press, 1975.

Rennie, Susan and Kirsten Grimstad. *The New Woman's Survival Sourcebook.* New York: Alfred A. Knopf, 1975.

Rossi, Alice S. *The Feminist Papers: From Adams to de Beauvoir.* New York: Bantam Books, 1973.

Rosaldo, Michelle Zimbalist and Louise Lamphere (editors). *Woman, Culture and Society.* Stanford: Stanford University Press, 1974.

Rowbotham, Sheila. *Women, Resistance and Revolution: A History of Women and Revolution in the Modern World.* New York: Vintage Books, 1972.

Rowbotham, Sheila. *Women's Consciousness, Man's World.* London: Penguin Books, 1973.

Ryan, Mary P. *Womanhood in America: From Colonial Times to the Present.* New York: Franklin Watts, Inc., 1975.

Schneir, Miriam (editor). *Feminism: The Essential Historical Writings.* New York: Vintage Books, 1972.

Smedley, Agnes. *Daughter of Earth.* Old Westbury, New York: Feminist Press, 1973.

Silviera, Jeanette. *The Housewife and Marxist Class Analysis.* Pittsburgh, Pennsylvania: Know, Inc., 1975.

Stacey, Judith. "When Patriarchy Kowtows: The Significance of the Chinese Family Revolution for Feminist Theory," *Feminist Studies,* II, 64-112, 1975.

Washington, Mary Helen (editor). *Black-Eyed Susans: Classic Stories By and About Black Woman.* Garden City, New York: Anchor Books, 1975.

PERIODICALS

Camera Obscura: A Journal of Feminism and Film Theory. 3 Issues/$9. Box 4517, Berkeley CA 94704

Feminist Studies. 2 Issues/$8.00. 417 Riverside Drive, New York, NY 10025.

Frontiers: A Journal of Women Studies. 3 Issues/$9.00. Women Studies Program, University of Colorado, Boulder, CO 80309.

The Lesbian Tide. 6 Issues/$5.00. The Women's Building, 1727 North Spring Street, Los Angeles, CA 90012.

Off Our Backs: A Women's News Journal. 12 Issues/$6.00. 1724 20th Street N.W., Washington, D.C. 20009.

The Second Wave: A Magazine of the New Feminism. 4 Issues/$4.00. Box 344, Cambridge A, Cambridge, MA 02139.

Signs: Journal of Women in Culture and Society. 4 Issues/$12.00. University of Chicago Press, 11030 Langley Avenue, Chicago, Ill. 60628.

Sister: West Coast Feminist Newspaper. 12 Issues/$5.00. The Women's Center, P.O. Box 597, Venice, CA 90291.

Women: A Journal of Liberation. 4 Issues/$5.00. 3028 Greenmount Avenue, Baltimore, Maryland 21218.

Quest: A Feminist Quarterly. 4 Issues/$9.00. Box 8843, Washington, D.C. 20003.

Selected Bibliography on Gay Male Liberation

BOOKS

Altman, Dennis. *Homosexual Liberation and Oppression.* New York: Avon Books, 1971.

Hobson, Christopher Z. "What Is It Like to Be the Mother of a Homosexual?" *Gay Liberator.* (Fall 1975), 4-7.

Hoffman, Martin. *The Gay World: Male Homosexuality and the Social Creation of Evil.* New York: Bantam Books, 1968.

Jay, Karla and Allen Young (editors). *Out of the Closets: Voices of Gay Liberation.* New York: Pyramid Books, 1972.

Jay, Karla and Allen Young (editors). *After You're Out: Personal Experiences of Gay Men and Lesbian Women.* New York: Quick Fox, Inc. 1975. (pp. 245-47 lists forty lesbian's and gay men's periodicals).

Lauritsen, John and David Thorstad. *The Early Homosexual Rights Movement.* New York: Times Change Press, 1974.

Richmond, Len and Gary Nogura (editors). *The Gay Liberation Book.* San Francisco: Ramparts Press, 1973.

PERIODICALS

A Gay Bibliography. Single Copy 25 cents. Task Force on Gay Liberation, American Library Association, Box 2383, Philadelphia, PA 19103.

Body Politic. 6 Issues/$5.00. Box 7289 Station A, Toronto, Canada MSW 1X9.

Fag Rag. 12 Issues/$7.00. Box 331, Kenmore Station, Boston, MA 02215.

Gay Sunshine. 12 Issues/$8.00. Box 40397, San Francisco, CA 94140.

Magnus: A Journal of Collective Faggotry. 4 Issues/$6.00. Box 40568, San Francisco, CA 94140.

R.F.D. 4 Issues/$4.00. 4525 Lower Wolf Creek, Wolf Creek, OR 97497.

Books from Times Change Press

UNBECOMING MEN: A Men's Consciousness-Raising Group Writes on Oppression and Themselves. This book reflects the struggles of a group of men who've come together because of their increasingly unavoidable awareness of sexism—how it operates against the people they most care for and ultimately, how it eats away at their own humanity. *Illustrated; 64 pp; $2.50.*

THE GREAT HARMONY: Teachings and Observations of the Way of the Universe—Edited by S. Negrin. This collection of teachings, drawn from Taoism, Western philosophy, "primitive" religions, Judaism, Zen and more, tells us that the sensory world is not an end in itself, but a path to knowledge. Understanding the laws of the universe is possible and leads to an artful life and ultimate self-realization. These teachings help illuminate the path. *128 pp; $3.50.*

HELLO, I LOVE YOU! Voices from within the Sexual Revolution—Edited by Jeanne pasle-green and Jim Haynes. Forty-eight pioneer-participants in the ongoing sexual revolution share their intimate, firsthand experiences with bisexuality, celibacy, erotic art, group sex, sado-masochism, gay and women's liberation. Here we have people taking risks to become more open and loving in a conscious search for better ways for us all to relate to ourselves and each other. *176 pp; $4.50.*

FATHERJOURNAL: Five Years of Awakening to Fatherhood—David Steinberg. This is a sensitive, unglorified account of a father who decides not to become "the second, somewhat foreign parent." Instead, he seeks intimate, nurturing contact with his child, and reveals for us the resulting emotional and sex-role conflicts, as well as the new levels of love and awareness that fatherhood opens to him. *96 pp; $3.00.*

FREE SPACE: A Perspective on the Small Group in Women's Liberation—Pamela Allen. *Free Space* is a good handbook for people wondering how to begin or restructure a consciousness-raising group. Developed by feminists, the small group is now being used by many people as a way of relating to different needs. *Illustrated; 64 pp; $2.00.*

JANUARY THAW: People at Blue Mt. Ranch Write About Living Together in the Mountains. Writing about relationships, work, parents, children, healing and celebration, these rural communards describe feeling their way toward a life that makes sense and feels good, in which people are more in harmony with themselves, each other, the earth and the universe. *Illustrated; 160 pp; $3.25. Cloth, $8.50.*

THE EARLY HOMOSEXUAL RIGHTS MOVEMENT (1864-1935)—John Lauritsen and David Thorstad. The gay movement, like the women's movement, has an early history, which, beginning in 1864, advanced the cause of gay rights until the 1930s when Stalinist and Nazi repression obliterated virtually all traces of it. The authors uncover this history, highlighting interesting people and events. *Illustrated; 96 pp; $2.75. Cloth, $6.95.*

MOMMA: A Start on All the Untold Stories—Alta. This is Alta's intensely personal story of her life with her two young daughters, and her struggle to be a writer. She tells of her efforts toward self-fulfillment and her battle against feelings of guilt—a story many readers will recognize as their own. *Illustrated; 80 pp; $2.50*

AMAZON EXPEDITION: A Lesbianfeminist Anthology—Edited by Phyllis Birkby, Bertha Harris, Jill Johnston, Esther Newton and Jane O'Wyatt. When lesbians within the gay liberation movement synthesized gay politics with feminism, they started a separate political/cultural development which thousands of women began to identify with. This is what this anthology is about. Culture, herstory, politics, celebration. Lesbianfeminism—one concept: the new womanity. *Illustrated; 96 pp; $3.00. Cloth, $6.50.*

THE TRAFFIC IN WOMEN and Other Essays on Feminism—Emma Goldman; with a biography by Alix Kates Shulman. Emma Goldman was a dynamic anarchist and so her feminism differed markedly from her suffrage-oriented contemporaries. Today the split between liberal and radical approaches to women's liberation are still not resolved. So these essays have an uncanny relevancy to problems now being dealt with. *Illustrated; 64 pp; $3.00.*

LESSONS FROM THE DAMNED: Class Struggle in the Black Community—By The Damned. This book describes the awareness of oppression as black people, as workers and poor people under capitalism, and as women and young people oppressed by men and the family. It may be the first time that poor and petit-bourgeois black people have told their own story. *Illustrated; 160 pp; $3.25. Cloth, $7.95.*

TO ORDER ANY OF THE ABOVE BOOKS

send your order and payment

(Including 50 cents postage & handling per order;

minimum order $4.00)

to:
TIMES CHANGE PRESS
Order Department
Albion, CA 95410

Times Change Press also produces
POSTERS
They are illustrated in our free, complete catalog.
It also lists all current titles and contains fuller descriptions.
To receive a complete catalog, write to:
TIMES CHANGE PRESS
ALBION, CALIFORNIA 95410